Prai...

"You have the soul of ... ..., your brutal honesty, imagery, metaphors and emotionality are so relatable. I look forward to reading your stories every day. You so vividly describe the epic redundancy of the pandemic while focusing on some of the most beautiful moments, the moments that make us human and why we cling to this precious gift of life." *–Therina Bella*

"It's very real and honest. It's refreshing for all of us trying to create a "real" summer and being reminded that it's different, and that's ok." *–Lesley Koehler Evans*

"Gut level, relatable honesty." *–Jennifer Gerard*

"Your complete honesty is like a breath of fresh air. You dig deep and come up with stuff most people would not bother putting down. Then there is your humorous side which is like dessert after a big supper. Do not stop." *–Tom Heinlein*

"Mix of vulnerability and gratitude." *–Phillip Johansen*

" this. They are comforting, vulnerable, clever, vivid, soft, honest and relatable. You have a way with words (and paint), my friend." *–Adrienne Miller*

"They are essential like air and water." *–Linda Mary Montano*

"I just love truth! We all have our own stories for sure... You are a beautiful writer in truth like your mom was…"
–Lorelle Mcbride Pugliese

"I love reading them. We are all living through this pandemic, but I have no idea what it is like to live through it with two kids. Your truthfulness is refreshing." *–Tanja Bungardt-Price*

Always and Still Here

SARAH CONRAD-FERM

Cover art by Sarah Conrad-Ferm
Cover & book design by Michele Walthers
Copyright © 2020 by Sarah Conrad-Ferm

For my Dear Friends, who read all,
most, or some of my letters,
and encouraged me to keep writing.

Author's Note

I started writing these daily letters on Facebook on the 9th day of my quarantine. At first, they were a way to connect to my community of friends as a whole. I missed them, and writing letters felt like a way to share the day and bring them nearer to me. It was a strange feeling those first few weeks. We were all isolated physically and at the same time insulated on social media in a way I had not felt before. Like we were all under a blanket with flashlights, whispering to each other. And there was nowhere else we were allowed to be.

I wrote my letters in a way that would feel, I hoped, that I was writing directly to the singular reader. But knew several of my friends were reading along every day, some friends reading now and then, some reading silently, some commenting. I asked a lot of questions along the way, hoping for responses. I did get answers sometimes. I also got a lot of love and support in return and a lot of encouragement to keep writing.

The letters became a journal of this strange historic time and I saved them in a file on my laptop to have for myself and my children when they are grown. A recording of this pandemic and what our lives are like. I thought I'd just print them and tuck them away. But the letters also became part of a routine for a group of us. Me writing and those reading. I would ask, "How long should I write these letters for?" And my friends would say, "Forever." They are good friends. Fine humans.

So I wrote and continue to write, most every night before bed at the end of the day. Reporting some of the day's events and the continued strangeness of this new world we live in, with it's ever evolving dramatic plots. So many twists and turns, and at the same time, such stillness. It is a strange dance, tiresome and difficult to master. But we plod along.

Here is a collection of all the letters from the first six months since the quarantine in New York began. I continue to write every night. I am not sure how long I'll keep writing. I suppose until the pandemic has been resolved, which right now feels like it's years away. But I don't mind writing, to you, my Dear Friend. I will always reach out a hand to you, gloved or ungloved, or an elbow to bump, or my least favorite, the air hug. Anything for you. Thank you for keeping me company through this strange time.

Sit with me now, let's talk a while. We've come a long way, but I think we have a long way to go. Let's not go alone, we'll go together. And by go, I mean, mostly just stay where you are. For now. I think we have plenty of time. Make yourself a cup of tea, I'll be right here when you're ready.

Always and still here,

Sarah

March 2020

March 20

Dear Friend,

Day 9.

Woke up too early this morning wondering if I should write out a will, and promising I'd get around to asking so and so if they'll take my kids if Joseph and I both die at the same time. Don't worry, it probably isn't you. And I might not get around to it. Seems too...bad harbingerish.

Got up with Sonny, got busy doing the usual chores. Putting things away from the day before, making tea, checking the ol' newsfeed. Felt teary looking at the posts, the news, my friends. Missing you. Had therapy on the phone. Sat in my hammock on the porch in my coat. Asked my therapist if all of her sessions sound the same now. She said not really. Go figure. Wondered if I should wash my coat.

Got to my studio. Started a David Sedaris audiobook. It occurred to me David and I were real whiners before this pandemic came along. We probably still are.

Ended up on the phone for a while with a friend who messaged, "Can I call you like it's 1989?" Yes, please. So good to talk to someone besides Joseph, Desmond and Sonny. I wonder how long it will be before I can get together with other people.

We made homemade pizzas tonight. An old friend from Brooklyn was passing through and stopped by to say hello. We stood outside, I at my front gate and him in the street. More than 6' away. Glad to see a friendly face but sad I could not get closer or hug him, invite him in, or make plans.

I blame this visit for the chocolate chip cookies I made but really, I had been thinking of them all day. I'll have to work on finding comfort in something besides carbs and staying up late watching *Better Call Saul*. Luckily, I think I am almost done with the whole series. Maybe I can take a break and read a book. Probably not though. I know that sleep is important for my immune system. I tell myself, "If you don't turn this show off, you could die." I keep watching. My favorite moment today was sitting on the hammock on the front porch watching it rain. It was so warm by the end of the day. But the mosquitoes are back. It's always something, with me and David.

I hope you are well. Write when you can.

Always and still here,

Sarah

March 21

Dear Friend,

Day 10.

Stayed up late last night, talking with Joseph in the kitchen, then barely keeping my eyes open to watch my show. He got up with the kids today and I managed to sleep almost until 9:00. So rare for me but I suppose I needed it. Remember when we were teenagers and would sleep until 10:00 or 11:00 in the morning?

I am having trouble remembering what we all did today, the days seem to blend together when nothing much changes day to day. Joseph went for a bike ride. I put avocado in my eggs. Fancy.

I did manage, just in time, to make it to a high school friend's live video stream of immunity boosting exercise and meditation. I had to keep asking the boys to "let Mommy do this, please!" but was able to be present enough. The video cut out before it was over but moving and breathing in unison with my friend made me teary, so desperate for connection with people. So grateful to have that moment.

This reminds me of when I visited Japan, a long time ago. How nobody hugged and how I couldn't wait to get home to hug someone.

Desmond seems to be feeling the isolation now too. He is quick to cry, easily frustrated. I managed to arrange a virtual playdate for him with his friend. He sat in front of the laptop in the living room talking about toys and music while I swept the kitchen floor and puttered around. He gradually built an enclosed fort around the computer so he was hidden away while he talked. Felt like he was trying to enter the virtual space they were sharing. I don't blame him.

He was sad again after his "visit", so we took a walk together into town to the bakery. The bakery is an "essential" store so it is still open. I'll say. What a delight to see all of their cakes, cookies, pies and soups are still there. We got clam chowder, iced sugar cookies and a piece of apple crumb cake. I bought Des a decaf coffee, which he always asks for and I never buy. And a tea for myself. Sweet to see our friend who works there too. A friendly face and well wishes.

In the early evening we drove to a new trail in the woods our neighbor told me about. So beautiful, the sun through the baby spruce pines, glowing green. A little running stream, fresh forest air. The kids whined and carried on, on and off. Joseph carried them one at a time, then both together. I took a lot of pictures.

Mac and cheese and leftover pizza for dinner. And then the obvious fail at avoiding sugar. Ate a sugar cookie and some handfuls of chocolate chips. At least I got 9 hours of sleep last night.

Practiced my cello, which sounds intermittently pretty bad and okay. I won't have a teacher for a while I guess so I'll just do the best I can winging it. Feels good to use my brain and feel the vibration of the cello in my arms.

Then a very hot bath to melt off the sugar, germs and worry. And then a letter to you. Sorry it is not more exciting. I suppose things may get more dramatic in the near future although I hope they don't. All in all, it was a good day. Hoping to find ways to increase connection to the outside world in new and interesting ways. Like this letter.

I have no plan for tomorrow. But I expect it will be interesting.

Sending you hugs, high fives and kisses on both cheeks.

Always and still here,

Sarah

March 22

Dear Friend,

Day 11.

It's the end of day 11 of our quarantine at home. Funny how something so strange can start to feel normal so quickly. I feel I am settling into a new normal. Today I seemed to spend most of my day talking on the phone or in a video chat. All of this distant socializing made it hard to get anything done. But I was glad for it and think tomorrow will be a quieter day.

Joseph goes back to work tomorrow after 4 days at home. I wonder what his day will be like at the hospital. I hope things there are on track for handling this virus as carefully as they should. Last week I was a nervous wreck. But what can I do? I am not sure how to answer that question, so I'll just keep doing what we're doing and try not to worry about things that haven't happened yet.

I have instated my face paint wearing. I think I'll wear some every day. At home war paint. Couch paint. I got to my studio to do some work today. I had to wait for the boys to be done with their virtual play date so I could take my laptop. I am so glad to have a place to go outside of the house alone to paint. Such a treat. Especially now.

I devised a test tonight to see if I have the virus. I thought if I danced really hard and fast to Joan Jet's song "Bad Reputation" and could still breathe afterwards, then I'm probably fine. The test was inconclusive. Or I have it. I was more winded than I expected. I also thought I should video tape this test and share it with you but when I played it back I could not believe how slowly I was actually dancing. I looked like my mom slow dancing to Tina Turner. I wonder if she thought she was dancing really fast too. Even though it is not an efficient test, I recommend dancing as hard and as fast as you can to this song because it does hold merit as a quarantine energy release. Also, I am reinspired to lose those 7, now 10 pounds.

Tomorrow is a new day and I will not bake cookies.

I hope you are feeling well. I will check in again soon.

Always and still here,

Sarah

March 23

Dear Friend,

Day 12.

As I expected, today was quiet and somehow passed quickly. Joseph went off to work and it snowed all day, on and off. The snow fell straight down in clumps. If it fell slower, it would have looked like feathers. It coated everything, but the day seemed gray and cloudy. It was pretty and gloomy at the same time, and like a camera filter; whitewash outside made the inside look like the saturation was pushed a little higher.

It's nicer when the weather outside is inviting so our "shelter in place" feels bigger. Felt like our world shrunk a bit today. I am hoping it melts away tomorrow and the sun comes back.

Nothing interesting to report. I feel as though I'm forgetting something, as if there was something I wanted to tell you but it slipped my mind. But really, I don't think so.

A few new virtual interactions today for Desmond. I can check off another day of minimalist face painting. I cleaned, I washed sheets, I cooked. I did not bake cookies but I did bake an apple pie. A healthy pie. Only 1/4 cup of honey in the whole thing and the crust was really more rolled oats than flour. Tastes like hot apples and crunchy oatmeal. It's just in the shape of a pie. But I like it. I kept thinking, "Man, this is the perfect pie for ice cream." But there was no ice cream. Thank God.

I have noticed that my friend's posts on Facebook have been getting more vulnerable. It's wildly endearing. They are singing and dancing. They echo in my mind throughout the day like jewels in my pockets and make me glad.

I hate to feel like I am just crossing days off the calendar. Wondering how I can create more...of a day within this same space. How to transcend limits. Makes me glad I am not in prison.

All of this weirdness has me constantly thinking, "It could be worse." I hope when it's all over I will think, "It could have been worse."

Do let me know if you discover some excitement. Please, not the virtual kind.

Stay well, stay home, wash your hands. Then moisturize.

Always and still here,

(My mom signed a letter to me that way once and I have it engraved in a bracelet I wear every day. Fun fact.)

Sarah

March 24

Dear Friend,

Day 13.

It was a long day. I wanted to go out but it was too cold and wet outside. Even though I think it was 50°, eventually. There was nowhere to go anyway. I felt sluggish and lazy. Everything moved slowly and with very little purpose. I'm afraid I'll end up agoraphobic when all is said and done.

Desmond has very little patience for Sonny these days. Did I mention that already? I can't remember. Sonny is mad at everyone. He has developed a new rage scream, that used to be reserved for when he was hurt and angry. Now it's just fury. He's mad at his stuffed animals.

We talk a little bit about what's going on. Why everything is closed. Why we are staying home. Maybe we should talk about it more. Or less.

Sonny is so young that you can really tell him anything and it all seems normal. Desmond is more aware of how odd it is. I think they are both disturbed by it but not consciously. And annoyed with each other.

And maybe I feel the same way. Increasingly nervous, just because. Like I'm rising up on a wave, not sure where it's taking me.

I was going to sew masks but then I read a study that says they may do more harm than good and at best they are 97% ineffective. I might sew some anyway.

Because I think they'll look good with my face paint.

I cooked some butternut squash in the oven early in the day and left it in there to make sure it was cooked through. I was going to make soup. Then I forgot it was there and made rice and beans for dinner. I guess it's lucky I remembered it was there at all and can make soup tomorrow.

I spoke with a friend this afternoon and she asked how our day had been and I could not remember. By 4:00, I thought I might fly out the door and make a run for it. But what would I do out there?

After dinner I took the boys in the car to our favorite nearby hiking trail. It was cold out, my hands hurt and my eyes watered from the wind off of the river. But we hunted for rocks and crystals. We found some quartz and I found a big tooth, I think. A funky fang looking thing. It looks like a bone in the shape of a tooth. We were there until dusk. That's a great word. It got real dusky. So we came back home.

Sonny told me he was going to lock me in the shower.

Joseph came home from work, exhausted. He's gone to bed. They have him going in extra early this week. I don't know what we'll do tomorrow. I imagine it will be a lot like today. I wish I had a better idea.

Sending you love and comfort.

Always and still here,

Sarah

March 25

Dear Friend,

Day 14.

Well, if it had been a two week deal, I could have said that went by pretty quickly. But here we are.

Joseph was off to work early again today. Screening people at the door all day for 14 hours. They are also preparing him to be ready to work in the ICU, he is usually in the recovery room. The PACU, they call it. I think that stands for People who Always Crap their Underpants. Just kidding, don't fire him. Maybe it's Post-Acute Care Unit. Hey, that might be right actually.

Ah, I asked him, it's Post Anesthesia Care Unit. So if you get knocked out, you get to wake up to Joseph. I wake up to Joseph all the time, it's really nice.

I made waffles for the boys. Sonny asked if he gets sick if I'd take care of him. He's worried he'll catch this virus. I reassured him it's not likely he'll get it and of course I would take the best care of him like I always do, as long as he hasn't locked me in the shower.

We went back to our favorite hiking, rock hunting spot this morning and then ordered bagels from the bagel shop and picked them up. They brought them right to our car.

Then we went home and watched a virtual tour of the Botanical Gardens Orchid Show. Felt like almost a normal morning with outings and events.

Put on a movie this afternoon and fell asleep on some pillows on the floor, which was heavenly.

A virtual acting class for Desmond this afternoon that I tried to eavesdrop on with Sonny's monitor from his room. It sounded pretty adorable. Desmond takes my laptop upstairs for privacy.

Played my cello while they wrestled and fought a bit. Finally played the C string, the lowest of the low. Thought I might conjure up a portal with that frequency, no luck.

Made butternut squash soup for dinner while the boys had a video chat with a friend in Florida who we love. That was sweet.

Got on a group chat with some grownups tonight and Sonny came in at the last minute to say, "I'm sorry but... her mom died." Oh man.

Heavy times.

So far everything is okay. But I still don't know what's coming. We never do I guess. Although the future seems suspect these days. Sonny sometimes asks me, "Is this the future?" "Is this today?" "Is this tomorrow?" Always the answer is yes.

See you tomorrow.

Always and still here,

Sarah

March 26

Dear Friend,

Day 15.

I went for a walk today by myself. No headphones, just walking and thinking. I haven't done that in years. I used to do it all the time. I thought of it as taking my brain for a walk. It's so true. And man did my brain need it. It had so much to say and I was so entertained.

I walked past a nursing home and could smell old lady perfume in the air. I walked past friends' houses and thought about throwing pebbles at their front porches so that they'd come to the door to say hello. How I would stand on the sidewalk and we could yell back and forth. I thought about just standing on the sidewalk and waiting for them to notice me and come out, I wondered how long it might take.

I passed a lot of FedEx trucks and I wondered how many delivery people will get sick.

I wondered why we aren't supposed to walk or ride our bikes on the left side of the street so we can see the cars coming. And if it's illegal to look inside someone's mailbox if you don't take anything.

I thought about vestibules and center hall colonials. If it would be more fun or less fun to walk with a friend 6' away from me. That the only things I was told were bad for me when I was a kid were TV and sugar.

Why would you pick up your dog poop in a green dog poop bag, knot it and then leave the bag in the grass?

I walked past a squirrel tail on a lawn and later a whole dead squirrel in the road that was perfectly intact except that its head was missing. Why are there detached squirrel tails around? Do they drop their tails in a fight like a lizard?

I looked it up when I got home. Their tails can be yanked off and they won't grow back. I have never seen a squirrel without a tail. I will be on the lookout. I prefer a tailless squirrel to a headless squirrel.

I thought about the 70 something set and the 80 something set being my most coveted people. About how when I was young, attractive men were what caught my eye. Now that I'm middle aged and married, it's people my parents' generation. I look at them longingly. I just want to sit in their kitchen with them and have tea. I guess it's the person that's missing in your life that you look for, whomever that may be. I won't say how I arrived at that thought, or where it took me. Not now.

I went shopping at Target tonight after trying without luck to find a store online that was doing curbside pick-up. It made me nervous. I wore rubber gloves; I was the only one. No masks, no gloves. Last time I went out people were wearing gloves and masks. Not today. It was so quiet there. Strange to see empty spots on the shelves here and there and an abundance of things beside the missing ones. I thought about all the people eating canned soup day after day at home. All the flour is gone but there's so much sugar. Are they baking bread? So much bread is gone. What is everyone baking?

I baked a healthy orange cake today. Whole oranges boiled and put in a blender with almond flour, eggs, honey, salt and baking soda, that's it. Poured it in a pan and baked it. Sonny saw it and said, "You baked ANOTHER cake??"

Saw a comment today "gaining the COVID-19".

I am trying to diet, and it occurred to me that maybe now is not the time. But my underwear is getting tight and I feel like that's a bad sign. Who among us will be bikini ready this year? I try and fail every year, I suppose this year won't be any different. I wear a bikini anyway. You know what they say. "The way to get a bikini body is to put a bikini on it."

I keep accidentally playing scary movies for the kids. Maybe they will just remember being afraid of the Fratellis', One Eyed Willie and *Jumanji* when they grow up, instead of this virus.

I've gone on long enough.

I miss you very much.

Always and still here,

Sarah

March 27

Dear friend,

Day 16.

Today I ate a banana with spots on it. The banana I love is the one that just turned yellow 4-minutes ago. Before that, it is too soon and it is hard to peel, chalky and bitter. And shortly after that it gets too soft and loses that sweet, bright flavor. My mom used to roll her eyes at me when I would turn down a banana with spots or bruises. "It's perfectly fine!", she'd say. "It's too ripe. It has spots," I'd say. She'd cut the mold off of bread and use it to make sandwiches. "You're lucky you weren't around during the depression," she'd say. She'd be so proud now. I only ate it because I didn't have anything else to throw in my bag to take to my studio. If I had been home I probably would have taken a bite, made a face and placed it gently on a shelf in the refrigerator. Let it die a slow death and then blame someone else when I would eventually have to throw it away because the peel had turned a dark chocolate brown and curled at it's open end like wilted petals on a tropical flower. Surely someone in my house would not be opposed to eating an open, rejected, spotted banana with a bite taken out of it. But usually that is not the case. In my studio I ate it slowly, a couple of dissatisfied bites at a time, thinking of my mother.

I have a memory of walking with my mom in the city when I had my own apartment there with my boyfriend. She must have brought up washing dishes and for some reason I mentioned that sometimes I didn't use soap to clean something, I'd just rinse it. "Sarah!!" she gasped. "Huh….," I thought to myself. To this day anytime I rinse something in the sink without soap I think of her being alarmed at the thought. And I wonder, doesn't everyone rinse without soap sometimes? I mean if you slice an apple and then just rinse the knife and throw it in the rack, isn't it clean enough? She must have rinsed things this way sometimes. Hadn't she?

I think the COVID reality has crept into my dreams now. Has it yours? There is more distance, there are more screens.

I thought about meeting up with a friend for a walk and maybe bringing a sheet so I could just throw it over her like a net and hug her.

I went for a walk again today but had nothing to think about. Maybe the key to not thinking is searching for thoughts. Empty cupboards today.

Desmond is digging a hole to China in the backyard. Why are children so enamored with digging holes? Maybe it is just the satisfaction of controlling their environment. I feel that way about raking leaves. Maybe he is looking for a way out. Or a way in…

I think it's time to set up the deck upstairs so we can sit in the sun on cushions. Add another room to our "shelter in place." Maybe tomorrow. It's Saturday tomorrow. I'm not sure if that means anything anymore. But we'll keep pace for when regular hours resume.

I may "accidentally" run into you somewhere and throw a sheet over you. If someone does throw a sheet on you and hugs you, don't panic. It's just me.

Always and still here,

Sarah

March 28

Dear Friend,

Day 17.

Today was okay. I think it was Saturday. I did not get the deck furniture put out as I had hoped because it was a rainy day. I can't remember all that happened today because nothing much did. I did get to my studio to paint. The last two days I have been there for a couple of hours at a time, I've been painting white plates. Nothing like trying to get the shadows just right on a couple of white plates for hours after weeks in quarantine.

Oh, brother.

It's actually fine, I enjoy being there. It's a change of scenery and I love painting.

I listened to a podcast where someone was talking to a zookeeper. She talked about how it is important that they introduce new toys to the animals to stimulate their minds while they are in captivity, and how this virus has sort of put us all in captivity. How can we find new things to stimulate our minds, to keep our children curious and content? How do we create variety in a long string of days where so little changes? Or settle into the simple pattern of being still...

I ate a proper and healthy breakfast and lunch but decided we'd order in for dinner. And since cold foods are not advised, I could not get a salad. I went out to the bakery for cookies, the health food store for a few things and then to the pizza parlor to pick up our food. Coming home I washed my hands 8 times just getting everything unpacked, put on plates, put in containers, wiping down boxes and bags. Threw my jacket in the washing machine.

Being out and going into shops, I was so confused about what I was touching, which hand I used, which sleeve. Were my keys contaminated? My credit card? Wiping things off in the car with disinfectant wipes in between stores.

I think about the people who live like this all the time, because someone in their house has health issues and is always at risk. Or people who are just afraid of germs all the time and are always vigilant. It's a lot of work. It's a lot of worry.

The workers at the health food store were frazzled. The bakery shelves were sort of bare. Strange seeing the chairs and tables piled up and pushed out of the way.

Desmond made his hole deeper today. He woke up last night complaining of his hands hurting from digging.

Tonight, I plugged in the party disco light that came in the mail and the boys danced around. I went into the kitchen to sneak cookies and Joseph sulked. He had a long day.

Got to video chat with some family which was nice and also strange. They are all far away. The video worked and then didn't.

Looks like rain for few days. Rain really shrinks our options for activities. Maybe a walk in our raincoats. ("What are we SAVAGES?", my brain screeches....) Too bad I was not a Waldorf kid. I can try.

Hope you're enjoying your weekend. Do people still do weekends?

Always and still here,

Sarah

March 29

Dear Friend,

Day 18.

For a while now I've been having trouble remembering my dreams. I wake up from a dream, know I was dreaming and can't for the life of me remember what was happening. It's so strange, and frustrating. It's like trying to remember a word or name that is on the tip of your tongue.

I sit in the evening to write these letters and I have the same feeling trying to remember my day. I did just have a day... what happened?

Oh, I finished sewing some cloth masks to wear when I go shopping, I guess. I made some for the boys too. I don't know if they'll wear them but they will be mad if they don't have one to reject. And of course, one for Joseph.

Most memorable today, I went out to buy food at the supermarket. I got tired of trying to do the online shopping, pick up thing. It was sucking my time and my life force. So I just went and did it. Actually, there is no "just go and do it" anymore. I wore things I wouldn't mind throwing right in the wash when I got home, not my cozy sweater I want to wear all day and such. I put one of my new masks in my pocket. I lifted the shopping bags off the front porch with two fingers and put them in the trunk. Touching the trunk door with one hand, not the hand that touched the bags. I wiped my fingers on a disinfectant wipe in the car.

Got my mask on before I left the car. Cleaned the cart handle with spray and paper towels supplied at the market door. Although that was confusing because

I knew I'd contaminate the handle once I started shopping. And on and on.

No one wore a mask. Maybe 2 people actually, but proper N95 masks. Will we be judged by our level of mask? As if your choice to wear a mask and the type you wear reveals something about your inner character, your knowledge or ignorance, your belief or suspension of it. Either way, it made me self-conscious and I was glad I didn't wear the silver sparkly one I had made and instead had gone with the teeny tiny flower print in a muted mauve.

They only had half of what I needed (or wanted) there, so I went to a second grocery store. Adams. Where I hadn't been since the last day I was out in the world with the boys, only sensing a quarantine on the horizon but decided the next day to stay in because my throat hurt and I didn't want anyone to die on my account. 18 days ago. It's my favorite. We were going every Wednesday after Desmond's acting class to shop and eat from their hot food bar. We'd sit in the green house and watch the turtles swim. Chicken fingers, salad and cookies for the boys. Soup and salad for me.

It was so nice to be there and also strange. The food bar was closed off on one side and an employee stood on the other side, there to fill containers for you. Same at the salad bar and the bakery.

I looked at the chocolate Easter bunnies in the candy section and thought about buying two for Easter baskets. What if everyone starts hoarding bunnies? What if I can't go out again until after Easter? But what if there's a speck of virus on that bunnies ear. I started to put jellybeans from the bulk candy bin in a bag but then thought, why is this the only bulk bin that's still open? Even though ⅔ of the flavors were empty. Of course they still had buttered popcorn jelly beans. Who eats those...I abandoned the beans and the bunnies. There's time, I thought.

I went and stood in the green house and pulled my mask down to take a deep breath of the rich green air and all the negative ions. I stopped at the little spinning rack of tiny ceramic animals that Sonny asks about every time we go. Always, can he get one? Mostly, not tonight. I thought I'd bring a couple home for the boys but incredibly like everything else, it was slim pickins.

Only cats, dogs and a couple of sharks. So many empty spots where all the more exotic animals used to be.

There was more confusion getting packages in the car, getting into the car, touching, wiping, removing the mask, not knowing where to put it.

By the time I got home I was exhausted, cranky and knew I had a good ½ hour at least of cleaning the groceries once I got them inside. Dropping my sweater, scarf, mask, shoes at the door. Carrying one bag at a time, emptying, cleaning. Contaminated pile and cleaned pile. Onions rolling on the floor. "Clean".

It's such a spoiled rotten thing to be annoyed that I have to clean my groceries. But here I am. I did not wash my oranges for 20 seconds each. They sat in a bubble bath, they got individually scrubbed, 5 seconds each max. Is it enough? Who's to know.

I am hating going out. It's confusing, worrisome and time consuming. I have enough cans of beans and a dozen white eggs to color for Easter. So maybe I can stay put for a while. Dang it, I should have bought the bunnies and beans. Sigh...

Always and still here,

Sarah

March 30

Dear Friend,

Day 19.

We had a family sleepover last night. It started with the boys fighting because Sonny would not be quiet and it was driving Desmond crazy. (Sonny's got my genes.) There were tears and Desmond moving back and forth, to and from his room, so I gave them both ear plugs. Of course Sonny was so excited to have ear plugs and was yelling because he couldn't hear himself. But they settled down eventually.

Sonny woke up at 1:30 and asked me to put his ear plugs back in. And was up early talking to himself so he got up with Joseph getting ready for work. Needless to say, everyone is sleeping in their own rooms tonight.

I wanted to make a rainbow for our window today but didn't get around to it. I cleaned the house all day. I scrubbed and sprayed, vacuumed and dusted. It reminded me of when my dad got cancer and all I could think to do was clean the house. Except this time it felt more productive.

Joseph sent me a message midday that he'd be in the ICU tomorrow with the 7 COVID patients. So I started panicking. At the end of the day he said he wouldn't likely be put there until later this week or next. So I am trying to put a hold on worrying and thinking about how things should change when he does.

I took a super hot Epsom salt bath and went to bed as soon as the boys were down. I felt nauseous all day and my chest felt tight. I can't tell if I'm just nervous or if I'm getting sick or am currently sick.

Listened to Joseph talk when he got home about the situation at work and it scared me more. How the virus affects patients. The WHO scoring system for who to save first.

I don't know what else to say today. I did not eat ice cream. I took care of myself.

Always and still here,

Sarah

March 31

Dear friend,

Day 20.

Rough start to the day but you were so kind and helped lift me up. I woke up really in a bit of a panic. I wasn't sure how I was going to make it another two months like this, worrying about every surface in the house, every object and Joseph coming and going at the hospital. But the day began and unfolded on its own and off we went like dinghies rowing to shore.

One dear friend called me to see if I was okay. She loves me. I love her too. My sister called. She loves me. I love her too.

I spoke on the phone with my midwife from when I delivered Desmond. She offered to speak with me and help me sort things out. I trust her. She's not an alarmist but she is wise. When I was pregnant, I asked her what I should and shouldn't eat. She paused and then said, "Eat whatever you want. Just don't eat high fructose corn syrup." See what I mean? She gave me sound advice today too. As I spoke with her on the phone I felt her moving me through this time and space, just like a birth. She helped move me forward just by talking to me. Isn't that something? She offered to bring Joseph medicinal grade bone broth that she made tomorrow. I said yes. She loves us. I love her too.

Another friend called and was so encouraging and loving. She knew me when I was Sonny's age. I don't have my mom anymore, but I have found mother love in some women over the years. She is one. She loves me. I love her too.

I reached out to another friend, more like family. Another mother love. My mom's best friend. We spoke about doing the best we can, being in the day. She loves me. I love her too.

The boys played, they made videos, they saw their friends on the computer. I cooked and baked. We got Desmond's room ready for Joseph when he starts in the ICU. We went for a walk around the block after dinner.

I don't know how I will do this for 2 more months. Or longer. But I did it today. And I can do it tomorrow.

I really miss you. And we are all uncomfortable. We are not meant to live in captivity. We are meant to wander around Home Goods.

I hope you laughed today. I hope you cried if you felt like it. The kids saw a funny video with someone saying, "Happy Quarantine!" at the start. And they were running around saying that all day. It's a nice way to look at it.

I wish you a Happy Quarantine! And it's April Fool's Day tomorrow. Be careful out there...I mean in there...

Always and still here,

Sarah

April 2020

April 1

Dear Friend,

Day 21.

The sun was shining today after a few days in a row of rain and clouds. What a relief it was to see life in full color again.

I was in such a deep dream state when Sonny woke me up, calling for me on the monitor. It's so strange when that happens. To shift from one reality instantly to another. Feeling so disoriented and groggy.

Joseph was already gone. He is waking at 5:30 in the morning to get to work earlier than usual. He spent a few hours in the ICU today with COVID patients. When he comes home from now on, he'll come in the back door and throw his clothes in the wash, put on a robe and take a shower in the upstairs bathroom that will be just his for now. He's sleeping in a separate room. And the rest will be as we've been going along so far. Washing hands a lot, cleaning surfaces, not sharing towels, napkins, or food.

Sonny was afraid to touch him last night when Joseph went to kiss him goodnight. And Desmond cried when he saw a picture of him on the computer today. So we talked about how Daddy is doing a really special and important job. A hero's job. And so we are too.

We got outside today and went to the river to walk and feel the sun, listen to the water. There were a few cars when we got there but lots of cars in the lot when we left. We hung Sonny's jacket on a bench by the water when it got wet, to grab on our way out. When we came back that way, there was a couple sitting there. I said I was sorry and that I had to grab his jacket, they said that was okay. They were so sweet. We talked for a little bit. They said their names were Jerry and Pam. Sonny said he has a Grandma Pam but she died. He held up the tooth he found. And told them about the picture frame that mysteriously moves in our house. They were lovely. It was so nice to talk to people in person.

Such a strange moment in time where every person is experiencing the same major event. We didn't know each other but we took a minute to check in and acknowledge the difficult twist our lives have taken. How are you doing? Eh, okay, you know... how are you? Okay, hangin' in. So nice talking with you. Take care.

How much more those words mean now. Take care.

We came home and ate lunch while we watched cougars live at the Houston Zoo. Did you know cougars are mountain lions? I didn't realize that. Or I forgot. I am never sure if I am learning or relearning something. I guess it doesn't really matter.

We are down to our last roll of toilet paper. We've had this subscription for recycled toilet paper for a while now. They were supposed to ship our box of 30 rolls on the 28th but today is the 1st and they haven't shipped yet. Guess we'll have to hunt some down, or see if a neighbor can spot us some that we'll replace when our ship comes in.

We ran out of eggs today too. When did I go shopping? I can't remember.

It occurred to me today that not only can I not figure out how to shop for two weeks worth of food that we normally eat, but I don't know how to shop for 2 weeks worth of food in this new world where I also have to prepare every meal every day. Dinners AND baking. That's so much food.

Joseph grabbed some groceries on the way home. Had to hit two stores to get all of the 10 or so things we needed.

He is home now until Monday. And since he doesn't have to get up early tomorrow, we can watch more *Tiger King*. I just want to know how he ends up in prison. Don't tell me.

Always and still here,

Sarah

April 2

Dear Friend,

Day 22.

Another day in the books. Another day closer to freedom. I don't know when freedom will come but I imagine it will come eventually. What is the first thing you'll do when we have the okay to resume life as we knew it? Or will it be gradual? Will we go back to restaurants but with less tables and more distance? Discreetly pulling our masks from our mouths to retrieve food from our forks then replacing them while we chew? What small freedom will come first?

If we did get total freedom back all at once, would we all be too nervous to do what we wanted?

Today I heard of a friend who is a Dr. and is quarantining herself from her family until this is over.

And I was told I should wear a mask in the woods.

I read an article the other day about how in China people were not allowed to leave their houses at all, not even to walk their dogs. How they separated children from parents with the virus.

I don't know what the exact right thing to do is. I don't want to die and I don't want to be responsible for anyone else dying. I've altered my life pretty drastically, pretty quickly, to try to be as safe as possible without creating too much unnecessary trauma or panic in myself or my small children. I am watching my neighbors and my community. I feel like I am stepping in line with my fellows.

We went to the woods for an hour today. There was no one else there. Then we came home.

Desmond unearthed an old brown beer bottle deep in the hole he is digging. Evans Ale from Hudson NY.

I put the deck furniture out upstairs.

I ate too many cookies. My pajamas are tight.

I am also feeling like I am failing at engaging enough with this vast cache of live internet events. I don't have any more time on my hands than I have had for the last 10 years. Getting things done seems harder for some reason. But I am constantly doing. When we used to go out, to the playground, to a friend's house, out to eat, there was time to rest then. To sit and talk and to just be. Now that is gone. I am home and there is always laundry, always stuff to put away, meals to prepare, requests to fill, fights to break up, tears to dry, noise to quiet, surfaces to disinfect, groceries to wash..

Still feels like everyone else is living a bigger more social life than I am. I just can't get around to it. I wish I could.

Sonny and I sang a song together today. And Desmond is making funny videos.

You know what it is? I feel like I am doing so much and trying so hard and some people will always think it's not enough. Including me.

Anyway, I'm gonna finish watching the *Tiger King*, which honestly is not fun, so I can start watching something more enjoyable. I think I'm just watching it out of solidarity.

Always and still here,

Sarah

April 3

Dear Friend,

Day 23.

Hey, hey. What happened today? Beats me.

Really nothing that didn't happen yesterday, or the day before...

I did get to my studio today for a few hours. That was quiet. Started a new audio book with British accents.

I'm making ice cream.

Almost had a panic attack when the ice cream maker wouldn't turn on. Then I realized it was plugged into an outlet that hasn't worked in 6 months.

TONIGHT we will finish the *Tiger King*. I thought we were done last night but there is one more episode. I am not thrilled.

The sun did not come out today.

I watched a live video from a museum about George Washington's physician. It was an actor playing the role, answering questions. Joseph and the kids wandered over to watch and then wandered away so I was watching it alone. I am looking forward to lying down tonight. That's a nice part of the day.

I hope you are feeling well and finding things to do. I wish I could do things with you.

Always and still here,

Sarah

April 4

Dear Friend,

Day 24.

When my mom got cancer, when I was 17, suddenly cancer changed from something that happened to other people, to something that happened to my person. Mental, emotional plates shifted in my cosmos. Cogs turned. I was fundamentally changed. I had the knowledge then that this is possible. When a terrible thing becomes a reality, it becomes a possibility from then on and changes how you experience life.

When my mom died from cancer, I was 21, death walked into my life and my psyche. Those plates shifted again. The cogs turned. This became a new possibility to live with, and changed my fundamental experience of life again. I then carried the knowledge that at any moment, anyone you know, including you, can die. It was my first experience with death and I learned what death meant. It was not temporary, gradual or subtle. There was no nuance. There was no presence afterward. No ghost. There was nothing. Complete absence.

This was a new world to live in. Living with this possibility is worrisome. It affects how I live, the choices I make, the company I keep, the way I love, the appreciation and gratitude I feel, the worry and fear that always has a back seat in the theater of my mind. It sits in the back eating popcorn, waving at me. Even if I don't look at it, I know it's sitting there.

This global pandemic, which until now, had not even been on my list of things to worry about, is our new reality. For me, the plates are shifting again, the cogs are turning. This is possible now. And maybe more likely to reoccur in the future. And because we are all experiencing it together, I wonder how it will change us collectively. I wonder how it will change me and how it will change my kids. Is there a before and after? I imagine there will be more for some than others. The more traumatic this event is for some as it unfolds, the more "possibilities" open in someone's mind.

There is so much to worry about in this world of ours. In this country. I worry about so much. Mostly the things that affect the health of my family and myself. Health is everything, health is paramount. Without health, there is little else.

I can go down some rabbit holes that have no end. I try to step gingerly around them. I do not want to miss this precious day that I have. I can do what I want with it. I can fill it up with love and light or I can trash it with monsters and throw gasoline over it, light a match and watch it burn.

I want to choose love and light over and over. I don't know what's coming, I never have, I never will. I only know where my feet are at this moment. And this moment is usually just fine.

I want to delight in my family. I want to admire what's beautiful. Like the pile of folded blankets in the sunlight stacked on a velvet footstool, Sonny's dimples, the swoop of Desmond's hair, Joseph's eyes, the little circles of light that fill the dining room when the sun hits the mirror ball on the stairs.

I might lose it all in a flash, or in a slow burn. But I won't be the one to light the match. And before the flames get here, I am going to do my best to savor everything that's good.

It's easier said than done some days. But I try.

I hope you find yourself admiring something beautiful today. And that your mind comes back to it again later on. That it sustains you. I hope you feel loved and safe in this moment. I hope there is something soft to touch, delicious to taste and magical to contemplate.

My heart feels open and I am teary because I love you so much. And I feel your love too.

One day at a time,

Always and still here,

Sarah

April 5

Dear Friend,

Day 25.

Yesterday was a gift. We spent a lot of time outside in our yard. I set up finger paint for the boys and a little picnic of snacks. Our big navy blue umbrella with the white fringe open on the grass to cut the glare on a long piece of bright white paper rolled down our front walk. A blanket and pillows on the lawn. Neighbors walking by, saying hello. The sun felt hot and good.

Today I was hoping to go for a walk with a friend who I did not hear from. And then almost went on a different walk with a different friend that didn't pan out either. I thought we'd sit in the sun again at home but the sun did not show up.

I wanted to go to a spot I like to walk this weekend, I wanted to go to the new rail trail to ride our bikes together. We didn't.

In a panic I rushed out of the house this morning with Sonny just to get outside, to be by the water again. But then I missed the live gym class I was hoping to do. And the tide was so high, the sky so gray and there were more people on the trail than I have ever seen before.

I ordered soups and croissants over the phone from the bakery to pick up on our way home. I grabbed some cookies from the day old dollar bin. And then ate too many of them after lunch and crashed in bed for a nap.

I knew I had to go grocery shopping today and made a deal with Joseph that I would do it if he decontaminated the food when I got home. I was anxious about it all morning.

So I got up and went food shopping. Two stores, only missed three things I needed. Maybe next time. I saw more people with masks today but not everyone wears one. I noticed people taking the social distancing more seriously. Giving each other a wide berth. Red tape X's on the floor for the check out line so you know where to stand.

Came home to a delicious dinner that Joseph managed to put together even though I thought we had no food. Tofu, a bean casserole with fried eggs on top with zucchini slices and roasted beets.

Our neighbor dropped off a cheese cake she made.

Desmond was still in an aerial yoga hammock that a friend gave us yesterday. He was doing a "work out" in it when I left. He said he took a 10 minute nap in there today too.

Turns out I stayed up too late last night because Sonny got up too early. Always a roll of the dice.

I am feeling antsy, tired, frustrated and claustrophobic. My usual cabin fever with a dose of apocalypse.

This is really intense.

Funny how the small differences in my day make a bigger difference now. I feel my world shrinking and if feels like I am shrinking with it.

I guess I can look at it like we are contracting before expanding. Feels like I am curled into a tight ball. I hope my life can expand again as big as it was before.

How was your weekend? What have you been up to? I do hope you are feeling well.

Always and still here,

Sarah

April 6

Dear Friend,

Day 26.

26 days! Look at us...

Today was a good day. The sun was out and we were outside to enjoy it. I rolled out the paper again in the front yard, emptied packs of markers into a bowl and opened a package of plastic dinosaurs from a friend. We traced their shadows and colored for a bit. Then the boys took the dinosaurs to the hole in the backyard. I gave in and turned on the hose so they could fill the smaller of the two holes with water for the dinos to drink and swim.

I went upstairs to sit on the deck where I could watch them and have a few minutes to myself. But as soon as I announced myself from up high, they clambered out of the hole and into the house to come join me. They came with their snacks and Desmond's trumpet. Desmond played some songs out over the railing, into the neighborhood and I wondered who would hear it.

Yesterday I felt terrible. Today I felt fine.

Joseph worked his first full day in the ICU today. I got just a few messages from him. Sounded like he was very busy, with just a 10 minute break in his

12 hour shift.

I cooked a lemon chicken dish in a cream sauce for dinner, while Desmond blew up a huge beach ball that looks like a watermelon and we listened to ghost stories. Sonny ate crackers and salami.

After dinner we took a walk to the ice cream parlor down the road. The benches were taped off with caution tape to prevent people from sitting. The door was propped open and there was a sign that said two people inside at a time. Yellow tape on the floor to show where to stand and sheets of plastic that made a wall in front of the counter, the length of the store. It certainly seemed appropriate and efficient but made me sad.

We ate our dessert as we walked home and I marveled at the colors of their ice cream and sprinkles, glowing in their hands. Desmond's bright green pistachio and Sonny's pink and blue cotton candy, both covered in rainbow sprinkles in golden cones. Wildly bright in the end of the day, sideways light. My clear plastic cup of coffee ice cream and cookies and cream, drab and delicious.

When we came home, the boys threw and kicked the enormous watermelon ball around the yard. The sun lit up the forsythia.

Joseph is home now, showered, in his pajamas, eating his dinner. I love him so.

Good night, good night.

Always and still here,

Sarah

April 7

Dear Friend,

Day 27.

Sitting outside on my deck, listening to the birds sing, dogs barking, a car drives by. We live in a little town with houses close together. I can hear my neighbors' doors open and close, kids' voices, motorcycles in the distance. I think I smell a BBQ.

The kids are downstairs, watching the last of a Peter Rabbit movie. Sonny is just up from a nap and they'll go outside again and kick their big watermelon ball around soon I guess.

We went out this morning to our walking spot. We were so happy to see our friend's car in the lot. So good to see people we miss so much, to see they are well and happy. Such a treat. We kept our distance but I felt comforted just being near them. Near enough.

It feels like magic to be outside. Winter seems to be gone. The world is getting greener and greener. The smell of fresh air in the house is one of my favorites.

Joseph is in the ICU again today. I got a note from him that he has his own patient today. Last night he was worried that next week they'd expect him to have his own patient, instead of working beside another ICU nurse. He said he would not be ready by next week. But he sounded like he is okay today. Taking it in stride. It's an extraordinary amount of work expected of them. So much to know and to manage. With so much on the line. Now more than ever. I don't know how he does it, honestly.

Feeling very much like life is like the movie *Groundhog Day*. Every day I get to do the same day in a different way, with different results. Every day resets. Did I write that already? I may have. I can't remember. I think I just mentioned it to someone. But how true. Today I heard Cuomo say it on the radio and thought, hey, that's my line. But it's exactly right and all of us are having the same experience of repeating our days with very little variation.

I am so grateful to be in a happy and safe home. It's not a bad day to be stuck in for a while.

There's not much to say.

I haven't practiced my cello all week. Maybe today.

I bought some steak to cook for dinner. I was reminded when I bought it why I never buy steak. So intense looking. Dead body parts. I'm a little scared to open it. I don't know why we can't have cake for dinner. If it really were Groundhog's Day, I would totally eat cake for dinner. I would use a cake as my pillow.

Thinking of you and wondering what you're up to. I hope I remember to look at the super moon tonight.

Always and still here,

Sarah

April 8

Dear Friend,

Day 28.

It's only 8:20 but I can go to bed now, so I will. Of course I'll be watching "TV" until 11:00 or so, but I'll be lying down which is really all that matters.

Today was almost the same as yesterday.

I still love you.

Always and still here,

Sarah

April 9

Dear Friend,

Day 29.

Tomorrow will be 30 days. We should probably bake a cake or something. Hardy har.

I had another walk planned with a friend this morning, but it rained. I think that's the 5th or 6th time I've had a walk planned with someone and it's fallen through. I have not walked with a friend at all, except for the one time I bumped into a friend, but we weren't really walking. We just sat on some rocks and talked for a little bit.

I went grocery shopping today and my heart leapt when I heard someone say my name. I looked up to see a good friend, wearing a mask, 8 feet away, behind her shopping cart. I gasped and we both started to cry. We stood at a distance looking at each other, crying. And then talked through our masks for a few minutes. I think we both felt such frustration with it all. To be so isolated and to finally see a friend but having to keep a distance. Something about only being able to see her eyes too and knowing she could only see mine.

We've bumped into each other in the same store before. Always with big smiles and hugs. This time not allowed to get close. Our smiles hidden. I was scared to touch my eyes to wipe at my own tears.

I am angry this week. I am angry at every suggestion. Every great idea. No. No to everything. I scroll my newsfeed and want to comment on every post. Nope. Nope. Nope. I can't even finish reading anything.

Tonight, Desmond was too afraid to brush his teeth alone because of his dark playroom beside the bathroom. Joseph was aggravated. I've had a splitting headache all afternoon. I sat with Desmond while he brushed his teeth. Then talked with Joseph about how Desmond has not been anywhere besides our house and our one walking trail in 29 days. How he is scared to go anywhere. He hears the news, he hears us talking. Of course he's scared of the dark.

And of course Joseph is aggravated. Not only is he showing up for work at the hospital to treat patients with this deadly virus, he is suddenly an ICU nurse. After one 12-hour day on the floor shadowing an ICU nurse, with just a 10-minute break on Monday, was given his own patient Tuesday and Wednesday. He's exhausted. His job in the recovery room that he has had for the last 9 years, is not the job he has now. His weekly schedule he's had for years is done now. He will be given a new schedule and it will likely include nights.Monday, they said he would have to work nights, Tuesday they said he would not, today they said he will. But nights will not happen for a few weeks. In the meantime, we'll be hoping that something changes.

And what then? He is already not sleeping well. I worry that his immune system will be too taxed.

We are moving through it all day by day.

Every day there are choices to make. Suddenly the mundane choices and the big choices seem like life and death.

Do I put fresh cilantro on my dinner? Isn't Joseph risking enough already? Do I have to wash this apple again? Can I leave my mask in the car or should I bring it inside and wash it? Should Desmond go for a bike ride around the block with a friend? Can I take Ibuprofen for my headache?

I cannot even write some of the fears I have. The words have too much energy.

I feel like I've said too much already.

I don't know what this letter is for. I wanted to keep a record of our days. And I wanted to share them with you. To bring you closer to me. These are our days.

They are simultaneously full and empty. They are sped up and then stretched out too long. They are busy and boring. They are a mixed bag of big and little terrors and delights. Like life usually is but it feels as though right now we are just sitting with them all in the same room, on our laps, in our hair, falling to the floor. We just kick them out of our path on our way to make a cup of tea, but there they sit. And they all pile up, don't they?

I keep opening the windows, to air out the house and the day. To let some of it out. Trying to make space.

I really look forward to seeing you again. Three feet away, after I hug you.

Always and still here,

Sarah

April 11

Dear Friend,

Day 31.

I did not write last night because I was busy highlighting my hair and watching the rest of *Unorthodox*. If you haven't watched it, it's a great palette cleanser after the *Tiger King*. If you still haven't watched *Tiger King*, good for you.

Tomorrow is Easter. Every year we go to My Great Uncle Joe's house on Long Island, in Franklin Square. My mom's family gets together and Uncle Joe makes a treasure hunt, an egg hunt and we play our annual game of wiffle ball. We spend the weekend on Long Island with my almost family. If we're lucky, Passover lands on the same weekend and we get to celebrate Passover too. We see so many people we love. And eat so much food. I am sad to miss it this year. But my family has agreed to celebrate Easter when the quarantine is over. This summer, I hope.

So tomorrow we get to make up our own Easter at home. Of course there will be Easter baskets for the kids. Luckily, I had picked up some goodies before this all began. I did finally get some chocolate bunnies at Adams this week. I overheard the women working behind the chocolate counter talking about how much they hated *Tiger King*. I bought an extra bunny for my friend Linda who lives around the block and left it on her doorstep.

I made some milk and honey bun dough today and it's in the fridge. Tomorrow I'll bake buns that may or may not look like bunnies. I may even make deviled eggs that look like chicks. I thought I'd make a bunny cake. I can't decide. And I pulled an old recipe from my recipe box for a 70's sort of salad. A recipe from my Long Island almost family's friend, Sybil. So it is called Sybil Salad. It's layers of salad vegetables and has hard boiled eggs, bacon, and mayonnaise mixed with sugar on top like icing on a cake.

You'd love it.

I have already been informed that Joseph did not buy me any Easter treats. That's okay. We can just break his Easter bunny in half, like a wishbone. Good thing it is solid chocolate.

Today I felt a little bit like a tightrope walker. I thought it was Thursday, then I thought it was Friday, then I realized it was Saturday and that I would not get to do the things I wanted to do last weekend, again.

I signed up for a 7-minute workout program and then could not for the life of me access any 7-minute workouts. It took me an hour, while I listened to the Easter fire truck drive around my neighborhood with its siren blaring.

Is rage a symptom of the virus?

I needed to leave the house, desperately. We all went for a walk in the woods at a trail we have not been to before. It was an old rock quarry and a gorge. It was boring. I hate everything.

Desmond and I ordered burgers from the diner and brought them home for dinner. That was really good. A cheeseburger with sweet potato fries.

After dinner I left the house alone. I went to the supermarket in town to get mayonnaise for our Sybil salad. No luck. I suppose I'll make mayonnaise tomorrow. There's a first time for everything.

Then I headed to the river where we usually walk and I look for crystals. And that was where I needed to be. The river calms me right down. The sound of the water. The way it smells, the trees, it's so quiet and so peaceful.

There were little boats on the river today, the first of the season that I've seen.

I wish I had a boat.

And no one was there. I found little crystals and watched the sky grow darker and the water turn bluer, the tide slowly moving out. And dusk came and all the contrast in the light of day disappeared and flattened out. And darkness started to fall into the nooks and crevasses. When it was dark enough, I took out my phone and tried my flashlight on the rocks and wouldn't you know, a whole new way to look for crystals appeared. The little bright light running over the rocks lit up each tiny facet.

Until a voice in my head said, "Go now! It is dark!" And that voice was right. I walked on the dark trail, imagining terrible things. I scrambled up our steep shortcut hill in record time and came home.

It's late already now. And I have Easter baskets to put together. I told Desmond I have to put on my Easter Bunny head to put these baskets together. He thought I had a real bunny head and got upset that I wouldn't show it to him. Finally, I confessed that it is invisible, but I envision it when I make Easter baskets. He asked if he could have one too. I told him he has to make an Easter basket for someone. He said he would. And as he walked in the woods today, he created his imaginary bunny head. I watched him do it. He's magic.

If you're wearing your bunny head tonight, I salute you. Have a happy Easter tomorrow. I hope you find the golden egg and that someone lets you break the ears off of their chocolate bunny. Or just do it when they're not looking. I won't tell.

Always and still here,

Sarah

April 12

Dear Friend,

Day 32.

So strange to be home today for Easter but we made the best of it.

The boys were happy to wake up to their Easter baskets full of goodies and started their day with candy, as all Easter days should begin.

I spent the day in the kitchen cooking and baking and that was okay. I didn't really feel like it was exactly what I wanted to be doing but I really didn't have anything better to do, or anywhere else to go. I got all the things made that I had in mind. Things I thought would make the day feel special. And they did, it was nice.

I made milk and honey buns shaped like bunnies, deviled eggs that looked like chicks, a very fattening salad and a sugary frosted bunny shaped cake for dessert. And we ordered pizza because it seemed like the right thing to do. I ate too much and was so full.

We put on the movie *Hop* for the kids and Joseph and I fell asleep. Woke up in time to catch some friends on Zoom and then some family as well, right before the boys went up to bed.

Not too much time to worry today. Just a little.

I am glad it's time for bed. Tomorrow is supposed to be a rainy day and I hear a very windy one to boot.

Batten down the hatches. Stay home I guess? Ha ha. Sure.

Always and still here,

Sarah

April 13

Dear Friend,

Day 33.

Today was warm, rainy and windy, just as we suspected. The wind whistled and it blew so many pink petals off of our cherry trees which reminded me of the same thing happening last year. I feel like we get a lot more windy days than we used to.

That's funny, that sounds like something an old lady would say. Well.

Today Sonny asked if it was still Easter and was sad when I told him no, it is the day after Easter now. But we still have our Easter decorations, chocolate bunnies, food and bunny cake. So it may as well be.

Last night at about 7:45, he ran into the room where Joseph and I were sitting and said, "Mama, is it still Easter?" And I said, "Yes," and his face lit up. "Great!," he said and ran out of the room.

I made the kids finish eating the cake tonight. After I ate enough of it to make my teeth hurt and want to take a nap.

I was thinking about how I write a lot about the food we're eating. And I think it's because it's one of the few things that changes day to day. I wish we had more pizza left. That was so good.

Last night I spent most of my TV time, show shopping. Trying to find something to watch. Somehow I ended up watching *Cagney and Lacey*. Of course I have heard of *Cagney and Lacey* but I didn't realize they were women. I had a vague idea that they were detectives. Anyway, that was sort of a weird hole I fell into but not an unpleasant one. I could not stay awake though to finish an episode, so I'll try again tonight.

I played the cello today after a string of days not playing. Maybe a week and half. I am just as bad as I was before. I'll try to be better about playing it daily. I do wish I had gotten a few lessons in before this all happened. I hope I'm not doing it all wrong.

I got to my studio today. Got a few successful hours in. Listening to Stephen King's *The Outsider*. Exactly like the show.

I wondered what Stephen King thinks about the virus. And David Sedaris. I wish I could call them on the phone. I'll have to do a search, see if they've said anything about it. I hope King writes a book that takes place during quarantine. It's just right. It's chock full of potential stories. It feels like we're in a book, doesn't it? More and more all the time. Maybe because it seems so far-fetched. But here we are.

I can't believe it has been 33 days and I wonder how much longer this will go on. It's so strange.

I wonder what tomorrow's version of the day will be. Oh man.

Always and still here,

(Although I'd really like to go someplace else. Just for a little while.)

Sarah

April 15

Dear Friend,

Day something or other.

I sit here, breathless after yelling at my 4 year old to go to sleep an hour after I put him to bed. The volume on my laptop up as loud as it will go, playing classical music on YouTube in another window.... so an otherwise unremarkable day, just ended badly.

If this was Groundhog's Day, tomorrow I wouldn't ask Desmond to unload the dishwasher because I'd know the dishes were dirty. And I wouldn't have to take the dirty dishes out of the cabinets and sink to put back into the dishwasher.

I wouldn't try to teach Desmond to do a headstand because he may have broken his fingertip.

I wouldn't tell Desmond and Sonny that the man who is going to assemble the trampoline Pop-pop bought for them is coming, because he doesn't show up.

I wouldn't stay home all afternoon waiting for the trampoline guy to show. I would take the boys for a hike.

I wouldn't read my texts from Joseph so I wouldn't have to worry about him in the ICU alone with 2 patients all day. Or see the marks on his face from his mask.

I would take 15 minutes for myself to play the cello.

I would not read the crappy news.

And I would not yell at Sonny when he calls me back upstairs just as I finally sit down to write this.

But today was today and we'll all remember it. Desmond's pinky may still be broken tomorrow. We'll wait a second day for the trampoline man to come and I'll listen to the boys ask about it until he does. And we'll likely stay home again in case he shows. And I'll know that tomorrow Joseph will likely have 2 patients of his own again. And his face will be bruised again at the end of the day. And Sonny will know I yelled at him the night before.

For now, I will sit and breathe. And listen to this music. And cry a while. Because today was enough.

Always and still here,

Sarah

April 16

Dear Friend,

Day 36.

Today was a much better day.

I am glad I get to wake up with Sonny in the morning. Even though he wakes me up and I'd rather sleep in, it is fun to get up with a 4 year old. I don't always realize I like it. But when I sit and think about it, I feel lucky. He is such a character. I do appreciate his fourness.

This morning the boys and I geared up and went to CVS to get Desmond a splint for his injured finger. They have not been anywhere besides the woods for 36 days, so it felt like a big deal. I was worried I might get yelled at by shoppers in the store. But I also worry that if they don't go into a store for 18 months, after 18 months, they'll be broken. I did give them the option of staying in the car, but they wanted to come. So they wore their masks and I told them not to touch anything. We got a splint, a Frisbee and a set of bubble wands with bubble juice. Success.

Desmond was very pleased with his splint and felt better right away.

Just being in the car with them, out of the house, out of the yard, going Somewhere, felt like relief. I didn't want to go home so soon when we were done at CVS but there was nowhere to go.

After Sonny's nap we met some friends for a walk in the woods along a stream in Woodstock.

I won't tell you that my friend and I did not last 5 seconds without agreeing that we should throw caution to the wind and just hug each other, tightly, with tears. I suppose you might frown on that sort of thing.

It would be so nice to take an hour break from all the rules after 36 days and be near a friend and let your children be close to their friends and touch each other, to help one another out of the mud, or to even play tag. That would be such a gift and so healing for everyone involved. And the freedom and connection and love in that hour could outweigh the worry and risk of that touch.

I think so. I'm not saying that happened. I'm just saying, I think that hour would be tremendous and like a balm.

And I feel better today.

After dinner, while I ate a warm blondie I baked yesterday with some almond ice cream I made, I watched a video of a very happy man talking about how "something good will come of this." He said it over and over. And I smiled with him.

And then we went outside for awhile and drew on the sidewalk with colored chalk. I watched Sonny as he drew a beautiful abstract line drawing in the street.

I got the boys to bed. Joseph came home. He fell asleep in an armchair while I was showing him videos of Sonny drawing outside with chalk, wind chimes in the background. And then went up to bed.

So here I am with you. I liked this day alright. I made a point to focus on what might lift me up.

I hope you found something today that helped lift you up or maybe you will tomorrow.

I like this part of the day. I wish you a restful sleep and dreams without rules, limits or fear.

Always and still here,

Sarah

April 17

Dear Friend,

Day 37.

Up with Sonny this morning, digging through the Lego bag trying to recreate a "battle droid" he'd been carrying around all week. No matter how many times I encourage the boys to leave the Legos at home or in the car, they never subscribe to this idea. "They are so tiny, they will get lost..." I plead. "No, they won't," they say. And of course they do. Not always, but sometimes.

Yesterday on our walk with friends, Sonny put his Lego battle droid on a very small blanket I was sitting on, unbeknownst to me, and when we were leaving, I picked up the blanket and off we went. When we got home, he asked me where his droid was. I said I did not know and asked him where it was. He said he put it on my blanket. Le sigh.

There were tears and encouraging words suggesting we could build another. And if that didn't work, maybe we'd drive back to Woodstock in the morning and see if we couldn't find it. Because I do love finding lost things.

We found a lot of droid pieces in our collection, but half of them broken and in the end, not enough parts to build a whole fellow.

Joseph and Desmond wanted to stay home, so off Sonny and I went for a drive. We walked onto the field where the boys had been running and I had sat with my friend in the grass. We looked around for a minute or two and then I told Sonny what we needed to do was close our eyes, put out our hands and ask Grandma Pam, Grandpa Bob and the Universe to help guide us and see if we felt a pull in a certain direction. "Let's hold hands," he said. So we did. And then he looked around and I felt a pull forward and forward some more and there was his droid. We were so happy.

Then, even though I could not get in touch with his pottery teacher, we drove to Mt. Tremper to see if his pottery pieces were still outside where she had said they would be available to pick up for a week, even though that was 12 days ago. And they were indeed there and that made us happy too.

While we drove we listened to a ghost story podcast and chewed bubble gum, like we love to do in the car.

We stopped at Sunflower to buy some milk and he got his small bag of cheesy popcorn he used to get when we'd stop there after pottery class. We wore our masks and I wiped his bag down with a disinfectant wipe before I gave it to him.

Now when we go out, everyone is wearing a mask. Cuomo announced this week that we should all be wearing masks in public when we can't keep the 6' of distance.

When we stood in line to pay, standing on the piece of tape on the floor that marks the proper distance, Sonny reminisced about the time we were in the same store and a man he did not know gave him a high five. Now everyone's face was covered and he held onto my leg.

I wanted to cry and took a moment to think about why. Why is it so sad? Seems obvious I guess but at the same time, not really. Everyone seemed jovial enough, looked healthy, everything was normal, except for the masks, and the distance. It's sad because it's dangerous to be there, in the health food store.

All of a sudden. Besides the old hat dangers, fears and anxiety about being out and about, like being shot, attacked by a strange man, or breathing in chem trails, now there is a deadly invisible virus. What a world...

I can't seem to find organic salted butter or organic shredded mozzarella cheese.

Everyone's home baking and making pizzas.

The trampoline installer was a no show, no call, and fired apparently. The new guy assigned to our case couldn't come until the 27th, which is 10 days away. No way was I going to make it 10 days of listening to Desmond pine for his trampoline. He called the company 5 times over the last two days, besides my

3 phone calls, trying to get it taken care of. He was very polite for a 10 year old in quarantine for 36 days, waiting for a dream to come true. The lamenting was more than I could bear. So I told him to start unpacking the boxes. He, Joseph and I managed to get it put together. The boys bounced and bounced.

I finally headed out to my studio to get some painting done. And then to Hannaford to finish the grocery shopping. When I came home, they were bouncing again and bounced until it was dark.

All in all, it was a good day. It was good to get out, find something lost, collect some-thing we had been waiting for, replenish our food supply, build an amazing bouncing contraption, spend time with my guys and paint a cake topping.

I think there's still time for a very hot bath. Tomorrow I get to sleep in so I can stay up late and watch TV...

If you had told the 13 year old me that I would have a small, flat, wireless, antennaeless, color TV that I could take to bed with me and have access to hundreds of thousands of shows and movies without commercials, I'd have peed my pants.

I'd still trade it in for a time machine though.

Always and still here,

Sarah

April 18

Dear Friend,

Day 38.

I got to sleep in today, so good to sleep and wake up when I'm ready. And then hide in bed as long as I can, until they trickle in to find me.

It snowed a little last night and it was cold this morning. Joseph told the boys they can't jump on the trampoline because it's too cold and it will break. I looked it up on the website and it says it's fine to jump in the winter and snow. So out they went with towels to dry it off. They love it so much. It's fun to watch them bounce.

Got to my studio again today. Some animals were running around in the ceiling, squirrels I guess. They were so noisy and I was worried that they were going to push the air vent out of the way and tumble into the room. I was so distracted listening to them.

I tried to make a video to show you but it ended in delirium. I couldn't tell if it was funny or worrisome. And after a while they seemed to settle down and I went back to painting.

I reworked a piece of the painting I had started the other day. Changing the colors and wondering what I was doing and why I was spending so much time on this little section again. But when I stood up and looked back at the painting, I was so excited to see I had created a fold of frosting with a shadow and light reflected back on itself. I was sort of stunned. And delighted.

I came home to soup that Joseph made and the boys still jumping on the trampoline.

Tonight, I sewed more masks to send to my sister in Florida. I don't have any elastic but thought I'd sew the fabric part and send them her way. Maybe she can find some or use some string or something or other.

Joseph went up to bed shortly after the boys. He is back to work tomorrow already. His old Monday, Tuesday, Wednesday schedule is out the window. Our days are changing and I won't know what day it is for a while, I suppose. Besides looking at the calendar, there are not a lot of ways to recognize the days of the week anymore.

He is tired already. I hope his day is not too challenging tomorrow. But I guess it's sort of a given that it will be.

I don't think I'll get the boys out of the house. I think they'll be stuck on the trampoline. I'll have to come up with some things to do. Besides baking.

It's supposed to be warm and sunny. Maybe I'll get a turn to jump for a bit. I'll try not to hurt myself. I am tempted to go jump on it now, in the dark.

I don't think I will. But sometimes I surprise myself.

Always and still here,

Sarah

April 19

Dear Friend,

Day 39.

It was a warmer day today and the sun was shining. The boys played inside this morning and I have no idea what I did. Laundry…dishes…sprayed surfaces and handles with disinfectant…fed the kids…had tea…

I got to do an exercise class on zoom with a favorite gym instructor and friend. That was nice. I won't burn enough calories to cover the calories I'm taking in but I can at least attempt to make a dent.

While I made lunch the boys went outside to jump on the trampoline. Sonny twisted his ankle and couldn't walk. So I brought him a bagel with cheese and told him to eat on the trampoline and rest. He felt a little better after his bagel and some apple slices. He walked inside but then wouldn't walk upstairs for a nap. I carried him up and he slept for an hour or so.

While he was sleeping, a friend stopped by to drop off a prize I won for a nature photography contest in a Facebook group. Such a treat and so nice to see her and talk and laugh. A candle, a balm and a face mask.

When Sonny woke up he was complaining so much so I put on a movie for him and had him rest on the couch. That seemed to help. I brought him an ace bandage and said I could wrap his ankle. He said he would do it.

Another friend stopped by to pick up a toolbox that he had left at our house. He stood at the bottom of my front stoop with a mask on and I sat on my porch and we talked a while. We talked about the virus, the government, politicians, movies, families, allergies. The kids, who love this friend and are always climbing all over him, said hello and then scattered. Sonny went back to his movie and Desmond was busy talking to his friend on my laptop.

After he left, Sonny said he had wrapped his ankle with the bandage and then took it off and it fixed his ankle "good as new."

I lost two of my 5 quarantine pounds and then this morning discovered I had gained 3. I celebrated by eating pizza and cookies for dinner.

The kids wanted to order a pizza. I placed the order and we walked to town to pick it up. I pulled Sonny's old stroller out of the shed so he wouldn't have to walk with his hurt ankle. After the pizza parlor I stopped in the bakery and bought some treats. Because it was open and we were passing by...cookies, banana bread for Joseph for work tomorrow, cupcakes in the day-old dollar bin, and a blueberry muffin for Sonny. Our sweet friend who works there would not let me pay. Such a nice gesture. Three friends in one day AND a prize and free cookies? Unusual Sunday in the days of quarantine.

We came home and ate the pizza at the table in the backyard, and the kids jumped some more.

The kids had a bubble bath and I put some of these light up flashing plastic toys in the tub that we had not put in the tub before. The lights in these things are so bright, they hurt my eyes. But the kids aren't bothered by them. They make me nervous.

When I let the water down, the tub was coated with tiny black dots. I could not for the life of me figure out what it was but now as I sit here thinking about it, I think they were burnt bubbles. I think it was the lights burning the soap. Can that be? Put those toys right in the donation bag after the bath. I should just put them in the garbage.

I was afraid that our water had been poisoned as I scrubbed the tub. It was like sticky soot.

Once, shortly after I had given birth to Sonny, I was nursing and using nursing pads. They are like little cloth pancakes you put in your bra in case you leak milk. One day I took my bra off at night and the pad fell on the floor and I thought my boob had fallen off. And I was not terribly alarmed. I thought, "Oh man, now I have to clean that up." My body was doing this series of unbelievable, outrageous, reality bending things. So the thought that a part of my body had fallen off felt like a probable possibility.

That's what the tub was like. The thought, "Oh, now the water is poisoned," was not far from my new reality. When all sorts of attack feel possible. Maybe probable. In this sci-fi story line we seem to have slipped into. Good Lord.

Well, I hope I didn't damage my children with those laser toys. They seem okay.

I turned the calendar page tonight to get ready for Monday. Totally blank pages for the week. Made me laugh. Meh.

Always and still here,

Sarah

April 21

Dear Friend,

Day 41.

Sorry I didn't write yesterday. My day ended with no room to spare.

It was a full day, just busy around the house, the usual stuff.

I highlighted my hair a week or so ago and it was too light, so I lowlighted it yesterday and now it's too dark. C'est la vie.

I trimmed it again. I thought I should make a video about how to cut your own hair. I have an impulse to make a video about everything now. I just want you here with me, or to be there with you.

I have never seen myself so much on video in my life with all of the facetiming and zoom chat rooms. And I am thoroughly surprised by how old I look every time. Which has made me think of my mom. She was just 48 when she died and I am 45 now. And I think of how she looked, how she had aged. Am I that old already? I am. I am that old now. I am close to the age she was when she died. I look a lot like her. And what will I look like when I am older than she got to be? Will I think of her then as very young? How I wish she were here so I could talk with her about it. All of it. Aging is so strange and it scares me. It makes me feel like I am running out of time, and losing myself.

I decided yesterday to take the time to play a board game with the boys. I remember loving Yahtzee so I took that out, but I couldn't remember how to play and I couldn't get my brain to understand the instructions, nor did I have the patience to concentrate long enough to read them all the way through. I thought the boys would get upset if it took too long so I abandoned that idea. We played Clue Junior instead, which was torture. I could only roll yellow over and over and had all the yellow clues already. We played out in the front yard on a blanket. I brought out a bag of pistachios but they turned out to be unsalted. Much to our dismay.

I felt like I was doing a good thing. But Desmond was a stickler for the rules, Sonny had no regard for them and I was doing my best to cheat so the game would end. I was glad when it was over. I curled up on the blanket and fell asleep for a few minutes, waking to Sonny crying on the trampoline. So many bumps and bruises these days.

I thought about the people walking by our yard, walking their dogs, seeing me curled up asleep in a pile of Clue Junior pieces.

I cooked chicken, noodles and heated up leftover pizza. Put out veggies and salad dressing and hummus for dipping. The usual fare. It takes me an hour to cook dinner and 5 minutes to eat it.

After dinner we went for a ride to the river to walk in the woods and be by the water. We collected things to make mandalas at home and when we returned, we made them on the front walk, racing the setting sun.

Sonny has discovered *Scooby-Doo*, but it's a newer version. Very similar to the old one but slightly updated. It's pretty good, very spooky, never a real ghost or monster. I was always so disappointed when I was a kid that it was always someone in a costume. Real ghosts are so much more fun.

There were arguments, negotiations and tears about who's turn it was to sleep in my room. When they were finally up to bed, I sat down to pay the bills.

Joseph came home, frustrated and exhausted. Not wanting to return today but he promised his patient he'd be back. He's got a heart of gold, that one.

Today is a rainy day, not much going on. It's a little after 3:00 but it feels much later. It's dark out. Waiting on a thunderstorm. Hoping to get to the post office to mail my sister some masks I sewed for her. It would be a nice walk, if we don't get hit by lightning.

Always and still here,

Sarah

April 22

Dear Friend,

Day 42.

Joseph is home today after a long week of work and will be home for 11 days. He had put in for vacation time months ago. This week we were supposed to fly to South Carolina for a week's vacation, visiting family we haven't seen in a long time. Then we were going to drive down to Florida to see more family and fly home from there. When talk of the virus was new, I suspected it might not be a good idea to buy tickets because if we did fly, we might get stuck quarantining somewhere, or our flights might be canceled. I did not yet know we'd be sheltering in place this whole time.

It's the first year in a long time we won't be going to Florida. We make a yearly pilgrimage to visit the Dads, mine and Joseph's and my sister and her girls. I wonder if we could go this summer or perhaps in the fall. Maybe if we drove it would be safer. Or maybe next year. It's hard to say.

I did not make it to the post office yesterday, or today. Which is usually how I am with the post office. It's two blocks away. My trips there are eventual.

We made mandalas out of food in the house yesterday. I am trying to make a mandala every day this week. I have yet to make one today. Yesterday we used snacks, cereal, beans, nuts, lentils, popping corn and a few radishes. The kids really enjoyed making them. And then eating them. They did not eat the radishes.

I ate well yesterday as I do most days, but it all falls apart after dinner. I ate handfuls of chocolate chips, trying to replenish my reserve of calm. Chocolate is supposedly an irritant. But that's bad science.

After I got the kids to bed, which took an hour and a half, I sat down and watched a movie on the couch. The new *Ghostbusters* movie with the women. I have wanted to see it for so long. It was so fun. I loved it. Have you seen it? It was long and I got to bed late.

Up with the kids this morning so Joseph could sleep in.

Sonny was so angry with me after he watched his two episodes of *Scooby-Doo*. He sobbed and yelled at me for a long time. How he hated me and he's not my little boy anymore.

So I took a paint sample book and my laptop and the phone out onto the back stoop in my robe and slippers, and watched snow flurries fall. I picked out colors of paint I needed for this town butterfly project I am supposed to be working on, and called Home Depot to order them. I don't know how I will get this butterfly done in the next few weeks. But I guess I'll figure it out. I waited so long to buy paint because I didn't want to go to Home Depot.

Joseph got up, probably because of all the crying. Sonny apologized and I headed out to two grocery stores and Home Depot. All in all, it took me two hours, not including the time to unpack and wash all of the groceries when I got home. I did not have my antibacterial wipes in my car, which made everything much harder. I was so hungry and bought a snack and then realized I couldn't eat it because I couldn't use my hands. I carefully pulled a plastic fork from my glove compartment so I could scratch my face with its handle end.

So ridiculous.

When that was done, I took a nap and slept for three hours. I dreamt I was with friends, meeting new people, shaking hands.

And here I am now, writing to you. Listening to Joseph put dinner on the table for the boys. Too late for the post office.

I am going to set my alarm for 4:00 tonight so I can get up and see if I see the meteor shower. Hoping the sky will be clear.

I have a mandala to make today. I bought chili from Mother Earth to have for dinner. I will try not to eat chocolate chips. Maybe I can sand the butterfly wings tonight and get it ready for paint.

I hear May 15th is a projected day for opening some things back up. That's Joseph's birthday. I wonder if they will and I wonder what exactly that means.

I asked Joseph what his favorite cake flavor is and he said lemon. I've been with him for 17 years and I've never seen him eat lemon cake. Who knew.

I hope you are doing well. I've been meaning to call you, but I am always so busy with the kids and chores, it never feels like there is time. And when there is a little time, I seem to want to be alone. Sometimes talking feels hard.

But I'm thinking of you. Wishing we were carrying on without all this worry. I am glad warmer weather is coming. And lemon cake.

Always and still here,

Sarah

April 23

Dear Friend,

Day 43.

43, 43, 43...

I set my alarm for 4:00 this morning so I could check on the meteor shower, but woke from a bad dream a little after 3:30 Sonny woke from a bad dream at the same time. I was dreaming about a rotten little boy who was going to kill an invisible dog. The boy and I found the dog at the same time, I placed an arm over it as he put his hand on it and then we could both see it, standing still, right up against a wall. I had to pin the little boy down to keep the dog safe.

Sonny dreamt I was fishing with a fishing pole upside down and when he turned it around for me so that I could fish with him, I disappeared. And he called and called for me but I was gone.

I read somewhere once that the most boring things you can talk about with someone are your health, traffic and your dreams.

After I consoled Sonny, I grabbed a coat and blanket and sat outside on the deck outside my bedroom and watched the sky. I saw 4 shooting stars in 20 minutes.

It was cold out and I could hear the train and I guess the hum of the thruway. Why such a hum at 4:00? I came back inside and climbed into bed. Then got back up to take the paint I bought off the porch because it was so cold outside.

I watched a scary movie before I went to bed. I had to check under my bed to make sure no one was there. I guess I shouldn't watch scary movies while Joseph is sleeping in another room.

I slept so late this morning. And the day was uneventful. I wrote Desmond's quarterly school report for the district. And finally sat down and went over his schoolwork. I left his math book for Joseph.

Then Desmond and I read about lemon balm in his *Herbs For Kids* book. I learned a lot and it made me wish I had some. Tomorrow we read about fennel.

I am sad I didn't start my tomato plants indoors yet. Maybe tomorrow. I feel so unmotivated to do much of anything. And overwhelmed by all that needs doing.

I don't think I'll get up again to check the stars. The sky looks cloudy now. And I'll be up early with Sonny tomorrow morning.

I did not make a mandala today, but I did get to the post office. Which was equally as weird as everywhere else. Tape on the floor to show you where to stand, plastic window guards up at the counter, everyone in masks. The woman working at the window said it's been super busy there ever since the quarantine started. Like people must be pulling things out of their closets and mailing them off. That's a strange theory. But I was glad to hear they are getting a lot of business.

I did not walk to the bakery. Even though I wanted to.

I watched the first episode of this British show called *Years and Years* today. It takes place in 2025 and Trump has been reelected and in his last 10 days of his presidency, dropped a nuclear bomb somewhere near Vietnam. Scared me so much. When impossible scary things are true and happening, that scenario feels too terrifying to think about. I wonder if I will keep watching it. I should find a good comedy to watch.

Lots of things I "should" do. But don't.

I had a flash tonight of what it would feel like to take the kids to Coney Island and the Aquarium...How wonderful that will be, when we can do things like that again. How sweet that freedom will be. I think. I get scared we won't get it back. It's hard to see from here.

But I expect we will. I will keep imagining it. Imagining the good. Calling it to me. Expect wonderful things. Big faith. Hold tight.

Always and still here,

Sarah

April 24

Dear Friend,

Day 44.

I did not leave the house today. Again.

I ordered what I could find online to become Jillian Holtzman from *Ghostbusters*.

I sanded and painted the butterfly's wings.

I made a healthy coconut cream pie.

I gave Desmond a haircut.

I continue to sweep the floor.

In some ways it was a fine day, in some ways it was not.

Nothing terrible happened.

Trump is more and more ridiculous.

Miss you.

Love you.

Always and still here,

Sarah

April 25

Dear Friend,

Day FORTY FIVE.

Honestly, I think it's strange I haven't caught this bug yet. Do you feel that way? Could I really not have come into contact with this virus at all? So many cracks it could have slipped in. And I wonder too if I had it already when this all started. I had a bad sore throat for a couple of weeks right from the get go. Maybe that was it, and that was all. Who knows.

I don't even really know anyone who has had it. I was so afraid so many people I know would get it and people I know would die of it. But that hasn't happened. Yet. But 45 days seems like a long time to wait for these things to happen. I am grateful I live in an area of NY that's not a hot spot. Our ICU is not over-run. Or even full.

I've heard of friends of friends having it. But not many. It still seems so distant to me. Though I have heard how bad it is on Long Island and in the city. How full the hospitals are, the morgues...feels far from here.

But here I am. Just having my uneventful days at home, day after day. It's okay.

I'll take that over the alternative.

Last night I had such a craving to go out for breakfast. And decided this morning I would make scrambled eggs, bacon and buttered toast. When I woke up, Joseph had made bacon and all the eggs were spoken for. So while he ran out to buy more eggs, I practiced my cello. He came back with eggs! Two dozen, just like I asked.

My breakfast was very good. But not the same as going out.

Today I also practiced dressing more like Holtzman of *Ghostbusters*. Desmond kept asking me where I was going. I kept saying, "Nowhere." I just stood outside on the front lawn, bare feet in the grass, hands on my hips, watching the birds.

I decided to cut the grass with our little push mower. I think I mowed a couple of four-leaf clovers that I didn't see until it was too late. It reminded me of accidentally vacuuming up spiders when I see them too late. I had the same feeling when it happened. Small heartbreaks.

I brought my butterfly project outside and started painting. Desmond helped and he was so proud and happy to be part of the process.

Heard our favorite ice cream shop, Alleyway, was open today, just selling pints. So we all walked to town to buy a couple and see our friend Julian, who owns and runs it. So nice to see him and say hello. He gave us the ice cream for free because Joseph is a health care worker. He's been donating ice cream to local hospitals. That was so nice. And it felt good to walk in the sun, look into the shop windows, holding Sonny's little hand. The boys and I all wore straw hats, which also felt light and jaunty.

Back at home Desmond saw some friends ride by on their bikes and he decided to get on his bike and go find them. He hasn't wanted to go out on his own at all. I was glad he was able to do that today. He wanted to wear his mask because his friends were wearing theirs. So off he went.

Joseph is struggling after his weeks working in the ICU with everything going on. I think it's a lot to process, and completely exhausting on every level. I won't say much about Joseph but for the sake of recording this strange time, I will just say it is difficult. I imagine it's a little like a soldier coming home from a battlefield. I think many of us may have a little PTSD when all is said and done.

Listening to Desmond and Sonny solve the latest *Scooby-Doo* mystery, is a highlight of my day. (It's happening right now.) I'll have to take a video of them talking about an episode. It makes me laugh every time.

I feel like there is something I am forgetting to tell you. But it's more likely that I am just wishing I had something to tell you. I often feel that way when Joseph comes home from work. Maybe it's a feeling of something good on it's way...

Always and still here,

Sarah

April 28

Dear Friend,

Day 48.

Sorry I haven't written in a few days. Been feeling a bit... crumbly. Everything is the same, the same, the same.

Was desperately sad last night after finishing the 2nd season of *Afterlife* with Ricky Gervais. Have you seen that one? He makes some really deep, emotional, lovely shows. *Derek* is another one that was just beautiful. *Afterlife* is about death and grief, and love. Just wrecked me, the last scene of the last episode at about midnight. Had to get up and pace the dark house. Looking for answers, looking for clues. I don't know what I was looking for. Ghosts. Lights. Proof. Relief. I didn't find anything, as usual.

Today the sun is out. I am dying to go do something. I have to get out of here. Joseph is trying to hook up a bike trailer to the car so we can go ride on the new rail trail. I think it may be crowded and we'll wear our masks. It doesn't sound very appealing. I don't know what else to do. It looks like this will be the only sunny day this week.

Took the kids to Adams yesterday to get a few things. But mostly to let them pick something from the bakery and visit the turtles. Sonny picked out a cupcake with a plastic dinosaur ring on top and Desmond picked out a Happy Birthday cupcake. Sonny also said he needed a watermelon and a bag of cheesy popcorn. They each picked out a little ceramic animal and we watched the turtles and koi fish swim for a while. It was so nice to be there with them and they were so glad to be there too. They watched the turtles for what felt like a long time.

I went to my studio yesterday, late in the afternoon. I don't like being there when it gets dark, but I needed to get out and wanted to paint. I've been listening to *The Shining* as an audio book. I read it in high school I guess. So long ago. What a great book. Listening to it as it got dark in my studio wasn't the best idea but really, what else was I going to do? When I leave my studio, I have to turn out all the lights and walk down the hall in the dark and out the back door, down the black iron fire escape stairs to my car. I jumped into my car like it was pouring out. And was sure someone was going to jump up out of the back seat and I would drive into a telephone pole. But that didn't happen.

I heard the birds have been singing louder because we've been quieter. I thought maybe there were more birds, but it might just be that the birds are louder. Maybe both.

More of the trees are getting their new leaves, tight and chartreuse green. My chocolate vine is growing wild around the porch like a scene in *Jumanji* and the flowers are opening. They smell so sweet. Not quite like chocolate, but sweet.

I am dreaming of the summer and of the things we want to do. The doing seems more complicated now and more baffling than usual. Sort of like traveling with a new baby if you've never done it before. How will we do all of the things...As we do them, we'll know.

Joseph is hoping to be back in the recovery room by the time he goes back to work after his vacation time is over. If the census is low in the ICU he won't have to work there, and he won't have to work nights there, more importantly. We're keeping our fingers crossed.

Hope you are feeling well today. Enjoy the sunlight and the warm day. Crack a window, slice an apple, think about your summer plans.

We should hang out.

Always and still here,

Sarah

May 2020

May 1

Dear Friend,

Day 51.

I took a too hot bath and can feel the blood pulsing in my body. Is my blood boiling? I was hoping to sweat off the handfuls of chocolate chips I ate tonight. I crave a hot bath at night, I think they keep me healthy or at the very least calm me. Something about heat. Hot tea, the warmth of the sun, a hot bath, a warm fire, a space heater, hot food...so satisfying.

I am waiting for a broadcast of a theater playing *The Turn of the Screw* online. It's coming on late, it's coming from California, I think.

I am doing my best not to check the news or my Facebook newsfeed much. It is too frightening. I would like to think this virus was a naturally occurring event, horrible and challenging as it may be. But it seems it may not be. That scares the b'jesus out of me. There's a chain of nightmares that come with that possibility, including nightmares in wait.

I just want it to fade and go away. I want to be able to go back to our lives. I'm scared we won't. All the news feels like doomsday. All the speculation is terrible.

I am surprised they still don't seem to know much about this virus. What it is, how to treat it. So much conflicting information. I cannot keep up. It sounds worse all the time.

I have to remind myself that in my experience, it's the projection that is so scary and can grow scarier by the day, but life has only gotten better, despite my worry and the worry of those around me. I am trying to hold fast to expectations of things ever improving. I tell myself all will be well, the world tells me something quite different. But I guess that is not new. I keep trying to bring my focus back to a positive thought, a flower, a smile, a hug, my feet on the ground.

Here comes my play. Oh, from Oregon. Have you seen it? I never have. I hope it's good.

My blood has settled down.

The play was pretty bad. May actually have been live, with actors in different rooms. So strange. Oh well. I found a movie version the BBC made in 2009, I'll settle for that.

The sun is supposed to come out tomorrow. It's been so rainy. I think I need a walk in the woods.

Did I tell you we went for our bike ride on the rail trail? It was not as crowded as I thought it would be. It was really nice. We picked up BBQ on the way home and that was really good. And then we walked to get ice cream. Felt like a vacation.

Cuomo announced today that NY schools will remain closed the rest of the school year. It doesn't affect us though. I imagine half of the kids are happy and half are sad.

Today we had a video chat with friends in England. I have a Facebook friend that I've never met from England and she has two little boys. Today we met up online for a visit with our boys. It was a lot of fun. I hope we can all go to England someday and have a real visit. So many places I'd like to go with the kids and Joseph. So many adventures await.

All will be well. All will be well.

Always and still here,

Sarah

May 3

Dear Friend,

Day 50 something.

Yesterday, Sonny was bit by a snapping turtle. I don't want to talk about it. There was screaming and I had to pry its jaws open. Three small cuts. The turtle was the size of a football. I was more deeply traumatized than Sonny.

It reminded me of the time I got caught in a rip tide and could have drowned. I don't like to talk about that either.

Such fear. Dread. A bad choice, a mistake. Consequences.

Sonny's finger is a bit puffy where it was bit. Hoping tomorrow it will look more settled.

The air is thick.

Attitudes are at high altitude.

I miss normal.

I heard someone say the handshake may never come back into fashion. How presumptuous.

I feel like, more than ever, we are living a life based on projection. All the terrible things on the way. I am not even looking for it and it seeps in all the same.

I was listening to a podcast that used to be funny. They were wondering if the last person's hand that they shook will be the last hand they ever shake.

Makes me want to lick people.

But don't worry. I am wearing my mask and washing my hands and staying home, except when I feed my children to turtles.

Thoughts :

The headline, the story, the pictures, the comments. If you stop at the headline, you miss it.

The title, the pictures, the ingredients, the instructions. If you don't read the instructions before you gather the ingredients, you'll regret it.

Never doubt nature.

Doubt the easy way out.

What are you thinking about? By the end of the day, my brain is empty as a bowl. A dirty mixing bowl.

Always and still here,

Sarah

May 4

Dear Friend,

Day 54.

54! What in the world...

Well, the good news is, Sonny's finger is healing very nicely. We had the antibiotic on hand but were able to treat it with natural remedies and that always feels so empowering and reassuring. Although he was very angry all day. I wonder if he didn't get a little turtle anger in his blood.

I did a chicken curry crock pot thing and I did a healthy no bake cheesecake thing. Neither were a great success. The chicken was very soupy. The cheesecake did not set, but it makes a nice pudding.

I heard of a friend's passing today. A very close friend of my sister's. An unexpected death of someone you know is so jarring. Such a surreal thing. This person is suddenly gone. So much floods in behind that thought. How the world shifts a little when someone leaves.

I read an article about the nano-chips they want to put into the COVID vaccine. "They". That really threw me off today too. Not a new idea or a surprise. I keep hearing about it. Dreading it. Hoping it won't happen. Funny, (not funny) how these days it does feel like anything scary is possible.

Also we have murder hornets now. That's fun.

What scares me more than murder hornets, is what this country will do to protect us from the murder hornets....

Did you know Polio is traced back to a moth that was released accidentally in Massachusetts? The government mandated the spraying of all farms with Paris Green, a highly toxic arsenic insecticide to try to get rid of this moth that was decimating crops. They added lead to it to make it stick to the fruit and vegetables better.... This on top of all the mercurial medicines that were all the rage at the time. Especially for teething... Oh boy.

Anyhoo.

Biting my knuckles.

I got to my studio but had a hard time concentrating. I did get to some painting though.

Everything feels all sorts of free solo right now. I don't know which end is up sometimes. Like I'm navigating some treacherous landscape. But like Mark Twain said, "I have been through some terrible things in my life, some of which actually happened." It's hard for me to tell what's really happening and not to worry about what might happen.

I do hope most of it will live only in my worried mind. And I hope I can find ways to turn the faucet on and let those thoughts run right out, to make room for better ones.

I wish I could go see a movie with you. Will you go see a movie with me some time? I'll let you pick. Just kidding.

Always and still here,

Sarah

May 5

Dear Friend,

Day 55.

It feels like it's been quite a long time now.

Every TV show or movie I watch, I watch in wonder. All of them filmed before the virus arrived. All of them in the world before, no one in a mask, everyone doing all the normal things we did in big crowds, parties in people's homes, rushing through train stations, sitting in restaurants, hugging, kissing, whispering in ears, shaking hands, clinking glasses, sharing forks...it looks almost perverse. I miss it so.

Today we drove all the way out to Ellenville, which is about a 50-minute drive. We went crystal hunting at a funny spot in the woods. You have to climb up big rock walls and meander around a path that leads to little tiny caves. More like rock pockets. I wandered up a path for a bit. The boys were calling for me to come down and I couldn't stop collecting tiny quartz points in the dirt. "I'm in a trystal crance!" I yelled.

I cut my thumb on a rock. It was a small cut but for some reason it bled a lot. I kept wiping the blood on my paper bag that was full of my finds. When I got down the hill, it was quite a show. Joseph had a first aid kit, I had one and Sonny brought his own in his own backpack, so we were well prepared. Joseph cleaned the cut, Desmond put Neosporin on it and Sonny put the band aid on. Desmond said he was hoping someone would get hurt so he could help them. Sonny said he was so glad I got cut so he could put a Band-Aid on it.

The farm stand that makes the trip out there extra special is only taking phone orders and I don't think you can go inside. It's such a nice spot to browse and grab lunch. They have sandwiches, soups, salads all packaged and ready to go. They have tables of cakes, cookies, muffins and ice cream. Books, little toys, pottery, and little tables to sit at to eat. We could have ordered something to pick up but it's just not the same. And we would have had to stop on our way as they were closing soon as we drove by. On the way home it was too late. I missed going. I wonder when we'll be able to go back and sit to eat.

We picked up pizza on the way home instead.

I visited with some friends on a Zoom meeting after dinner. Still such a strange alternative to really being with people. I do like to see people in their homes though. Their bookcases behind them or artwork on the walls, babies crawling around, or they're outside smoking cigarettes, or lying in bed, ceiling fans spinning over their heads, dogs in their laps. I sat in an armchair eating my no bake cheesecake pudding, looking at my wrinkly neck.

I've been thinking about how discomfort comes and goes. Every time I ask

Sonny how his healing finger feels, he says it only hurts if he bumps it on something. I feel like that about my woes. Like my mom, I don't walk around feeling bad that my mom is gone but when I bump into something like a song she loved, or see a mother and daughter, it hurts. Like bumping a sore finger. The virus is similar. I can forget, I feel okay, and then I bump into something that hurts. A news article mostly or thinking about something I planned to do but can't now, driving by closed shops, seeing people in masks. If I bump into too many things in one day, the hurt lingers. The hurt is disappointment, trailing fear. Like a lightning flash and the thunder that follows. Stormy days.

Joseph seems to be called off from working in the ICU. The numbers are low enough that he is not needed. Elective surgeries seem to be gearing back up so he may get back to the recovery room and his old schedule next week. That is a relief. I hope that keeps moving in that direction and the worst of it here has come and gone.

Last month, Sonny accidentally threw a pillow on a plant I had on the floor of my room. It broke the plant right in half. I was so sad. I had bought it for $5 at the thrift store in town. An Angel Wing Begonia. Just a small thing with little white spots spread across it's smooth, green, wing shaped leaves. I made it a pot in pottery class, transplanted it so it had more dirt and it was growing much bigger. And then it broke in half. I put the piece that broke off in water, in the sunlight. It's growing roots now in the water and I'm so relieved. When the roots look long enough, I'll pot it in its own pot. Looking at its roots in the sun, its strong healthy leaves up above, makes me feel hopeful. Even though we feel broken now, I think we can take our broken parts and nurture them so that our lives can grow bigger and in ways we did not expect. Soon I'll have two beautiful plants where I thought the one I had was ruined. It's amazing how much plants can do just being still.

Things grow, things you nurture grow. And it's likely that just sun and water will be enough for now. That is a comforting thought. I hope that comforts you too.

Always and still here,

Sarah

May 8

Dear Friend,

Day 58.

I do not much feel like writing, talking, trying or growing. I do feel like painting, sitting in the sun, being with my family, crying and making pancakes.

My heart is very heavy.

I don't know which way is up. I kinda want to get off this ride.

There's nowhere to go.

Always and still here,

Sarah

May 8

Dear Friend,

Still day 58.

I have entered a stage of being totally flummoxed. Utterly bewildered. Perpetually perplexed. Deeply dumbfounded. Stumped and stupefied.

I don't know what to tell you. I'm trapped in my house. So are you. I don't know what's going on. Neither do you.

I just opened a link from an email to a YouTube message from Desmond's dance teacher and ended up watching a video of monkeys reacting to magic. It made me want to cry. Monkeys in glass rooms, mystified.

Let. Me. Out.

I do feel like a monkey at the zoo. Staring at the walls. I wish the mailman would do a magic trick for me when he walks by my house. I guess I'll sit on the porch just in case.

A friend told me today it's okay to curse. At least we have that. Because there's too much we can't do. Like eat all the bread.

I guess I'll be here forever,

Sarah

May 11

Dear Friend,

Day 61.

Yesterday was Mother's Day. I woke in the morning from a scary dream. I was part of a sort of game, and a ride. Run by a couple of frightening people. It was a spinning flat disc, slow moving, like a merry-go-round but with stationary chairs. Myself and maybe 20 adults, dressed for a party, are sitting in the chairs, looking up at the ceiling. On the ceiling is a mirror but in the mirror, we are all dead. And we know that if we don't "play this game right" we will have to kill someone on the ride. With a hatchet. Someone leads me off the ride and offers me a bag of candy. I hesitate. The people running the game say, "It's ok," and smile, "you may have a small treat." So I take the bag. Then I am in a hallway, about to enter a cafeteria. I am not sure if that is allowed either but I am desperate to get out.

An obvious parallel, don't you think?

Right before I woke up, in my dream I was sitting with Desmond and Sonny with a box of photographs on my lap of my parents from before they had children. Sonny asks his usual real life question, "Would Gran'ma Pam have loved me so much?"

"Yes," I say, "She would have loved you so much. She would have loved to read to you. And she probably would have written a book about you and Desmond." And I don't know why that has never occurred to me before. Of course she would have. And it breaks my heart. And I wake. The day begins.

It was a fine day. My boys showered me with love and thoughtful gifts and gestures. We made my favorite breakfast. Waffles, fresh whipped cream and sliced strawberries, with bacon on the side. For Mother's Day we make the waffle recipe that uses a stick of butter. Heaven.

I worked on finishing my painted butterfly project for town.

Watched the neighbors visit with their children and grandchildren in their yard. In three separate batches. It made Desmond sad. He said he wished he had family nearby to visit. Me too.

We went to our usual spot by the river to look for crystals and be by the water. There were more people than usual, some with masks, some without. We found lots of little treasures and ordered Japanese food on the way home.

After the kids were in bed, Joseph and I started watching a new show. Called, *I Am Not Okay With This*. About a teenage girl who discovers she has telekinesis. Seeing her at a diner and a party, dancing with her friends, at a friend's house, made me sad and long for crowds of people.

We went to bed. For some reason, the image of speaking to my sister in Florida, and my mother and father, who are gone now, all together in a Zoom meeting, came into my mind. It was so upsetting to me in the moment. And then another thought came right behind it, even more upsetting. It was just, "I don't know what my future looks like." That thought felt like a sledgehammer. Like the root of all my worry. But now it seems strange and vague. Sort of like a song you make up in a dream that is so beautiful, or a joke that is so funny but when you wake, it is not at all.

But this aimless waiting... 61 days and still no answers to questions about this virus, the big questions and the small. Where did it come from? When will it go? How will it go? How should we treat it? What effect will this all have going forward? How do we go forward? Can we? When? I have no idea what happens next. And can't visualize what next year looks like, or the next.

Today Joseph went back to work. His usual job on his usual days. It is a relief to be back to some normalcy for him.

We ate leftovers today. The food we eat seems to be the only variety in our day. I ate leftover soup for lunch and dinner and it made me anxious. I feel like that tiger at the zoo that paces. I tell myself prison would be much worse.

The good news is, Desmond gave Sonny the marshmallow test today. You know the one concocted by a psychiatrist a long time ago. You put a marshmallow in front of a little kid and tell them if they can wait 15 minutes, they can have two marshmallows. Or they can choose to eat the marshmallow right away but then they only get one. Sonny waited and got two. This means that he has the ability to delay gratification and will do well in life. According to the study from long ago. Although there was an awful lot of whining until that timer went off. Desmond thoroughly enjoyed himself. Delayed gratification indeed.

Always and still here,

Sarah

May 15

Dear Friend,

Day 65.

I was trying to write you a letter but it was really awful. It hardly made sense and was all over the map. It's been 4 days since I last wrote and those days are soup now. Some things float to the surface but they don't match up with anything else nor are they very interesting. Like a bunch of single socks. Gray ones. Falling out of the dryer onto the floor. I can point them out to you, but who cares.

So I will just tell you my favorite thing in the last 4 days. Yesterday, Alan Chartok, on WAMC radio station, interviewed Governor Cuomo. Alan asked a few questions, and then Andrew mentioned that he is staying in the governor's mansion with his daughters, it has 8 bedrooms, they have lots of space. Alan says, "Is the mansion haunted?"

I felt like someone had handed me a beautifully wrapped present in that moment. Stopped me right in my kitchen tracks.

And then Andrew answers, "Yes, actually, it is. I've never seen anything myself but the staff that works there, that have been there for years, they say they have seen things. And my daughters say it's haunted. When I was a kid and my father was governor, I remember the staff telling me it was haunted then too."

Or something like that, he said something along those lines. And I really could not have been more surprised or pleased in that moment.

That is all. The governor's mansion is haunted, right from Cuomo's mouth. And it pleases me to no end.

I've stopped reading articles, or looking for news. It does me no good. I accidentally read an article today about how the sun is going into "lockdown" and we'll have snow in July and other travesties. Please, don't take that to heart, from the little research I did, it's not true. And if you think it is true, don't tell me about it. I really can't handle it.

I'll just be here, thinking about ghosts, Cape Cod, planting seeds for flowers, what Desmond will cook next, and getting to my studio tomorrow. My worry shop is closed. No room at the Inn. I'm leaving it for the folks who are better at it than me.

And now, I will stay up too late and watch some TV before I go to sleep. A goodnight to you.

Always and still here,

Sarah

May 16

Dear Friend,

Day 66.

Today Desmond cried because I've been wearing my hair up since I watched the new *Ghostbusters* movie, a few weeks ago. He said change was hard. He said he was glad he hadn't watched a movie that made him want to change how he dresses. I said, "What about the time you saw a kid with his shirt tucked in on the school yard in Kindergarten, and you tucked your shirt in every day for 4 years straight?"

"Well, then I realized that that wasn't me."

"But it was you at the time. Sometimes we see someone else doing or wearing something that we feel matches our insides and we try it out on the outside. Because it feels better."

He was not convinced. But I thought this was an interesting conversation.

We talked about all the loss we feel right now and that it's worth being sad about. We talked about grief and gratitude, it helps to notice them both, but not to let one outweigh the other.

Then he sat in my lap and cried.

When I went to college, I cut my long hair super short. When my mom went through chemo, I shaved my head. When my dad died, I cut my long hair to shoulder length. Something about change, loss, a new life, that makes me want to change how I look I guess.

So I decided to wear my hair down today for Desmond. That lasted a couple of hours. I was so uncomfortable. It has become a comfort to me to have my hair "put away".

There's left over cake in the house. It's so loud, that cake. I asked Joseph to cut pieces for the boys so I wouldn't have to get too close to it. I had already had a piece after lunch today. So he did, and then he left it open, out on the counter.... so I had more cake.

I wish I had an elliptical machine at home. I feel so... fluffy.

I got to my studio today. I never say, "I went to my studio today." Always, "I got to my studio today." Like a football player running down the field with the football, dodging defense players all the way to a touchdown. I touched down in my studio today. Spent a few hours trying to figure out how to paint shredded coconut on pink frosting. Talk about painting yourself into a corner.

Then I went to Ulster Landing where Sonny and I had the turtle incident. So beautiful there. I thought a lot about that turtle and walked the path with a fury, imagining stomping on its face. That's terrible, who said that.

I saw a couple of perfectly still frogs and they scared the crap out of me. I was afraid they'd attack. But no turtles. They felt me coming. I considered it all exposure therapy. Maybe we'll all go there tomorrow. It's a nice place to explore when the tide is out.

You should come too.

Always and still here,

Sarah

May 17

Dear Friend,

Day 67.

What's happenin', hot stuff?

I can't believe how fat I feel right now. I can't believe how much cheesy popcorn I stuffed in my mouth on accident at 9:00.

Hope you had an excellent Sunday. I saw some friends today and that was a delight. We met after dinner down by the river at low tide, on the sand flats. Our boys played in the water and the muddy sand. It was cold but they did not care. They ended up in their t-shirts and underwear, wet and oblivious to the cloudy sky and cool breeze. I sat shivering in my jeans, boots and sweater. They were so happy to see each other and to be exploring a new place. So strange and wonderful to see my boys with other children. I was so glad for them to have the hour or so. And it was so wonderful to see my friend.

We planned to meet and I ended up driving right behind her car as we got close. Her long hair was blowing out of the driver's side window in the wind. It was a thrill just to see her hair. How I miss my friends.

It was both cloudy and sunny today. Chilly and warm. Breezy and still. A fickle kind of day.

The boys filled the trampoline with balls, stuffed animals, pillows and blankets.

I made a Thai shrimp coconut soup with shiitake mushrooms for dinner. I did not eat more cake. But the boys polished it off this afternoon.

We ate dinner outside. Our Spring yard is feeling lush and green. It's shaping up for summer and that feels good. I feel lucky to have a comfortable home to spend all this time in, a pretty yard, the trampoline for jumping, and that the four of us get along so well.

I almost read an article on Facebook about some travesty. But I caught myself. Not today, Satan.

Tomorrow I'm making weight watchers bagels. Flour and Greek yogurt. Wish me luck. And will power, energy, motivation and fortitude....

Tomorrow the butterflies will be installed in town. I think we'll walk in, in the afternoon to see if we can spot any going up. I don't know where mine will be yet. I hope it gets a nice spot where you can visit it.

I think I should try to make more plans to see friends, to walk or sit outside somewhere. Funny how I long for connection and at the same time, lack motivation and the feeling of being at ease so I can be social. I feel like parts of me are on backward and I forgot how to walk. I should probably make the effort.

Do you want to go for a walk?

Always and still here,

Sarah

May 18

Dear Friend,

Day 68.

Today I started cleaning my basement. My basement is an unfinished basement but it is full of stuff. Shelves of food, holiday decorations, tools, cans of paint, all the things that a garage would hold since we have no garage and all the usual basement things. The attic has the attic things.

I made weight watchers bagels this morning but I'm not sure what makes them good for dieting except that they were small. Made with equal parts flour and Greek yogurt so a fair amount of protein compared to a regular bagel I suppose.

The boys requested waffles so I made those too.

And then I made these cinnamon, raisin, oatmeal rolls I have been eyeing. Those turned out really good.

Ended up with a stack of containers on the counter full of carbs. I am terrible at dieting.

Cleaning the basement out felt good. Makes me feel like more things are possible than I imagined.

I let the boys watch a movie this afternoon. It was a cloudy day. We didn't walk into town as I had hoped, to see if my butterfly had landed somewhere with all the others. Maybe tomorrow.

Leftover soup for dinner. Fish sticks and noodles for Desmond, yogurt and noodles for Sonny. Sliced cucumbers that are still sitting on the table. Meh.

I cut my hair last night. Have you cut your own hair yet? I have been wearing it all pulled back every day, but I took the section on top and cut it a little shorter, all the same length and used thinning shears and a razor to thin the ends. I don't think it will match up with the rest of my hair if I wear it down but I don't care right now. It was not a great improvement as far as I can tell. Those 11:00 haircut urges are hard to ignore.

Joseph has an unexpected day off tomorrow. Maybe I'll get to my studio. But probably I'll just get to go grocery shopping.

I miss thrift stores. I am thinking about a yellow ceramic bowl that was like a woven basket that I had passed up a couple of times at the thrift store in town that we used to visit most Mondays, unsure of what I could put in such a bowl. A bowl with so many holes. Today I realized I could have put fruit in it. But now as I think of it, I remember it being too small for fruit. What would you put in a small ceramic bowl with holes in it? Thrift store things. Thrift store thoughts.

I heard Florida is opening up stores now. That feels promising. Their numbers have been so much lower than ours. Makes me hopeful that the warmer weather will free us up some.

I do love some freedom.

When I went down to the basement today I asked Desmond to stay downstairs to be close to Sonny who was in the bath. I told him he could do whatever he wanted to, besides screen time, watch TV and eat marshmallows. He was so excited at the thought of being able to do whatever he wanted. He may or may not have taken off his clothes and ran around with his pajama pants on his head.

I have excellent company at home, I must say. But I wish you were here.

Always and still here,

Sarah

May 19

Dear Friend,

Day 69.

Highlights:

Sonny bathing in a bucket of water in the sun.

Planting flower seeds. Poppies, zinnias, goldendrums... nope... gladiators... nope.... glassbottoms... ....MARIGOLDS!

A neighbor playing jazz music that reached my yard while I was placing seeds in the dirt.

"Seeds are like wishes, Sonny. You plant what you intend to grow."

Put my tomato plants in the garden boxes. They are small and we likely won't have tomatoes until August. Purple, yellow and red cherry tomatoes.

Walking into town to see all the butterflies installed. Sonny's excitement at each one.

Desmond's beautiful furrowed brow.

Eating healthy food.

Going to a Zoom meeting.

I did not get to my studio but I did go food shopping. I bought ingredients to make two new dishes this week.

My feeling of the day was monochromatic, until I sat down to recall it. It was actually pretty sweet.

Always and still here,

Sarah

May 21

Dear Friend,

Day 71.

Yesterday we went for a morning hike at Esopus Bend Preserve. Just me and the boys. We picked garlic mustard because I read that was something worth foraging, but I kept calling it mustard greens. I brought it home and it's sitting in the strainer basket that rests on one side of my sink. I'm not sure what to do with it now. I also scooped up 3 varieties of baby ferns to bring home and plant in our yard. Sonny touched a stinging nettle and howled like a monkey. He wanted to go home but was soothed with a band aid and some BBQ potato chips I had in my backpack. A first aid kit and a bag of BBQ potato chips go a long way.

We saw an orange butterfly and a black snake. Our boots got sunk deep in creek mud and I had a panicked moment where I thought we wouldn't get out. I did not find the clay I was hoping to collect.

Desmond started to talk in a scary voice saying, "I am Satan! The Christian Lord of buttockses..." It was the same voice I used to use when I was a kid that made my sister laugh. So we made her a quick video and texted it off to her. "THE VOICE...Lmao," she texted back.

The path was longer than I anticipated and Sonny whined a long way until we reached our car. He does not last long on a walk. He gets very tired. When we got home he went straight to the trampoline and jumped for 9 hours straight.

Desmond went for a bike ride with some friends around town. They used to wear their masks on their faces, now they wear them on their necks or in their pockets. I am more afraid of angry townspeople yelling at them than I am of them getting sick riding bicycles in the sunshine. The anxiety I feel about not knowing what to be more anxious about is wearing away. For that I am glad.

Desmond had his Zoom acting class and I made dinner while Sonny played in the dirt with dinosaurs and trucks. Chicken salad with pecans, celery and grapes. Sonny, who had basically eaten bread all day, came into the kitchen and said, "Ohhhh! I can't wait to eat that CHICKEN SOUP!!" Which he doesn't usually eat. So I threw together some chicken soup too but made the dreadful error of adding peas. So he ate buttered toast. I think he actually ate a few spoonfuls of the soup. He was very kind and said he'd eat around the peas, but his bowl was still very full when he refused to come back to the table.

I promised them ice cream sundaes at Mickey's Igloo after dinner. Sonny said he would eat a carrot stick so he could have ice cream, so I peeled an enormous carrot and he ate it on our walk there. He kept saying he was going to get a "Sunbathe". I would ask him what flavor ice cream and he would get exasperated. "Bathing!" he'd say.

I said, "Well, Desmond is getting something called a Sundae, with two flavors of ice cream, a topping, whipped cream and sprinkles."

"I'll have what Desmond is having."

I brought my own spoons. That's two less plastic spoons in the world that I am responsible for.

I paid the bills and went to bed early. 11:00, which is better than my 12:30 these days. I am staying up later and later. After the kids are in bed and sleeping by about 9:00, even though the process starts at 8:00, I finally have time to myself. It's not much time if I go to bed early, which means I blink and it's time to serve them again.

This morning Joseph is home and up with the boys. I was able to pack a lunch and head out for my studio. I am here now. It is nice to be alone. The quiet is good. I'll work on the shredded coconut in my painting. I am close to finishing this piece. I should write the date on the back of the canvas when I begin one. I don't know when I started this one, seems a long time now.

On my way here I saw three women in the parking lot of a storage place, their cars side by side, their trunks open. They were all in workout gear and they were all hoola-hooping. Only in the time of COVID does this seem normal.

Sorry this is so long. Two days worth of not much to report sure does fill a page.

There is beauty all around you, Grasshopper. Go find it.

Always and still here,

Sarah

May 22

Dear Friend,

Day 72.

This morning Sonny woke up early and we started the day together while Desmond and Joseph slept. I made more of these weight watchers bagels I'm hooked on now. I get so tired of eating the same things that when I find something new, I eat it until I hate it. I will likely eat these bagels every morning for the next month and then never eat them again. My last repeat breakfast was one hard-boiled egg with salt. This was part of a diet plan. The bagels were a welcome change.

I took the boys to the river later in the morning to meet up with my friend and her son. The same friend I had bumped into at Adams very early on in the quarantine, both of us with masks on, pushing our shopping carts and stopping short 10' away from each other, each of us starting to cry. Today we sat together on rocks by the water with no masks and no fear, our boys exploring the beach. What a change. Such relief.

I was thinking this morning of how the fear has left me. That panic early on, sure that people I knew would get sick, would die, that Joseph and I would surely get it, hoping we would not end up in the ICU and that we wouldn't get sick at the same time. Who would take care of the kids? What would the one mistake be that I would make that would bring the virus to my mouth, or nose, or eyes...How would I carry on with so much worry, disinfecting every surface every day, being afraid to be near my husband? It has not at all been what I feared it would be. And now it feels like we are just patiently waiting for the outside world to be ready to begin again.

I am still wearing masks in stores and wiping my hands, phone, car key, and car door, with disinfectant wipes in the car. Cleaning things that come into the house. But not with the same worry I felt before. Now I trust that these precautions are enough. I know I could still get sick, but it doesn't feel as likely as it did at the onset. Feels like we are somewhere in between dodging a bullet and being sold a bill of goods. I can't tell which. Mostly bullet I guess. But so much is still unclear and confusing. I don't read articles about the virus anymore. I'll wait till it all shakes out. Let me know how it ends when it's over.

Went to Target today which felt very exciting. It's the only place I can shop for anything besides food. Got pool toys for the kids and not much else.

Got to my studio for a little bit, it was hot there today.

Came home for dinner but Joseph was busy putting the pool up and dinner wasn't a thought yet. Our pool is a put up, take down sort and I suppose we've had it for maybe 6 years? 7? This seems to be its last. Joseph started to fill it but it is leaking and he is trying to patch the holes he can find. I am wondering if it is full of holes now and if it's done for. Not sure how to find the holes if they are on the bottom of the pool. There are no bubbles. Do you know?

I foraged some wild violets and garlic mustard again, as I had thrown out my last bunch. I had let it sit out too long and it all withered. Tonight, I pulled off all the leaves and washed them, put them away in the fridge for pesto tomorrow. The violets I put away too. I will make a violet infused something, or a salve.

Tonight there was a fire truck and ambulance parade through town. They came up Washington Ave., across Main St. and down Market, the usual parade loop. It was for the health care workers. Their sirens were going, their lights were flashing. This town loves loud noise, they love their fire trucks. I am usually an old biddy about it, rolling my eyes. But I found myself teary as I watched and listened to them go by a few blocks to my left, listened as they passed a few blocks ahead and then watched and listened some more as they passed a few blocks to my right. Joseph and the boys walked down the block to see them up close. I stood at the front gate in my pajamas, waiting for them to come back.

When we came back inside Sonny said, "I don't wanna say this but...I don't like parades." He was disappointed they did not throw him any candy and said that's really the only part of parades he likes.

I also found out today that it's Memorial Day weekend. Who knew? Every year I hope I will be invited to a BBQ, but I never am. I think this year will be no different.

Tomorrow our farmer's market is opening up and I'm very excited to go. Not sure how that slipped by but I'm glad it did. I will be there with bells on. Or face paint.

How are you feeling these days? Are you less afraid too? Are you opening up your shutters a little bit? I imagine we will all emerge in our own time. And that's okay.

Always and still here,

Sarah

May 23

Dear Friend,

Day 73.

I am feeling blue. Missing my mom. Uncomfortable in my own skin. Self-critical. Surprised. Disappointed.

Nothing in particular happened, besides one of those occasional gut punches of grief. It's like a mugger jumping out of the shadows and just sucker punching me, grabbing my heart and running off, leaving me to pick things up off the floor in a panic.

Another parade tonight, this one for the graduating seniors. We were more prepared than last night and walked down together to the corner to watch. Fire trucks and police cars, flashing lights, sirens and horns. After the trucks, came the seniors in cars, sports teams and more sports teams. Honking horns, hanging out of windows, standing up through sunroofs, waving out of windows. Balloons and painted signs.

It made me think of my high school. My teenage self and my life then. My small group of friends. How much I hated school. How mean a lot of the kids in my class were.

And then a silver Honda accord went by with a parent driving their kid in the parade and that was that. That silver Honda accord. My mom's car. The summer after my senior year is when my mom found out she had cancer and started chemo and radiation and nothing was the same after that. Thanks, parade.

I could still hear the parade with the doors and windows closed when I walked home alone. Snare drums started up and they felt like forks scraping my bones.

Right before I sat down in bed to write this, I tried on a bathing suit that came in the mail. Because I ordered it. Why would I do such a thing?

Who is this person in the mirror? I feel at a loss.

Other than that... I did go to the farmers market today which was bizarre and not at all farmer's markety. There was none of the usual easy breezy, meandering and chatting. There was a very official roped off line, a bouncer of sorts, painted marks on the ground, and not many people. We bought some cookies for the boys and left. It was hard to breathe in our masks, the day was warm and so humid. Sonny was whining that he could not breathe and I had a window into what summer will feel like with masks. My heart sunk.

I took out summer clothes and sheets from the attic, did laundry and more laundry.

I went to the river alone after dinner and looked for crystals and talked out loud to myself.

So, I'll put myself to bed now. Sort of defeated.

There's always tomorrow.

Always and still here,

Sarah

May 24

Dear Friend,

Day 74.

I was up early with Sonny this morning. Waking from another night of dreams full of eventful outings. I never wear a mask in my dreams. I am always with friends.

We left a couple of windows cracked open overnight to cool the house down after such a hot day yesterday. Joseph put our air conditioners in the windows too, in preparation for the heat coming our way this week. He patched more holes in the pool. We may end up with a big sprinkler of a pool sooner than later. Like a cartoon, with new spouts of water bursting here and there each passing day. Hoping to get one more season out of it. And then move to a mansion with an in-ground pool and central air.

Today a friend came by to give me a horseradish plant he had offered me a while ago and an unexpected bonus Amaryllis to cheer me up. I asked him if he wanted a hug and he said of course he did. So nice to see a friend and give them a hug. He said he could not remember the last hug he had. These little moments feel like light seeping back in.

Desmond has rejoined his few friends on the block, playing outdoors, riding bikes and swimming in pools, pizza on the porch. I fear I will not see much of him until snowfall. Today he was the bravest boy to investigate something floating at the bottom of his friend's pool and dove down to scoop up a dead squirrel with a skimmer net. Earned himself the nickname "Savage". I'm so proud.

Walked over to pick him up tonight and sat on the porch and talked with his friend's mom in the dark for a while. Something about being outside with people now, after being inside alone for 74 days feels just about right.

I went to my studio today and installed an air conditioner there too. Plugged away at painting the shredded coconut for hours and left with it looking pretty much the same as it did when I arrived today. Oh well. Still a worthwhile stroll around the paint pallet.

Headed to the supermarket before I went home and realized when I got there, I had forgotten my mask. I dug around in my car and after rejecting a pouch for headphones with a draw string that seemed a likely candidate but just hung on my ears, I found a pair of Sonny's pants and tied those around my face. It worked well enough and I came home with almost everything I needed for a few more new recipes this week.

It does seem that the summer season has arrived on little cat feet, suddenly in my lap, purring and lazy. I don't mind it at all. It feels like a pleasant surprise.

Always and still here,

Sarah

May 25

Dear Friend,

Day 75.

Today was Memorial Day. Fireworks keep popping around town in the dark. The dryer is spinning. Everyone in the house is asleep.

Desmond is giddily happy. Long days of swimming and bike rides with his friends. He had a giggle fit at bedtime. Bliss.

I am so grateful for his happy childhood. It fills me up.

Sonny and I went over to hang out with the boys in the pool and sit on the porch for a little bit. They had an Alexa dot on the porch and we asked it to play the theme songs to *Superman*, *Spider-Man*, *Batman* and *Star Wars*. Sonny laid on the cushioned porch swing with his small bare feet with multi-colored painted toenails propped up on a pillow, listening to the music.

Funny how more freedom has arrived unexpectedly and part of me wants to reel it all back in and hide again. Something about the safety of having everyone in sight is comforting. Less decisions to make, more routine. Home. Let's stay home.

Desmond seems charged up. Like his battery is at 100% now, when it's been at about 62% for a long while.

Sonny is so sweet and loving but in his spare time seems to work on finding things to say that are like little daggers in my heart. That my mom was mean. Or that he'd like to live on the street alone. Or insisting that it's his fault my dog died before he was born. I am doing my best to navigate those waters. Sometimes he leaves me in tears. Today he did make me cry. And he spent the rest of the day apologizing and telling me how much he loves me and that I am beautiful and gracious. Man, oh man.

I made oven baked falafel and Joseph was home in time for dinner. We had it with arugula and sliced radishes. Sonny ate buttered bread and pistachios. We ate in the backyard at the table. The pool is up, patched and full of water. The triangle shades are up over the table. It was a very beautiful day.

I feel a little unsure of myself today. A little anxious. I almost read a couple of news articles. I skimmed one. Decided it was none of my business. I have been so much less afraid since I stopped reading news articles online. And then I had a panicked thought that maybe I should be afraid and I am just lacking enough information to be scared. But nothing I read made sense, it just left me in a general state of panic. It didn't seem useful. I'll keep doing my best with what I know for now. It's enough.

I have not had sugar in 8 days. I want to eat a cake. I think about getting ice cream with the boys. It's something to do. Something fun, to delight in. When there's not much else to do. Makes me sad not to. But I know I feel better when I eat well. It's just sort of boring. What else can I do? There must be something.

"If that's all there is my friends, then let's keep dancing..."

I feel like I need to crochet something.

Always and still here,

Sarah

May 27

Dear Friend,

Day 77.

It was a day for blowing up pool floats, washing them, patching them and blowing them up again, then setting them afloat in the pool. Then stacking them to skim the pool, then pondering throwing them all to the curb because I feel like E.T. in a pile of stuffed animals now in my backyard. There is quite a lot of clutter back there all of sudden. But it keeps the kids busy, and so it is.

The boys have been bickering for days and driving me a bit mad. I've had a headache that comes and goes. Yesterday was a very long day, so I did not write you a letter. I took some Advil last night and laid in bed with my tablet to watch season 2 of *Homecoming*. Have you seen it? So glad to have a story to immerse myself in when I find one. So blue when they end.

The boys and I set to scrubbing the outside of our pool this morning. Which in reality was me scrubbing 85% of it, Desmond leisurely giving it a sponge bath and Sonny disappearing inside. But it's clean now.

Got the kiddie pool in working order too. Now we have two pools. And a trampoline. Not much else fits in our yard.

Sonny took a nap today which was a treat for me. I made use of this quiet time by exercising and cleaning out my fridge.

Luckily, I had leftovers for lunch and dinner, which were delicious enough to be looked forward to and made more time for getting other things done.

Desmond came and went again today. Off to be with his friends. Swimming, biking, Dallas Hot Wieners, Domino's pizza and a king sized Kit Kat. How can I compete?

I, on the other hand, have not had sugar and eaten healthy food for 10 days straight. Hurray for me. So boring.

I was thinking about how it was so uncomfortable entering quarantine, so much anxiety, confusion and adjusting. And it makes sense that it would feel the same way on the other end, trying to come out of it. We are entering phase one of opening here, which is nothing that will change what I've been doing. It includes construction, fishing and hunting, things like that. Although for sure it feels like I've entered phase one socially in some ways. And it is uncomfortable. There is some relief and some worry. Same as figuring out how to stay home at first. Just in the other direction. What a ride.

Sonny asked me again today if my mom would have loved him so much. I talked to him about how he's made up of Joseph and I, and I am made up of my mom and dad, so part of him is made up of my mom too, in his genes and his DNA, in his blood. Of course, this made no sense. And when Joseph came home, he told Joseph about how he is made up of some of Grandma Pam's parts. Sort of like Frankenstein to hear him tell it. Just as well.

Tomorrow is Thursday. Joseph will be home. Maybe I'll get to paint. I got a new bicycle helmet in the mail today. Maybe I'll go for a bike ride or wear it on a walk to town. It has a magnetized, removable visor. If it had a magnetized, removable mask, I'd be all set.

How are you feeling these days? On the brink of change again...this emerging.

I fear I will lose some friends who decide to do it differently and decide that I am doing it wrong. I do hope we can all support each other through it. We are all captains of our own ships, navigating through some dense fog. We're not likely to all make the same choices. And our vessels are all so different, not to mention our crews.

I'm trying to leave a small wake.

Always and still here,

Sarah

May 28

Dear Friend,

Day 78.

All you really need to know is today I bought a peony pink jumpsuit on sale at Target. It was an XXL but I am washing it in hot water and throwing it in the dryer and it should be perfectly oversized. Then I will have reached a new level of Holtzman.

I have a headache again. I made some healthy cookies and popped them in the oven. Joseph made carrot soup.

When the kids go to bed tonight, we're going to watch a scary movie.

Last night I watched episode one, season one, of *Unsolved Mysteries* from 1989. Remember that show? How come that show isn't on anymore? They solved so many cases. I guess the internet does the same thing now. But it's not as much fun. I was fascinated by how old it looked, how outdated and nostalgic. There must be a club for people who want to go back to the 80's. Or a club for people who are working on a time machine. Or a club for people who are looking for people who are working on a time machine. I would like to join all those clubs.

I think Home Goods may be open in two weeks. I am not sure what it says about me that I am really excited to be able to go to Home Goods. It certainly says something about where I live. There's not a lot of places to shop around here. Or a lot to do, I guess. Or I'm terribly boring. And I have small children and can't go very far, for long.

Having small children is a sort of quarantine in itself. I have felt like I'd been grounded for almost 11 years now.

Anyhoo, I think more than anything else, this experience just shook me up, spun me around blindfolded (and masked) and I'll be stumbling around for a long while. I'm still not sure what happened, or why, or what's happening now. But I'll keep showing up.

Always and still here,

Sarah

May 29

Dear Friend,

Day 79.

Today was Friday. I got up with Sonny and made some waffles. I love making pancakes and waffles. I don't eat them, I just love making them. I would love to eat them too but I am too old to eat them apparently. Nobody tells you when you're young that when you grow up, any carbs you eat will become a layer of play dough on your belly and thighs. So, only on special occasions, like Mother's Day do I eat waffles, and then I make them with melted butter, so they are really worth it. Pancakes make my upper arms swell up like water balloons. That's not completely true. Well, sort of.

I ate a weight watchers bagel. Still satisfying.

I had a phone therapy session which I started in my bedroom. I went out on the deck and noticed a woodchuck waddle into my back yard and start eating my mulberry bush. I ran downstairs and out into the yard to shoo him away, but he was gone by the time I got there. So I skimmed the pool while I talked. I told her I was upset that no one calls me to check on me. She said she does. But that doesn't count. Orphan problems.

I made it to my studio today and I think I am done or almost done painting the shredded coconut and pink frosting. I wish I could stay there longer and go more often. So many things I wish I had more time to do. Or more discipline. I'm never sure which of the two I need more.

Sonny's being a real pill. Grumpy and demanding. Not napping. Fighting with Desmond a lot.

Desmond is spending so much time with his fellow 10 year olds, he seems to have lost his patience with Sonny when he is home.

I came home for dinner, Sonny was in a mood, Joseph looked defeated. After we ate, I played a card game called Spot It with Sonny. Then I walked with him over to "see the big boys" at our friend's house where Desmond was. We walked with umbrellas, the sky was dark and the wind was blowing the leaves in the trees. We could hear thunder rumbling. As soon as we got to their porch it started to pour. A heavy summer downpour, the wind blowing the rain onto the porch, spraying us all, the boys shrieking and laughing, hiding under their pool towels.

When the rain stopped, they waited a little while and then jumped into the pool. Sonny and I stayed for a bit and then headed home; past his bedtime by then.

Getting him to bed was rough. I always panic when I tell my kids to do something and they refuse to do it. It doesn't happen very often and it always throws me off kilter. Joseph took him up to bed. There were slamming doors and yelling. Patience was lost. But before it was lost, it was in great supply. As it usually is. But kids have a way of stealing your reserve. Especially Sonny, lately.

I had such a craving to climb into bed early today, before it got dark. With the windows open and just a sheet on the bed. I was so nostalgic for that feeling I had when I was a kid.

I wish I could be a kid again. Seeing Desmond with his friends, so free, relaxed and happy reminds me of what that felt like. I wish I could have some of that somehow.

I did not get to bed early. It's late and dark out now. Everyone's gone to bed angry. The upstairs is like a black licorice cloud now. Not the rainbow I wanted to float on.

Ah, well.

Always a still here,

Sarah

May 30

Dear Friend,

Day 80.

Well, I kinda made it to bed early. I had to rush around to get up here in time while the light was still fading. Not exactly what I had in mind but there's always tomorrow. I opened the windows to a cool breeze and the sound of our neighbors. Someone dribbling a basketball behind our house. Our next door neighbors talking with friends on their porch. The smell of smoke from a fire pit. Even some frogs trilling from somewhere under the low green of our yards. Joseph on the phone downstairs.

What a day. What a world. What a strange time. The news comes right to my lap and glows on a screen, or into my kitchen from the radio. I adjust my surroundings, I shift uncomfortably, I write things, I say things, I focus on the proverbial plant that pushes up through the cement. I don't know. I keep trudging along.

Years ago, I sewed a red, white and blue peace sign flag to put out for the 4th of July. I decided today I want to sew a "Black Lives Matter" flag to put out this year. The letters in fabric a variety of skin colors on a red, white and blue background.

They are like prayers, these flags. The making of them and the displaying of them. I want so much to heal what's broken. I think it will settle something in me to make it. And maybe settle the hearts of my neighbors who see it. I am always soothed when I see signs of love where I live. Bumper stickers, signs in store windows, in people's yards.

Besides the collective angst that is swimming around, the day was a good one.

My small grape vines are growing wild and I tied them to a wire that I hope they will travel.

For the first time in 80 days, I had a friend over and we sat in the backyard and talked, ate snacks and drank herbal iced tea. Joseph made pesto out of the garlic mustard I picked in the woods and it was so delicious.

I made creamsicles from orange juice, plain Greek yogurt, maple syrup and vanilla. I sat with Sonny in the hammock after dinner and we ate our creamsicles together. He in his damp bathing suit, I in my favorite summer rainbow dress I found in a church rummage sale years ago.

All of Desmond's friends shaved their heads. With no barbers, their hair had grown wild. One boy shaved his head and it spread like wildfire. All of a sudden, they all had peach fuzz noggins. Desmond asked to shave his too but I talked him into shaving the sides and back and leaving some long on top. He looks summery and can feel the breeze on his scalp.

Now that I've gone to bed early, I just may get up and go back downstairs. It's dark out now and the breeze is getting cooler and cooler. I think Desmond's come home. Somewhere dogs are barking and motorcycles are passing us all by.

Always and still here,

Sarah

May 31

Dear Friend,

Day 81.

I am writing and deleting. Writing and deleting. I don't want to give myself away as the weirdo that I am. So I shan't.

Although, by now it may be too late.

I will just tell you one story.

Today I ran some errands. My Sunday food shopping before Joseph heads off to work so I don't have to go shopping with the kids in tow. I went to a few places to try to find everything on my list.

Heading to Target, which is at the mall, I pass empty parking lots. And in the one just before Target's lot, there was a black man, in his late 40s, maybe 50s, on a skateboard. He was alone and his eyes were closed. He was moving slowly in a dance while he coasted on the board. Just moving his arms through the air, his legs bent at the knee. His face turned towards the sun.

It made the most amount of sense. It's what art does. When nothing makes sense, art fills the space where sense should be. And it brings relief.

I tried to glimpse him over my shoulder as I drove by and saw his green shirt there still. I parked my car in Target's lot and got out and looked that way but he was gone. Like a ghost.

I only saw him for a few seconds. But the vision of him was solid enough to carry with me. Like a talisman.

I am tripping over the empathy I feel. It's blustering in me like a sheet on a clothesline, whipping in the wind. I had a hard time being out in the world today. And if I keep writing, I'll say all the wrong things. I think it's best now to just listen.

Always and still here,

Sarah

June 2020

June 1

Dear Friend,

Day 82.

A happy June to you. Perhaps.

The calendar said the day was Monday.

I organized my spice racks that hang on the inside of our basement door. Made a shopping list for all the spices we are short on, noting how much we need so I can buy the proper amount from the bulk section at the health food store. I used diagrams, arrows and parentheses.

We lured some of Desmond's friends over to our house with promise of ordering food. They jumped in the pool even though it was freezing today. They jumped on the trampoline. We ordered a pizza pie, half pepperoni and they ate most of it and disappeared again. Sonny and I stayed home and ate creamsicles.

I sat Sonny down so I could trim the hair around his face. He said he wanted the same haircut as Desmond and I couldn't bring myself to do it. His hair has grown long and the ends have started to curl just a little, reminding me of when he was a baby. I told him maybe next time.

Desmond came home earlier than I expected so we took a ride to the river to be by the water and looked for crystals again. There was a sailboat moored in the water. There was nobody there at all. The sun comes sideways through the trees that time of day. The beach is in shadow and the river is lit up, the trees on the other side aglow.

When putting the boys to bed I said, "Today was Monday, so tomorrow is..."

Desmond finished the sentence for me, "Tuesday."

"Yes," I said.

"So what does that mean?" Sonny asked.

"Nothing really. It's just the day after Monday."

Always and still here,

Sarah

June 2

Dear Friend,

Day 83.

I'm feeling pretty defeated. Trying very hard to do the right things right now, say the right things, show up at the things, support the right things in the right way. But at every turn, it seems, I am criticized for doing it wrong. Heard there was a #tuesdayblackout today, post a black box on your social media spots to support the Black Lives Matter movement. So I did that. Now it seems that was wrong. Because it's taking away from something. I can't keep up.

And so. Regardless. I am going to keep caring and keep showing up the best way I can figure in the moment. That's really all I can do.

It feels like a lot of "Come here. No, not like that."

Maybe nothing will feel like enough. Because nothing will be enough.

Today Desmond got out a big piece of paper on his own and some black paint and painted a Black Lives Matter sign, with little black smiling faces all around it. He wrote a speech asking people to help end racism. I was glad he was moved to do these things. He wants to go protest, he wanted to read his speech on social media. His heart is big and open and he's upset by the injustice and he wants to help.

Sonny painted a green sign. He mourns the loss of his last life on a planet where he had green skin and a green dog. Green lives matter. But I don't know where they are.

Our town has started a nightly vigil for George Floyd a few blocks from our house. So, we'll go tomorrow evening. We'll wear our masks and stay 6' away from everyone.

I feel like I'm sitting in a chair in a dunk tank. But I'll sit there forever if it would help.

Always and still here,

Sarah

June 3

Dear Friend,

Day 84.

Indeed.

Today I started a new exercise regimen. And there's a diet too, but I have to read the book. It's called *Metabolic Renewal*. Supposed to fix me right up, like new again. Balance all my hormones and make me gorgeous. I'll let you know how it goes. I did the first 20-minute power workout which was exciting. Not really, but I did it. It was fine.

I ordered a pedometer because I am supposed to walk some intimidating number of steps every day. Not the kind with the GPS and the heart monitor. I don't want anyone to know where I am if I fall off a cliff. It's just a step counter with a lithium battery. Old school. I'll wear my Reeboks. Should arrive between now and October.

Desmond and I watched a documentary about Kemp's Ridley turtles, the smallest and most endangered species of turtle in the world. They travel from the Gulf of Mexico and wash ashore in the fall onto the beaches of Cape Cod Bay. They are too cold to move and are "cold-stunned" lying still on the beach. People come from all over to rescue them. They dig holes in the sand and cover them with beach grass, then carry as many as they can to their cars, drive them to the wildlife sanctuary where they warm them up and get as many of them well as they can. Some don't survive, but the ones that do are flown to Florida by the Coast Guard and set free into warmer waters. We made plans to become volunteers someday.

Desmond has mastered a yo-yo and was learning new tricks from YouTube videos.

I put together a craft, an "invitation" on the table, to make a collage rainbow. Sonny and I each made one. Desmond said he might make one, so I left the supplies out. A little late to the quarantine "rainbow in the window party", but better late than never.

I cooked dinner and left it on the table and we walked to town with our Black Lives Matter signs to join our little town's vigil on Main Street. There were about 30 people there. Spread out, holding up signs, facing the street, wearing masks.

A lot of cars honked as they drove by, some were silent and looked straight ahead pretending we weren't there. Some stared in disgust and shook their heads. It surprised the three of us. It was disheartening to say the least.

Sonny was upset that no one was looking at his sign. He whined that he was bored until he made friends with the couple standing nearby. He climbed a light post and talked with his new friend, Frank. I sent Desmond across the street to grab a few slices of pizza for him and Sonny and we walked home. We talked again about maybe trying to do one of the marches in Kingston. It might be more uplifting to walk with a large crowd and not just white people.

Staying the course, trying not to stick my head in the sand out of shame. I y'am what I y'am.

Always and still here,

Sarah

June 4

Dear Friend,

Day 85.

Today Joseph and Desmond headed out early for a drive to Connecticut to pick up a new bike for Desmond. Joseph hunted it down online. Bikes are hard to come by in a pandemic when quarantine means there's nowhere to go, but you can ride your bike. He'd been promising Desmond a new bike since last year and his birthday is next month. It's an early birthday present. It's a very fancy 10 speed bike, bigger than the bikes he's been riding. He already crashed into a stop sign somehow. I guess it will take a little getting used to. He was fine, bike's fine.

Sonny and I hung back at home. We went to the river and he played with toys in the pebbles and we sat by the water for a while. Then we came home and had lunch and collaged the other side of our rainbows. He took a nap and I filled the kiddie pool.

I was thinking about how some people shook their heads at us from their cars last night, as we stood with our signs. Maybe it was because we were gathered in a group larger than 10. That's easier to swallow. But I can't be sure. Either way, it doesn't make sense.

Joseph and Desmond came home with dumplings from Poughkeepsie. From the Dumpling Palace.

Sonny reluctantly tried the dumplings after some coaxing and really liked them. He gave Joseph a high five that landed his hand right in the dumpling sauce which splashed all over our fluffy new light blue pool towels I just bought. This is why we can't have nice things.

Sonny played in the kiddie pool and I read some of my new healthy diet book. Super depressing. So many vegetables, so little carbs and fruit.

I went for a walk this evening by myself for about an hour. Just around town, over the little red bridge, down a lot of hills and then back up. Then I sat on a lounge chair in the backyard and put my feet in the kiddie pool. The book says if you walk an hour that's 5,000 steps. I am supposed to walk 10,000 steps a day. In what world...

I made popsicles again with the creamsicle recipe but I used peaches. I guess they are peachsicles.

I'm so tired. It's a good night to curl up on the couch and watch a movie. I've been wanting to watch *The Goldfinch*. I loved the book. Have you seen it? I think tonight's the night. Unless I fall asleep.

I hope you are feeling at peace in your space. What a whirlwind we've been in for so long. I wish we could meet up at a party full of smiling people. I look forward to that sort of thing. And the zoo. I really want to go to the zoo.

Always and still here,

Sarah

June 6

Dear Friend,

Day 87.

Missed a day writing yesterday. I was at my studio painting. I went grocery shopping from there, came home to put the groceries away and then went back to my studio after dinner to keep at it. I am so close to finishing this cake painting. That shredded coconut has really challenged me. I was so close to being done with it yesterday and then did something that took it far from done again and I was pacing around my studio talking loudly to myself, "I don't even know what I did! What happened?!" Growling and moaning. So many frustrating moments, lulls and triumphs in painting. So many choices made along the way, lots of guessing, lots of false starts, attempts and failures. But sometimes, eventually, success.

I am frustrated with my paints and not having the right colors, not being able to mix the colors I want. I think I will try some different paints soon. Splurge on better materials. I wish I could study painting with a master painter. I always feel I am taking the long way about it. Like there are techniques and tricks I should know by now.

I watched the rest of *The Goldfinch* movie before I went to bed last night. It was very good. It was so much like the book I wondered if I had seen the movie before. Which is entirely possible, but I don't think so.

This morning I went to an auction house in town. They have had a few controversial sales on weekends. Some people in town have been upset with them opening to the public. But I think small businesses in our town should be supported and I don't see how it's different from shopping at Target. Except that it benefits a family in my town, instead of a big corporation. I wore a mask and it was not crowded. I bought a small wooden chair, a pink lamp and some brand new pillow cases. I miss treasure hunting in thrift stores and antique shops. So much about it is satisfying. And good for the Earth. I stared at two chairs there for a while but left them in the end. Now I think I may go back and get them.

I sat outside in a bathing suit to soak up some sun and it started to rain. Classic. Now the sun is out again.

Sonny has started to play Lego games with Lego men protecting black people from being hurt. We have been talking about all that's going on. I talk with Desmond about what has happened, what is happening in a broad way and in specific ways. The story in pieces. It's so big, so old, so monumental, so important. Desmond talks about how he feels, what he thinks. Sonny hears it all and repeats back to us what he thinks we are saying. I am glad he speaks what is on his mind so I can correct him when he is off track. Better to say the wrong thing with me in the kitchen than in the middle of the grocery store. His refrain today was "Killing black people should be illegal!" "It is illegal, Sonny. But..." Explaining America to a 4 year old is good work. Constantly clarifying, boiling it down, trying to keep it simple but honest. And hopeful. I am hopeful we change. Clearly, this country is hopeful. Protests are carried out with great hope and desire for change. Someone pointed that out to me and I was glad to hear it. Sometimes I feel hopeless. But it lifts me up to think of so many people believing change is possible. I can be hopeful too.

There is not a lot of talk about COVID-19 these days. I wonder what the numbers are like now. I did see there has been a jump in numbers in places like Florida where more things have opened up. But numbers seem to be down in New York. We're still keeping to the same routine.

I may get back to my studio today. I downloaded an audiobook yesterday before I went to paint that is pure bliss. It's a whodunnit set on Cape Cod. Can you think of anything better? All things Cape until I get there. Can't wait to go back.

Always and still here,

Sarah

June 7

Dear Friend,

Day 88.

I've gone back to the auction house twice since I last wrote. Once to get the two chairs yesterday and once today to poke through boxes they had opened up along the sidewalk. A treasure hunt with a "pay what makes you happy" system, equals pure joy. I came home with a box of very special, new to me, old things. I miss that so much, it was so unexpected and so much fun.

On my way home yesterday I stopped in my friend's new bakery that she was just about to open when we were sentenced to quarantine. She has slowly been offering pop-up days of curbside service and I had yet to stop by. So nice to see all the work she's done, pick out some pastries for the boys and stay and talk for awhile.

The day had such a leisurely feel about it, the weather was so beautiful. After dinner Joseph, Sonny and I went for a bike ride around our neighborhood. Desmond was off with his friends again. We stopped to look at the fountain at the ice rink because the water was dyed blue. There were magenta peonies and I reached for one and was stung by a wasp or a bee, I couldn't tell which. No stinger, just a red dot in the center of a light circle on my skin. The bones in my finger ached but within the hour the pain was gone.

This morning, the four of us sat outside on the patio and ate fresh strawberries together. I had gone out to join Joseph, Sonny followed me out and Desmond came along soon after. We were in the sun, but Sonny wanted shade. There was all sorts of adjusting of chairs and bringing over an umbrella but eventually, everyone had the right amount of sun, shade and cushions. It lasted until the boys ended up on top of Joseph and he couldn't get out from under their shenanigans.

I went back to my studio today to paint the whipped cream on the last cake. I may finish it the next time I get over there. It was a good start. I was sad my Cape Cod mystery book ended. I wish there were more to listen to. I found one more that I downloaded but I felt like the reader was yelling at me. So I'm back to listening to my podcasts.

Have you listened to any good audio books lately? Or read any good mysteries?

Set in Cape Cod, perhaps?

Always and still here,

Sarah

June 8

Dear Friend,

Day 89.

Whew. Today wiped me out. Maybe I ate something bad. Maybe I'm getting the dread mahosis. Maybe just going for a hike for three hours with friends when Sonny usually naps just wore me out. I was too tired to make dinner so we ordered burgers from the diner and walked the few blocks to pick them up. Had a picnic on the front lawn in the dappled shade from the tall trees and the late day sun.

On the way to our hike we listened to the ghost story podcast we like, *Jim Harrold's Campfire*. It's just people calling in to Jim and telling their personal unexplainable or paranormal stories. This one had a man call in who told a story about seeing a creature that had the face of a child with stringy hair and white eyes with tiny black dots in the center. It was wearing some kind of jacket and had 8 legs, each with a small hand on the end of it. It was outside and ran up his apartment building wall. After it ate a cat. The host was so horrified. I am still laughing. It was an incredible conversation to witness. Of course, Sonny topped it with his own made up story as soon as the man was done talking, and Desmond was afraid to go to sleep tonight.

Equally as entertaining I learned about the black rain frog of Africa today. It "sounds like a squeaky toy and looks like an angry avocado." I hope you will look it up. It made me laugh almost as much as the crazy spider child story.

I restrung a wind chime that I found at the auction sale yesterday. Now I am waiting for wind.

And I am happy to report that my little town of Saugerties has arranged for a Black Lives Matter march on Thursday at 5:00. I'm so excited that someone took the initiative to coordinate the event. I will be there with bells on. Maybe you can come too. Meet me at the small pavilion at Cantine Field at ten to five. We'll walk together. Bring your mask and a sign. Or just a mask and your big heart. It would be so nice to see you.

Always and still here,

Sarah

June 9

Dear Friend,

Day 90.

They say 90 days breaks a habit. Also, it may be true that 90 days will turn your kids against each other and then turn them against you as well. Just a thought.

Today there were tears, whining, so much name calling, toy throwing, door slamming and yelling. There was a missing 10 year old, cold dinner, a bee sting, an elusive centipede, flying corn on the cob and the TV wouldn't work. I got called a loser face.

But I hung a hummingbird feeder, we made dinosaur bones and swam in the pool. I planted things in pots and mowed the lawn. We played tic-tac-toe and went for a bike ride.

I'm afraid of tomorrow. I might break down and eat ice cream or a whole cake. Lord help me. I hope you had a better day that I did.

Always and still here,

Sarah

June 10

Dear Friend,

Day 91.

I woke from a dream last night that I was with a group of people. They were talking about how the virus is everywhere now, we will all have it and we will all likely die from it. I was so terrified thinking of Joseph and I dying before Sonny does. Who would take care of him? Who would comfort him when he was sick and dying too? "Good luck," they said as we were leaving, "Hope to see you again." As I was waking I remembered that most people recover from the virus. I woke up confused and nervous.

Some anxiety is creeping back in now, with more options to be around more people. More events with crowds. Desmond's friends have started hanging out inside and at the skate park. We rode our bikes by the skate park when they were there, the day I got stung by the wasp. And there was a crowd of teenagers there, without masks. And I get confused. And nervous. So no more skate park for a while. And I've told Desmond to just play outside. He's not happy with me. But he doesn't give me a hard time either. He's just sad. Everyone is going at a different speed. I think I'm somewhere in the middle. And as before, I am not sure how necessary my precautions are but I don't mind giving it a little time to wait and see.

We went for a hike with our friend we have seen before during quarantine, with two other moms this time, with their boys, people we haven't seen. I thought we could try to keep a six-foot distance but it was impossible. So I let it go. But I came home exhausted. The worry, whether I acknowledge it or not, simmers beneath the surface like a pot on a stove. It takes so much energy to simmer that pot. And I get so tired.

Desmond came home late yesterday from his friends, so I told him he could not go out today. He is here now, telling me how glad he is I made him stay home, how nice it is here, how he loves our pool and his family and how beautiful everything is. So much for making him think twice before he comes home late again. Living his best life wherever he goes.

Joseph took Desmond for a hike today and Sonny and I stayed home. I gave myself a haircut and Sonny played so nicely with blocks by himself. It was a nice break from the bickering of late.

Planning on getting to my studio soon. Maybe today will be the day I finish the cake painting.

Ahhhh, my wind chime is gently chiming...

Off I go. Enjoy the rest of your day today.

Always and still here,

Sarah

June 11

Dear Friend,

Day 92.

Today we joined a Black Lives Matter march in our own little town. I am so glad we were there. It was so affirming and moving. It was a hot sunny afternoon. I taped our signs to the side of our red wagon so we could pull the boys. Put some cold cans of fruity seltzer in the cup holders, threw in a container of cheese crackers, wet some bandanas with cold water for their necks and gave them a big umbrella to hold for shade and off we went.

There were speeches, powerful speeches. It felt so good to be able to cheer for the passionate words spoken right there, not a video, not read on a screen, but right there. And I could yell "YES!" and maybe be heard by the people speaking. I clapped and yelled and cheered and wiped tears away over and over. Yes to everything. Yes, yes, yes. Thank you. Everything, anything, let's do it. I'm here.

Someone said they thought there were 300 or 400 people there. It seemed like a lot, I wish there had been more, the whole town, but it was a good turnout all the same. So many young people. Lots of signs, lots of masks, and loud chanting. I saw some friends. It's funny with everyone in masks, it takes an extra minute to recognize people I know.

The most memorable speakers were two black mothers and a black man who was a local preacher. All of them brimming with such determination, strength, and anguish.

The preacher spoke at the end of the march. He had trouble speaking at moments, it was so emotional. He asked us to kneel for 9 minutes, the length of time the officer knelt on George Floyd's neck. And we all knelt in silence. But I could hear the microphone picking up his labored breathing. I looked up and could see he was crying. Beside him was the other preacher from his church, a white man. And he reached for him and they supported each other. This tableau was just the opposite of the event we were reflecting on. And it was the way it should be, and I was glad to see it. And I cried too.

I noticed when I stood listening to their speeches, I swayed back and forth on my feet. I could not stop myself from moving. It reminded me of when my boys were babies, always rocking. Even when I was alone, on line at the grocery store, I'd still be rocking, back and forth. I felt this great flood of mother energy, nurturing, holding space and a great desire to comfort. I have seen signs in pictures at marches that say "When George Floyd called out for his mother, all mothers were summoned." That sounds about right.

I am so grateful I got to be there. That I am invited to help and join in this movement. I want to be in that wave, I want to help carry everyone to safety. How could you not?

Always and still here,

Sarah

June 12

Dear Friend,

Day 93.

I drove through town tonight and saw that the restaurants have tables set up outside distanced 6' apart. It was nice to see people in town and tempting to think of being served a meal. Such luxury.

I went to Mother Earth today in Kingston and the lights were on in Home Goods and a woman walked through the sliding doors. The Easter signs had finally been taken down and all the lights were on. My heart leapt. It's not supposed to be open for another three days. I parked my car and tentatively approached the door myself. A white piece of paper taped to the glass said, "This store is closed and is only allowing truck deliveries." Ah well. But excited about the truck deliveries...

I finally sat down and spent some time on a web site today for fancy Guerra Paints. I decided to upgrade my materials after being so frustrated with color in my last painting. These paints are emulsions? Dilutions? Delusions? Oh yes, "Pigment Dispersions". Concentrated pigment that you mix with a medium to make your own paint. In such rich colors.

I scrolled through the color chart, pausing at the names of the colors. It made me think of my mom, how she would have loved these words. She was a writer and a lover of new words. She had a t-shirt that listed all the names for groupings of different animals, like a murder of crows, a clowder of cats, a smack of jellyfish. She bought an old sailboat and learned to sail, I think mostly because she loved the language of sailing. Trimming the shroud, ready about, for and aft, port and starboard.

If she were around, I'd have sent her a list of these colors so she could delight in them with me.

Benzimidazo golden, midazo orange, perylene scarlet, zander orange, anthraquinone red, flaventhrone yellow deep, quinacridone pink madder, bone black, Van Dyke brown, hansa yellow, bismuth vanadate, and zanderin golden...

I looked them up.

Midazo is a drug used to produce amnesia in anesthesia, as well as a dye for pigment. Benzimidazo has a wide range of medicinal purposes. Anthraquinone is derived from plants like rhubarb and also makes a good laxative. Quinacridone is such a high-quality pigment, due to its weather fastness, it is used in automobile and industrial coatings. Bone black is made from bone charr, which is charred animal bones. Van Dyke brown was made famous by Sir Anthony Van Dyck, a Flemish Baroque artist who became the leading court painter in England in the 17th century. He used soil to make his brown but now they use asphalt and iron oxide to make the same color. Bismuth is a chemical element that has a half-life more than a billion times the estimated age of the universe, which is estimated to be 13.8 billion years old. So that paint should last a while.

There's so much to learn, everywhere you look. I heard about a father who every night at dinner asked his kids to tell him something new they learned that day. And if they couldn't think of anything, they had to go look something up. Such a brilliant way to live. Let's do it. Wanna? Imagine how smart we'll be?

Always and still here,

Sarah

June 13

Dear Friend,

Day 94.

Not much doin' today. I did get over to my studio for a little bit this afternoon.

Worked on my own color chart with the paints I have and wondered how I lived without one. Started a new painting from a photo I took at the beach last summer. A Long Island beach although I can't recall which one. Jones Beach or one on Fire Island. We had such a beachy summer last year. It was the best. I was thinking I would start my kitchen sink series from photos I've taken of dishes in the sink, but I'd much rather stare at a photo of a crowd of people on a beach. Tired of my kitchen sink after so much time in quarantine.

I was wondering where I might find some mulberries this year since the trail to the lighthouse is closed and that's usually where I get my fix. When I pulled into the lot for my studio, there was the telltale sprinkling of dark berries on the black pavement. And above them, a big mulberry tree. Problem solved.

On my way home from my studio I drove past my friends Bill and Patricia in town. I rolled down my window and yelled a hello. I called Bill and told him to come by and so they did. So nice to see them both and with hugs too! Sonny was so excited. We sat in the backyard with blankets and hot tea because it was so chilly. It was one of those days when it feels hot in the sun and cold in the shade. And cooler as the day went on. So much to talk about too, no shortage of current events to discuss.

Someone's setting off fireworks in town tonight. Big booms and crackly snaps.

There's another Black Lives Matter march in Kingston on Wednesday. I think we'll try to go. Joseph will be working but the boys have agreed to do it. Desmond is excited. Turns out he rode his bike to the front of the march on Thursday after we swung by our house so I could switch shoes and he could grab his bike. He led some chants when the crowd got quiet, shouting, "What do we want?!" The crowd answered, "JUSTICE!!" He called back with, "When do we want it?!" They yelled, "NOW!!" Could you imagine? Being 10 years old and leading chants at a protest? What a cool kid. I am so proud. He didn't even mention it to me until the next day, like it was no big thing. My friends told me about it before he did. I'm nervous to even respond to the call for a chant in a crowd. Hearing my own voice yelling makes me self conscious. I'm so repressed. I'm glad he has a strong voice in this world. And that he uses it for good. Blessed be.

Always and still here,

Sarah

June 14

Dear Friend,

Day 95.

First of all, I went to customer service at Hannaford the other day and the woman called me "Sweetheart" and I almost cried. Felt all parenty and stuff and no one ever calls me sweetheart, so if you want to call me sweetheart, I wouldn't mind.

Today I was downright exhausted. I declared I would need a nap at some point early in the day.

I went back to the auction house because they were doing their boxes outside thing again. I bought some more random treasures, including some model NAS-CAR race cars, "For adults. Not intended for children" and gave them to the boys, who were thrilled. I bought some blue ceramic fish chopstick holders, because everyone needs those. And a beautiful silver compact looking thing with the initials NA on the front. It opens to a very faded photo of an older woman on one side and on the other side is a little speaker and buttons. As if her voice is recorded there. Of course it did not work and I will try replacing the batteries but I have never seen such a thing. I showed Joseph when I got home and he said his mom had made one once with her picture and voice but he doesn't know what happened to it.

I ate my lunch outside and watched a squirrel try really hard to figure out how to get a drink of water from our pool. I brought out a bowl of water for it to drink instead. I hope it finds it. That reminded me to put out a shallow bowl of water with marbles in it for the bees to land on to drink water. I read about that online ages ago. I wonder if it's true. But it looks nice anyway. Surely some creature will enjoy it. Even if it's just Sonny when he discovers it tomorrow.

I did take a nap out on our deck upstairs under the shade of the umbrella with a pillow from my bed and earplugs in my ears.

Ran out for some groceries when I was up and ran into one of my favorite friends and her family. We stopped to talk and she kept telling me what her face was doing under her mask. "I'm grimacing!" she said. Then, "I'm smiling!" I love her.

The boys had gone to the high school track to run. When they came back Desmond wanted to go out with his friends and Joseph, Sonny and I went to town to sit down and be served a meal. It was amazing. First time back at a restaurant where Joseph and I could both sit and eat a whole meal together that neither of us cooked and not be running back and forth to the kitchen for things for the kids. You remember restaurants. I'm mansplaining restaurants, it's been so long. Sorry. It was so great.

We went to Diamond Mills, a fancy hotel, restaurant spot in town on the creek beside the waterfall. Sat outside. It wasn't crowded and we wore masks to and from the table. The server wore a mask. It was weird but mostly because it didn't feel weird. It just is. The weirdest part was the inside of the restaurant was sort of emptied out, some of the tables moved outside.

I told Desmond we were going out to eat and he chose to be with his friends. But he called my phone sobbing as we were finishing our meal, saying he had come home and didn't know where we were. He saw my car was gone and the back door was wide open and he thought someone had stolen us all.

I reminded him we had gone out to eat in town and he said he thought we'd be back by now. So he walked back to his friend's house and I picked him up there on the way home. He was so regretful he had not come with us. Especially when he heard Sonny had birthday cake ice cream with his meal.

Growing up is hard. So many little lessons along the way. Little regrets that inform future decisions. All these choices we make every day. Hoping we make the right one. Intuition, impulse, hindsight. A lot of that going on these days.

I ended the day back on the deck on the phone with my best friend from college, catching each other up on our lives since quarantine started. She lives on Long Island where the numbers of COVID cases have been so high. She helped her parents who are in their 80's move out of their home into a small apartment this month. She talked about how they are slowing down, more forgetful, less capable. I wonder what that is like. I won't know. I think it is valuable to see your parents age, something about it might help you to understand your own aging and future when it arrives. I am three years younger than my mom was when she died and it makes me feel like I am at the end of the line. What comes after is a blank. Like I will turn 100 in three years. I can't imagine or compute what's further than that because I didn't see my mother do it before me. Sort of an abstract thought that's hard to pin down. I am feeling it all the time these days. Like I'm in some weird time warp. Seeing my mother through my eyes as a teenager, seeing me through my kids' eyes. Wondering if I am just like my mother was then. Am I that old? I suppose I am.

Anyway, glad to be here, aging and all. We are all home safe and sound. Everyone in the house is asleep now. I should be too.

Always and still here,

Sarah

June 15

Dear Sweetheart,

Day 96.

Funny how the day unfolds. Midday I thought I could write to you but nothing at all had happened. I had made pancakes. Strawberry for Desmond, Blueberry for Sonny. And the rest of the usual morning things, swept the floor, threw in a load of laundry. I cut the grass and raked it. Really nothing. The weather was just like the day before. Everything the same.

But the day really picked up after lunch time.

I pulled our old stroller out of the shed and wiped it down to get it ready for the march in Kingston on Wednesday. We walked to Stewart's so I could put air in the tires. Then we headed over to Mother Earth for a few things. They have a funny plexiglass window set up at the cash register with two small slits at the bottom to pass money and receipts through. I had to hold up each item for the cashier to scan. That was a new one.

When we got home, Desmond mentioned wishing he could hear Grandma Pam's voice. My mom passed away when I was young and although I am sure I've played videos for him in the past, he had forgotten what she sounded like.

My mom made a video four months before she died. She had a friend record her in our home, reading three of the children's books she wrote. The first one on the couch, the second on the deck outside her bedroom and the third on her bed. She made it for her someday grandchildren that she knew she might never meet. She wanted to be a grandmother so badly. She loved children, she loved babies.

I had been thinking of playing it for Sonny, and Desmond, although I had played it for Des when he was small and he was unimpressed. When Desmond asked today, I figured now was a good a time as any.

It took a while to get the VCR hooked up, the tape located and everything ready to go. The boys sat and watched, we paused it so we could get the book she was reading so they could follow along. They sat still for the first story and then started wandering around the room, chatting, playing with other things. I sat transfixed.

I was scared to watch it. It was lovely to see her face and hear her voice. I was surprised by her Long Island accent which I thought she had lost at some point but I guess not. Maybe it was just me that lost my own. Joseph says it comes out when I am mad. How did she look so healthy when in such a short time she would be so gravely ill?

At the very end of the video, she is on her bed. She finishes the last book and closes it. She says, "And now it's time for your nap," she lifts a throw blanket from her bed and lays it out flat. She pats it with her hand and says, "Come lay down here with me." And her face crumbles as she does her best not to cry and the tape ends abruptly.

And my own tears spilled down my face. I covered my face with my hands and cried quietly. The boys asked why I was crying. I said I miss my mom. They told me it was okay and not to cry. So I got up and cleaned my face.

I put salami on crackers and called it dinner.

I went out and cut the grass some more. And a friend called. Joseph came home and took the boys to the track to run again.

I feel a little shell-shocked. Like someone beat me up. Grief is like that. So punchy.

I'd say I'll probably dream about my mom tonight but I rarely do. When I do, they are bad dreams, I realize she's been alive this whole time but won't talk to me.

My yard is very tidy now.

I should like to watch a show and be somewhere else for a bit.

But, I'm always and still here,

Sarah

June 16

Darling Friend,

Day ninety-seven.

Should we have a party on the 100th day of quarantine? And by party, I mean shall I celebrate alone?

Today was a really nice day.

The most interesting part of the morning was discovering Desmond has really been slacking on his schoolwork, so we had some reconfiguring to do today. More work for him and for me, but mostly for him. Some lost privileges but he takes everything in stride. A pretty even keel on that kid. Hard to know how mad I should be. As long as he gets it done and knows I'm disappointed. He hates when I am upset with him. I remember feeling that with my mom. She never really punished me but just her disappointment in me felt awful. She had a disappointed face she'd wear. I wonder if I have one too. I must. "Oh, Sarah..." she'd say. With that face.

This afternoon a friend came over with her daughter. The kids played so well together and my friend and I got to sit outside and drink iced tea and talk in peace for almost 3 hours. It was so glorious and I can't remember the last time that happened. Such a treat. It made the day feel different than all the other days. The kids played outside and inside. Other than one other friend we had in the house to use the bathroom last week, that was just the second time we've had anyone in the house since the quarantine started. My friend came inside for a tour since she'd never been to my house before. Of course Desmond had taken forever to unload the dishwasher so the dirty dishes were still piled in the sink. I was not expecting we'd come inside. But it felt so nice anyway, mess and all. I miss having friends over. We promised to do it again soon and I hope we do.

By the time they left it was nearly dinner time so I walked to town with the boys to get them some pizza. We came home and they sat outside and ate while I went inside and made myself a salad. No pizza and no sugar for a month and the scale doesn't care. Getting old is nonsense.

Our yard is feeling super sweet, green and delightful. Desmond has taken to counting our 5 blue jays in the morning and throughout the day. He set up a bird watching station in the back corner of the yard with a little table and chair, a sketch pad and binoculars.

Our life has shrunken a bit but it is as sweet as ever. I am glad for these days.

Tomorrow we march again in Kingston. Should be a lot bigger than the one in our town. Desmond started to make a Black Lives Matter drawing with chalk on our sidewalk in pinks and light blue. I get anxious about showing up in big protests but my anxiety is a tiny thing compared to the fear so many Americans live with on a daily basis because of the color of their skin. I'm so glad we are able to go. It's the least we can do.

Always and still here,

Sarah

June 17

Dear Friend,

Day 98.

It's interesting that the 100th day of my quarantine will be Juneteenth. Feels like I should have seen this coming.

Did you hear Cuomo today say he is going to make Juneteenth a state holiday? That's pretty cool. Executive orders for state employees this year and state-wide next year."...so New Yorkers can use this day to reflect on all the changes we still need to make to create a more fair, just and equal society." Good, good.

The first part of today was preparing for the second part of the day. Taking my 3 guys to march in Kingston required lots of provisions for comfort, restlessness, hunger and thirst. It was a hustle to get there on time and all together, with dinner in tow and a stroller, signs, drinks, toys, a scooter, masks, wipes for our hands, water, sunscreen, hats....oy. Totally worth it. It was a beautiful day for a walk with our fellow humans. Less speeches at this one than in Saugerties. A little more waiting in the beginning and a pretty quick ending when the march was done. I couldn't tell how many people were there. It seemed like a lot. I could not see the start or end of the March, we were somewhere in the middle.

When we started, we were in a big crowd of people. The closest we've been to a group of people in a really long time. Then we spread out as we walked. I soaked up those moments of close people energy. So strange to feel that after not having had it in so long. Watching crowds of people on TV and longing for that feeling, and then there it was, right where we left it. We all had masks on, but it still felt good to me.

Desmond led some chants again, which he loved. I had a really hard time not crying every time I opened my mouth. But I tried again and again. I kept it together pretty well.

We lasted beginning to end. And headed home to eat bagels and get ready for bed. The kids ate bagels, not me. Are you crazy?

Always and still here,

Sarah

June 18

Dear Friend,

Day 99.

Today would have been my mom's 73rd birthday.

My mom was my best friend. She was my first love and that love has lasted, even though she is gone. She was the most present person in my life for 21 years and has been the most absent for the last 24. Those two extremes live side by side in ways. The contrast makes the latter harder to bear. But what can you do.

I have been thinking a lot of her lately. She was an incredible power of example for me, I learned so much from her just being herself. The way she treated people, the things she talked about and cared about, the things she was passionate about, equality for all people, kindness, generosity, the service she did, the friends she had, her friendly way with everyone that came across her path. She found herself feeling lonely sometimes, as we all do. But when she died, I swear, everyone I talked to felt like they were her best friend. She was heartfelt and vulnerable with people. I don't know if you can BE heartfelt, but she was. She was very genuine and felt things deeply. She worried and she laughed. She loved so many things and so many people.

I have been thinking of a specific memory lately. My mom raised me to not see differences in people based on the color of their skin. She adopted a black baby girl before I was born, after several miscarriages. My mom was 24 or 25 years old, my dad was 25 or 26. They were altruistic people. They sponsored a Vietnamese family after the war. My mother's parents adopted a Vietnamese baby. My mother's brother married a Japanese woman. Her other brother married a Dominican woman. My cousin married a Puerto Rican man. My family is a beautiful blend of faces and colors.

Anyway, the memory I have been thinking of is of her and I at a park on Long Island where I grew up. I must have been about 10 years old or so. We went there because there was some tumultuous stuff going on at home. There was a seesaw there and it was missing a seat on one end. She told me to get on the seat and she sat on the other end without the seat, so she was straddling the circular metal pole with no seat. When I went down, she went up and flipped right over, or under I should say. Just spun feet over head and she fell on the ground. A group of 4 black teenage boys, the only other people in the park came running up to her to help her up and see if she was okay.

Now, the important part of the story is this—She confessed to me that when we got to the park, she was nervous when she saw them. A group of black teenage boys and no one else around. But she didn't say anything to me in that moment, and we did not leave. We went about our business of spinning her onto the ground on the see-saw. And she mentioned it after because she wanted to out herself and say she was wrong and look how it turned out. They came to her rescue without hesitation. I don't think I would have remembered this outing otherwise, even though she fell off the see-saw. What I remembered is what she said afterward. And what she didn't say out loud, but what I heard was "Don't be afraid of people. Don't judge them by what they look like, or by what you have been taught by society to think. That's nonsense."

I love that she shared her false judgment with me, that she was vulnerable and shared her faults and mistakes. So that I could learn along with her.

We're taught so much by our parents, but also by the society we live in. There are so many societal ideas that need to be ignored or repaired in our minds. I learned that from her too.

Love everyone, be kind, help people, find your passion, follow your bliss, life is a mystery, babies are miracles, expect abundance, don't eat too much sugar, dance, sing, write things down, make art, be by the water, go for walks, bring a friend.

I desperately wish all the time that she was still here. There is a huge hole in my heart and my life with her missing. Still. Probably always will be. I can't see how there wouldn't be.

So, Happy 73rd Birthday to my mom. Wherever she is. I am told she is around me. I do hope so. And I hope someday, a long ways from today, I get to hug her again and say thank you. "Thank you, thank you, thank you." And, "I've missed you like crazy."

Always and still here,

Sarah

June 19

Dear Friend,

Day 100!

100 days of strange and unusual. 100 days away from our old routines. Not a strict quarantine now but an emerging little by little. I don't know what you'd call this part, if not quarantine. It's somewhere in between. Things are not back to normal but some things have come back into our lives. What would you call it?

Our numbers in NY are very low now, I believe. As of four days ago, 0 new cases in our county. Haven't heard any news since then.

I know you've been wondering if I'm still eating those weight watchers recipe protein bagels made with Greek yogurt for breakfast. I haven't been. My new diet plan says veggies and protein for breakfast, no starch till dinner time. I miss those bagels.

I haven't lost any weight but I lost 2¼". Whatever that means. I'm not shorter, the inches came from my waist and my neck of all places. Didn't know my neck was fat. Now I know.

I've also stopped wearing my hair pulled back from my face every day. I started wearing it down again when phase 1 of opening happened. So weird. And only interesting to me probably.

I've heard that it is unlikely that we can catch the virus from surfaces, but I can't stop cleaning my groceries when I bring them home. Now they just seem dirty if I don't. Will I be stuck cleaning my groceries forever? This concerns me. It's very time consuming. When will I know for sure I don't have to clean my groceries? Maybe I need to see a video of the Dr. who did the video that showed me how to clean them, telling me I can stop.

I've discovered on my protest marches, that were on really hot days, that if you soak your mask in cold water and ring it out before you put it on your face, it stays nice and cool. Just a tip for your summer.

I went grocery shopping yesterday and walked past two white policemen talking to a very upset black man just inside the doorway of the store I was entering. He had had some sort of confrontation with people who worked at the store, it was hard to tell from what he was saying. I asked an employee inside too and it was still hard to know for sure. But it sounded like he had been in several times, upset over a cashier grabbing money from his hand. So the store manager called the police. He was complaining about the police being called at all, about all that is wrong with this country. The police listened to him, patiently but I could see they were annoyed. Like a parent with an upset child. I walked in past them, stood and waited. Another white woman stood nearby and waited too. We nodded at each other. I felt like I needed to be there just to bear witness. I don't know if he cared that we stood there and waited; if he appreciated it or hated it. I didn't expect anything would go wrong but I didn't feel like I could leave him either. They told him he was asked to not come back to the store. That made me sad. Seems they could have just told him to stop harassing the staff. If he was. I waited until he walked away and the police got back in their patrol car.

Staying vigilant and loving.

I bought a package of little cupcakes for the boys and we sang Happy Birthday to my mom in the afternoon by the pool. Sonny said we should save one for Grandma Pam. It's still in the fridge.

In the evening I was checking my voicemail on my cell phone and I had a message from my dentist. I touched the play symbol on the screen and put the phone to my ear and the phone stayed silent. So I took the phone away from my ear to look at it and it was dialing my sister. I like to think my mom was connecting the two of us and saying hello.

My pedometer finally came in the mail, but sadly I only walked about 2504 steps today. Far from the recommended 10,000. I mean really. But I do like the pedometer. It seems like a good friend to have.

My new paints came in the mail too. I brought them to my studio today and lined them up. Now I have to figure out how to use them. It's sort of like dye that you mix with medium.

Worked on my new beach painting and listened to an audio book about a haunted house. It's okay. Not as great as the Cape Cod whodunnit. BUT! I also got in the mail, a book that is another Cape Cod whodunnit mystery, written in 1931 by Phoebe Atwood Taylor, who went on to write a whole series of them. She was only 22 when this first one was published! It reads like an old Alfred Hitchcock movie. So charming. Of course it is called, *The Cape Cod Mystery*.

Okay, I've gone on too long. Sleep well. Miss you.

Always and still here,

Sarah

June 20

Dear Friend,

Day 101.

I forget what happened today. I've been in bed for a few hours with back pain. I don't know why I was messing with the pool ladder, because it wasn't "even". I tweaked my back trying to even it out in some weird OCD nesting episode.

Desmond got me a tiny arnica homeopathic ball to put under my tongue, from the fancy set I ordered from England. And Joseph heated up one of our rice heating pads for me. I love the way they smell, kind of like oatmeal.

I was mostly at home "relaxing" today. I baked a banana bread for Father's Day for Joseph because he loves banana bread. I helped the boys make cards. I ran to Target to pick up a few things. You can't try on clothes in Target right now. You have to just buy them and try them on at home and then return them. Seems like the dressing rooms would be a safer bet.

It was super-hot and humid today. We were all in and out of the pool all day. So nice to have a little pool to slip into and cool off. Sonny has remembered how to swim with his puddle jumper floating device on and is loving the freedom of swimming around without being suspended in a float. He can touch the tips of his toes to the bottom of the pool now. He's growing so fast.

Today was the summer solstice, the longest day of the year. Summer is surely in full swing.

I made a reservation for an Airbnb in Cape Cod for August. Sad to wait that long but happy to have a date in the calendar. Anxious to get back there. It has such a pull for me, I feel at home there. So nostalgic and familiar from the first moment I arrived. Must have been my home in a previous life.

Tomorrow we are going to a friends for a BBQ for Father's Day. Just us and them in their yard. They prefer the 6' of distance so we'll do our best. I'm going to bake a raspberry custard and maybe even make those summer solstice cookies I have been thinking about making since last summer...It's possible I could.

I think Joseph has a friend visiting from Brooklyn tomorrow too, earlier in the day. Should be a full and busy day. One thing at a time, and it may go over without a hitch.

I hope you have a happy Father's Day, or just a happy Sunday. Fathers are complicated animals.

Always and still here,

Sarah

June 21

Dear Friend,

Day 102.

It was Father's Day today. With an apostrophe. We gave Joseph a little pile of gifts this morning and cards we made. The boys swam in the pool and hung out under the umbrella in the shade. Another very hot muggy day.

I finally baked those summer solstice cookies. The dough had herbs like rosemary, thyme and sage, with lavender flowers mixed in. The icing had lemon zest and turmeric to make it yellow. We had two edible flowers growing in our yard to place atop the icing. Perennial phlox, the tall kind is okay to eat, the annual low growing shrub is not. I happened to have some blooming tall lavender colored phlox and white clover flowers in the grass. I collected a few and brought them inside, cutting the stems from the phlox and the tiny clover blooms. Sonny helped put the flowers on the cookies. Adding a sprinkling of the dried lavender flowers I had in the cabinet. They were so beautiful and so delicious. Sort of savory and sweet. Desmond said they reminded him of Thanksgiving and Christmas. A new summer solstice tradition is born.

I also baked a raspberry custard. An old favorite recipe from Martha Stewart.

Joseph's friend from Brooklyn did not end up visiting after all.

We went to our friend's house for a BBQ at 4:00. So nice to see them and be fed, to eat outside somewhere away from home. I think that was our first meal at someone else's house since the quarantine started. So much more conscious of everything I touch, just noticing, paying attention to things I never did before. Not worried, just in the habit of watching now. It comes and goes, the noticing. It occurs to me and then I forget again. I think it will just fade away eventually.

Their neighbor was clearing out their garage. Placing boxes of toys on their lawn. Things left over from their three grown sons. Of course Sonny wanted every toy. Two pirate ships full of pirates, nine motorcycles, 6 planes, one teeny tiny car. Desmond made off with a black wool top-hat with a red feather in its band, a black velvet Islamic cap, a movie take clapper board and snow goggles. He let us know soon after he wants to make movies and that Joseph and I will be in his romantic comedy. I can't wait.

It did not occur to me to clean any of it. So things are getting better.

We came home late and there were bedtime tears and I had no patience. It's nice when Joseph or I are completely done and the other is there to step in. Joseph got them off to bed.

I am so tired. I managed to walk an extra thousand steps today according to my pedometer. No idea how that happened. But I'm glad I made it.

Always and still here,

Sarah

June 22

Dear Friend,

Day 103.

Thought it was Tuesday all day, but it's only Monday. Which means I didn't miss the 3:30 virtual talk about stings and bites with Coyote Peterson. That's nice.

Pirate ships all day for the boys. In the pool this morning, into a bubble bath and then back in the pool again. Sonny's named his ship The Blue Willow and Desmond has named his The Princess.

Today felt like a hustle all day until 3:00 when I had a friend and her kids over to swim. It was a day for staying in a bathing suit and climbing in and out of the pool. The pool's water temperature is up to 81° which is very warm for our little pool since it's in the shade by 4:00 or so.

My friend who came by has a little baby. So nice to hold a baby again and marvel at her little fingers and toes. And watch our gaggle of strong, big kids run, swim and jump.

I had a pizza delivered for dinner and ate some too. It was so good. I have not had pizza in a long while. No sides, no salad, just pizza slices by the pool.

Desmond has decided the first movie he makes will be a scary movie instead of a romantic comedy. Sonny's going to be a ghost child in the basement. I get to be the woman who tries to help him. We start filming tomorrow.

He's planning on making a craft services table and asked me if I'd like to get paid. I said I'd work for free but I hear Sonny is getting $1 an hour.

It's 10:00 and I just had to go take Sonny's flashlight and book from his room. He can't even read yet. Go to bed, kid.

Always and still here,

Sarah

June 23

Dear Friend,

Day 104.

Man, was it hot out today. And in. My house was so hot. We have one air conditioner in the living room window that is usually enough for the downstairs but today I had to hunt down a box fan to put on the floor and blow the air from the living room into the kitchen, which saved my life.

It was another day for staying in our bathing suits but Desmond had us dress up and start our work on his horror movie. It's called *Haunted*. He picked out my outfit and I was beside myself with worry. A fitted white tank top with black polka dots and short peach colored shorts with light blue crew socks with cartoon clouds on them that say, "Stop talking." And a beaded bracelet. I mean, they were all things in my closet but those shorts don't really fit me anymore and the combination was alarming. He also picked out a pair of mid calf high, leather, pale pink boots for a scene when we walk to town. I was simultaneously flattered and frightened. But I couldn't do it. I asked for different shorts and to be barefoot, not in town but at home, no socks. He is a very sympathetic director, thank goodness. He said as long as I'm comfortable, it's okay..

He dressed Sonny in a white tank top and brown pants. Sonny looked timeless and was excited that he looked like Obi Wan Kenobi. We put makeup on him, dark circles under his eyes and white on his face, black scratch marks and a pink scar across his eye. Sonny plays the ghost.

It was hard for me not to direct the movie myself. I tried not to give too many "helpful suggestions". But Desmond had a vision and we did our best to show up and make it happen. So the first scene is done. It took a lot of takes and there was no craft services table after all, and no one got paid. Yet.

We have plans to recruit people in town tomorrow.

I spent some time sitting outside by the pool unknotting and rearranging lines on the pirate ships. Reeling in anchors, untangling and adjusting sails.

While Sonny napped I grabbed some quiet time on my float in the pool with my Cape Cod Mystery book. My float was slowly deflating and my minutes afloat were numbered. But it was good enough.

I cooked dinner and heated the kitchen back up. A one pot recipe with chicken, rice and mushrooms. It was alright. It was hot.

After dinner we rode our bikes to the Senior Center to vote. I realized when we got there I did not bring a mask. I asked Desmond if he had anything in his pouch on his bike I could use. He had a paper napkin and I figured it was good enough. I hoped they would let me in. Sonny insisted on coming in and put his t-shirt up over his mouth and nose. Desmond waited outside with our bikes.

Lucky for us they had a box of masks inside. A huge tub of hand sanitizer and a box of rubber gloves. I skipped the sanitizer and took one glove and a mask for me and one for Sonny. I had not worn one of those disposable paper masks before. It was not as comfortable as the fabric ones I've been wearing.

Sonny was sure to inform everyone in the room who we weren't voting for and why. Good Lord. And got his first ever Werther's caramel hard candy. As we pedaled away on my bike he said, "How did those elector people make such good candy?" I told him Werther's made it.

And as always, I did not get a sticker.

Always and still here,

Sarah

June 24

Dear Friend,

Day 105.

Wooooweeeee........

Today we took an hour drive to Wurtsboro, which is out past Ellenville. Pretty drive on Rt. 209 all the way, fields and farms, old houses, cows and horses, little towns, repair shops, ice cream spots, hand painted signs, a dollar store and McDonald's thrown in here and there. So much green. Summer's green is my favorite. It's like we're in a lush green bowl wherever we go.

That's the furthest I've driven in a very long time. We listened to our ghost story podcast. Sonny fell asleep on the way there and the way home. He'll be up till midnight.

My friend is running a big old house from 1800, with additions that have additions, including an inground, indoor pool, a teepee in the yard, 124 acres of woods and a rushing stream that borders the property. She was renting it out as an Airbnb for retreats and groups before the quarantine and is just getting back to renting it again. It would make a great place for a wedding or family reunion. She's there with her son who's Desmond's age. Another friend of ours met us there with her daughter.

I remembered everything except for Sonny's puddle jumper for swimming. So I was a nervous wreck watching him run around the pool. He swam holding onto pool noodles just fine but without a floating device strapped to his body, I couldn't look away.

At one point I looked up and he was gone. I jumped up and ran around yelling, "Where's Sonny?! Where's Sonny?!" Everyone froze and Sonny sauntered in the door, said he was just warming up in the sun outside. I instantly had a headache that stayed with me until we got home.

We walked on a path to the stream and the kids waded in the water on the rocks, Sonny with his black socks and yellow sneakers on, Desmond barefoot, the four kids disappeared around the bend. I worked at being okay with them being out of sight. They are so rarely out of my sight these days, especially Sonny.

Between worrying about him around the pool and worrying about him in the creek, I wore myself out. When dinner time rolled around we headed out to the car where I could strap Sonny into his seat and relax. He fell asleep in the car and I watched him in the rearview mirror with his head tilted back, mouth slack and a piece of chewing gum leaning on the inside of his cheek. I told myself he would not choke to death. He did not.

We made it to Adams and stopped in to get dinner. I put Sonny in the shopping cart barefoot, since his sneakers were soaked and muddy. He shivered in the cold and I wrapped myself around him while we waited for my sandwich from the deli. Desmond got New England clam chowder and Sonny had 1 chicken tender with a package of oyster crackers. I felt revived after my sandwich, like I would live another day.

We made it home. Joseph arrived the same time we did. So nice to see his face at the end of the day. "My FACE..." he says. The N95 mask with the disposable mask on top of that one is driving him crazy. His face is free for the next 4 days, or mostly anyway.

Desmond had a hard time getting to bed. He got up to tell me he keeps thinking about the coyote from the ghost story podcast. The one who's joints bent the wrong way, who was emaciated and as he trotted off into the woods, stood up and walked on its hind legs as it disappeared into the trees. I told him I didn't think that coyote was creepy, just really smart and special.

I am really excited to lie down. If a coyote walked into my room, I'd still fall asleep. I am glad we have no plans for tomorrow. But I do have to get groceries.

Always and still here,

Sarah

June 25

Dear Friend,

Day 106.

Today Joseph was home so I got to sleep late. I woke up at 10:00, I think I really needed the extra rest.

I got to go out on my own to run errands. I went food shopping AND popped into Home Goods and Marshall's for the first time since quarantine started. They just opened back up four days ago. I was so happy to see the parking lot full. I surprised myself with the satisfaction I felt just looking for a parking spot. I yelled out loud in my car something like, "Hey! Look at this! Welcome back! You all came back!" Such a sign of normalcy. The way "it used to be."

There seemed to be an extra buzz in the air. A woman stood at the door of Marshall's with a thumb button counter in her hand, counting the people who walked through the door. She welcomed everyone with a big under the mask grin. As if she were welcoming you to your own birthday party. Shoppers chatted excitedly with each other, I kid you not. Strangers giddily talking about how strange it was to be back, overwhelmed at the sheer pleasure of shopping. It was sort of weird.

The bathing suits had been "toilet papered". Just a few were left, so sparse on their rack. The fitting rooms were closed which threw me for a loop. I held things up in front of a mirror, with my mask on. It was hard to tell, but I whittled my finds down to half. I bought a few summer shirts, one summery dress and some playdough for Sonny. Only one shirt will go back because it was a little scratchy. Not too shabby.

Home Goods felt the same, but no counter at the door. I got my chewing gum for the kids and some seat cushions for the dining room I had been thinking about all Spring.

I came home and cleaned the groceries again. I almost forgot and put a couple things away and then remembered and decided to stick with it. As annoyed as I was to do it.

Joseph headed out for his first group bike ride since quarantine started. He had been missing his group rides and was excited to go.

The kids decided to have a movie night and rent the new Sponge Bob movie and have popcorn. Remember when renting a movie meant going out to the movie rental store and browsing the shelves? I miss that. I miss Blockbuster. Funny that I remember it so clearly. Remember the Block Buster microwave movie popcorn you could buy there? Rewinding the tapes before you returned them?

You know microwave popcorn bags are super toxic, right? I hope so. I worry about you.

It's a beautiful night. Sitting on my deck upstairs, listening to the neighborhood. Reminds me of the Alfred Hitchcock movie *Rear Window*. The neighbors behind us are eating outside, plates and silverware clinking, chatting and laughing. Another neighbor a few houses down is playing jazz music. The birds are mumbling in the trees. Motorcycles are humming in the distance somewhere, on their way out, or home.

I haven't heard any crickets yet. But the lightning bugs are out again. So glad they are here with us.

I guess I should put the kids to bed. I wonder how long they'd let me sit up here. Sonny came up to see me and give me a hug, just to make sure I was here I think. Desmond was right behind him and then they ran back downstairs to their movie that they said wasn't over yet. Now I'm not so sure.

The sky is purple. Sweet dreams tonight. Until tomorrow.

Always and still here,

Sarah

June 27

Dear Friend,

Day 108.

I have a reignited fear of the virus. Someone posted something on Facebook about how it can have lifelong effects on your health. I looked that up. It's true. Scarring of your lungs, increases the likelihood of strokes, even in young people, neurological issues, other stuff. I forget. That will keep me washing my groceries and keeping to small groups of people or keeping my mask on.

Yesterday I got to my studio and mixed some of my new paints. Working on my 3 matching beach paintings in varying sizes. Shadows on clouds. Listening to another haunted house story.

After sitting for a few hours I went to the river by myself to look for crystals. Founds some really nice ones. One small super clear diamond looking one in the rocks. One nice sized point growing out of the mud in the woods on the way out. How do they grow there? It amazes me completely. I may as well be finding real diamonds, they are so special to me.

I stopped at my friend's bakery on the way home. Picked out a little chai crumb cake and a small flourless chocolate cake. Brought it home and cut them in fours and had some myself and shared them with the boys. It's been five or six weeks since I've had sugar. I am always afraid I won't be able to stop if I have some again. So far today I am doing okay. I have thought about sugar more than usual but have managed not to have any. I think I'm gonna make it. It's nearly bedtime.

Today it rained so much. We needed the rain, everything was so dry, the grass was cooking in the sun. I opened the windows and let the cool wet air drift into the warm house. Felt so nice.

It was a perfect rainy Saturday with nowhere to go. I finally made the sunscreen I had been wanting to make the last couple of weeks. Moving the pile of ingredients around in the kitchen from here to there and back again. Refusing to put them away so that I wouldn't forget.

It was so easy and quick. It came out so well. Feels good on my skin and smells nice too. I used zinc oxide and the other ingredients have some sunscreen properties too. Good nourishing skin food. Not to mention, so much cheaper than the stuff from the store. Even though I already bought some. Now we have enough for the whole summer and then some.

I spent a good part of the day looking at school curriculum for 6th grade for Desmond and Kindergarten for Sonny. Filled up a shopping cart of books online.

Walked to town tonight to poke around in the shops with my mask on. Everyone wears them. It's hard to recognize people I know. Picked up fish tacos at the Mexican spot in town and brought them home for dinner.

Joseph's in bed, trying to sleep. He hasn't slept well lately. The boys are hopefully sleeping or close to it. I'm going to watch a movie. I was hoping I could pull together a crocheting project too. The idea of watching a movie and crocheting sounds so good. But by the time I come up with something to make it will be too late for a movie.

Too bad all the county fairs have been canceled this summer. I have a feeling there would have been some amazing quilts and afghans this year.

Always and still here,

Sarah

June 28

Dear Friend,

Day 109.

This morning we had so many raspberries on our raspberry bushes that I made a spontaneous raspberry custard. I had made one to bring to my friend's house on Father's Day and it was so good and so easy to make, I figured why not make another. I made it with agave instead of sugar and a little less than was called for. So it is a sweet treat that won't make me want to eat the whole thing, which is nice.

Sonny was upset with me for taking so many berries and said he hated raspberry "cuspard". But when it came out of the oven, he jumped up and down asking for a piece.

I've been spontaneously cleaning things out. Bins, drawers, containers. Editing and clearing away clutter. Went through some papers today, saving directions to crystal hunting spots and Cape Cod brochures, throwing away school calendars and notes about things that have come and gone.

I took myself for a walk to the track at the high school, jogged and walked a mile around and then walked home, finding feathers where I walked, reminding me of my mom. I thought I'd do better running but it was harder than I expected. Nice track though, I had never been before. It's sort of tucked out of the way, far off from the road and is surrounded by trees. I admired the grass, the way the white clover flowers dot the green. A stripe of light green, soft, taller grass growing through the dark short grass with the clover.

I liked the blue and white hurdle on its black metal legs. Sitting off to the side of the red track in the grass. Sometimes everything looks like a painting to me.

After lunch I walked to town to help a friend work on a mural she's making to replace another mural she made. The last one blew down in a storm. Luckily it just landed on the flat roof below it. It was hung up high on the side of a building on Main Street. I started painting in some white clouds. So nice to paint so big, walking around barefoot on the painting, carrying a can of paint, a house painting brush, laying down bumpy, wispy white shapes in a light blue sky.

I have been thinking about making a video of our little town. I'll walk from our house to Main Street. Record all the shops, trees, cars and people. So that Desmond and Sonny, and I, can look at it decades from now. I can put in on YouTube so that anyone who wants to visit Saugerties from 2020 can. I know 2020 might not be a year we'll miss specifically, but I wish I could see a video of my town from when I was a kid.

I was thinking of an old store on Sunrise Highway that I used to walk through. I can't remember the name. Or exactly where Woolworth's was.

I will take a video of our house too. Every room, and even the yard. Little time capsules. Uninteresting until the future starts to needle it away from us, then we can visit as we please. Scoff in the face of the future. Take that, time thief.

Made some excellent fried shrimp for dinner. Coleslaw and French fries. Joseph almost took the boys to the track so he could run too, and I could cook in peace. But the sky grew so dark and there was thunder rumbling around. He drove them there, saw lightning and brought them back home, dropped them off and went for a run. They came back inside bickering and Sonny stormed upstairs crying. I went to his room to talk with him. He was upset that the high school had had a drive-in movie set up for graduation. I am still not sure why this bothered him so. Desmond called his friend who lied to him about where he was. So I sat in the living room, dish towel in my lap and talked with him a long while about that. Such a mom thing, to have a dish towel in your hand. Such important moments, the comforting and listening. Talking through reactions and options. Practicing empathy when there is no resolution. Letting that be enough.

Eventually I got back to the shrimp. I liked coating them in flour. Why is it so satisfying to flour something? It feels so nice. Like putting cornstarch on a marshmallow, goes from sticky to smooth. Flour, milk, breadcrumbs and into the pan. Gray shrimp, limp, soft and pale to tight, curled, crisp and browned.

Felt like a beach vacation meal. I am missing the beach so much. I'm worried summer will slip by and I wonder if we'll get to our favorite beach spots on Long Island this year. We usually stay with family friends. But that doesn't seem likely. And I miss my family friends. Almost family but not by blood. Family by time, generations and love. Chosen family. Missing them so.

Everything still feels in limbo. Just the meantime. Making do.

Makes me a little blue to think about it.

Always and still here,

Sarah

June 29

Dear Friend,

Day 110.

Today was a day much like the other days. Same characters, same scenery. Made waffles this morning. Sonny had his usual five breakfasts. Protein shake, waffles, bowls of blueberries, popcorn...he eats all morning. Not much of a lunch and dinner guy. If dessert did not exist, he'd skip them both. Thank God for "cuspard".

Not much happened today until about 3:00 when some friends we haven't seen since the quarantine began came over for a swim. So sweet to hug my friend and see her two girls. I love having women and girls over, their female energy in the house is like an unexpected color thread woven into the day. Her girls giggled so much, they made me laugh and want to be little again too.

That was the bright spot of the day. Really the rest of the day was the same as most days, but more so. Even more of the same as any other day. All of the things I do most days, I did today. Sweeping, laundry, dishes, blah.

That is all. I hope your day had a little more get up and go than mine.

Always and still here,

Sarah

June 30

Dear Friend,

Day 111.

Last night when I went upstairs around 11:30, the windows were open in our room. Joseph was already asleep. It was very dark out and there was a cool breeze blowing in over our bed. The head of our bed is right up against two windows, side by side. I climbed in under the blankets, laid down, and rested my chin on my arms, atop my pillows, to stare out the window. My wind-chime tolled a single distant note every now and then. The whispering of the leaves held me there. I stared at the blurred edges of the dark blue sky and the black outlines of the trees for a long time. There was a soft flicker of green in the center and I imagined a story of someone who sees a portal floating there, high up in their yard at night. How they would look for it every night, how they would try to reach it, where it would go. I could not keep my eyes open staring at the leaves moving, like reading a book in bed. The night was so beautiful, the air reminded me of a Florida night, a Long Island night, memories of other night air. Is it the thruway I can hear in the distance? Or is it trains? Always a low sound, a busy hum. I long for silence behind the trees. There are no crickets yet, no cicadas.

Looking out the window at the night, I thought, "Yoo-hoooo...." This is my constant internal call. "Yoo-hoooo..." Always looking for what's under the veil. Knocking on walls when I was small, looking for secret rooms. What else is there? What is just beyond this surface? I think if I look long enough, it will reveal itself to me. It never does. But it doesn't stop me from believing there's something underneath it all.

It was a nice way to head off to sleep.

Joseph was home this morning, which was unusual for a Tuesday. We all went to the track together after breakfast. I walked there and the boys went in Joseph's car. I ran around the track a mile and did not need to stop this time. Desmond joined me for a lap. Then I walked around a couple of times with the boys while Joseph ran. Then ran once more around alone. Desmond said this was his new favorite thing, walking with me and talking. Desmond and Sonny were extra cute together, holding hands and singing the alphabet, talking about numbers and letters. Desmond walked home with me and Sonny rode in the car.

The sky was ominous with clouds, and there was mist and a breeze. The high school looks like a prison and I am glad I never have to go to high school again.

I cut the grass when we got home. Between the track and the grass, I managed to put 10,441 steps on my pedometer. I am so proud.

As I got out of the shower today, Sonny woke from his nap, covered in pee. Somehow the mattress got wet too. The waterproof sheet not waterproof after all. Running him downstairs to the bath he yelled, "Bill's here!" And indeed, he was. Bill and Patricia came to say hello. They settled in the backyard while I took care of Sonny, then sent him outside while I took care of his bed and then joined them myself.

We had popsicles and somehow managed to lure them each into taking a turn on the trampoline with the boys. I jumped too and managed to knock my knee into Sonny's chin. Then I sat and rocked him in my arms for a while, while he cried. He looked up at me and said, "I still love you," through his tears. A small feather floated down from the trees onto his face and it felt like my mother was there. She was a collector of feathers and I always think of her when I find one.

We all sat in the shade and talked for a long while and then ordered delivery from the pizza parlor in town and sat outside to eat.

Desmond is almost done with his schoolbooks and 5th grade is coming to an end. I told him when I graduated from 5th grade, my mom bought me a parakeet. He wants one too. He loves birds. He said if he got a parakeet he would name it Paul, after our friend who has parrots and loves birds too. Joseph said he did not want a bird because it would be too sad to have it in a cage.

So Desmond took to making a habitat for a pill bug. And of course Sonny followed suit. Desmond researched all that a pill bug needs. I did not know you could tell a female from a male by its feet. Or that it can change from a male to female from bacteria. They do not bite or sting and carry no diseases. They eat decaying fruit, vegetables and leaves. They need moisture and breathe through gills. Easy pets. Desmond named his Mark. Sonny named his Roly, but then changed it to Another Mark. There was a lot of pill bug discussion at dinner and adding of more pill bugs to the habitats.

After the boys were in bed, I watched some parakeet videos on YouTube with Joseph, found a bird cage for sale on marketplace in town for $20 and made an appointment to go see it on Thursday.

I don't know if pet stores are open. Or if Joseph will come around. I'm not even sure if it's a good idea. But it's not the worst idea. I have fond memories of my bird, Watson. Time will tell. We have plenty of it.

Always and still here,

Sarah

July 2020

July 1

Dear Friend,

Day 112.

I woke from a nightmare this morning, it's too scary to tell you about.

I have decided after much deliberation and self torment, to go ahead and take the 22 hours of continuing education courses to keep my real estate license, even though I have not made much use of it. When I started, I thought I'd learn the ropes and when Sonny went to kindergarten, and Desmond was in school, I'd have so much more free time. But then we decided to homeschool the boys, and here we are. I wasn't very good at bothering other people in my office to have them help me. Not one of my strong suits. I felt a bit adrift. And then the pandemic came along. Anyway, I think it's worth holding onto, even if it's just to be able to go look at empty houses for sale by myself. Or with you.

The classes are very dry legal speak and make me feel like I've tossed my brain into quicksand. Then I try to pry it out with a stick. Then I try to pass the test. And do, somehow.

I sat in on a zoom office meeting today and learned that this month's sales are double what they were last year and the highest they've been in the history of the world, or at least, this office since 2012, which is probably the same thing.

The pandemic has made everyone decide that their home is not quarantine material apparently and they are looking for a better fit. People are moving out of the city and coming to the Hudson Valley. Which, I gotta say, is a really nice place to quarantine. I am so grateful to be here. With so much space, and so many places to hike and be in nature. To have a yard and a neighborhood to ride our bikes around.

We walked to town this morning so my friend could take a video of the boys eating cupcakes for an Instagram video for her new bakery. But the cupcakes were so good, the boys ate them in a blissful silence. Not really commercial material. After they ate their first cupcake, we had them split one more, in hopes of some more action, but they just inhaled those quietly too.

This afternoon the sky grew so dark and we had a couple of big thundering downpours. Desmond walked to his friend's house in his long black raincoat and ski goggles. Looked like he was headed into The Thunder Dome.

Sonny and I walked back to town to help finish up the clouds I had started on my friend's mural. I got to paint while Sonny ran around with my friend's daughter who is Desmond's age. It's fun to see Sonny play with someone besides Desmond and without Desmond by his side. Sort of a rarity.

We picked up some dinner at the bakery. Turkey chili, chicken salad and deviled eggs and headed home, stopping to pick up Desmond on the way. Sonny had to grab a wintergreen lifesaver he had hidden on our friend's porch, months ago. It was still sealed and still there.

I told him wintergreen lifesavers spark in the dark. So after dinner he went into his closet with Desmond and a mirror. But instead of biting into it with his mouth open so he could see in the mirror, as I instructed, he chewed it with his mouth closed and then opened his mouth to look in the mirror. Both of them were so disappointed. When they came out, I asked Des why he was holding a box of crackers. He said it was in case they got stuck in the closet. I could have slipped them crackers under the door.

They drove me to a breaking point with their bickering, whining and carrying on. So I took them to the river to look for crystals, to get out of the house, to be by the water, to calm down. It was a, "PUT ON YOUR SHOES NOW," exit. I asked them not to speak, but that didn't work. But oddly, I discovered that when I don't speak, it doesn't matter. They just carry on as if I were.

Thunder grumbled along the river the whole time we were there. Dark clouds mingled with bright white ones. A piece of a rainbow appeared and then faded away.

One of Desmond's pill bugs just had babies...Tiny white pill bugs all over the habitat. I'm equally flabbergasted and nauseated. The babies stay by their mom for the first year. You can keep a pill bug in a habitat for up to five years.

I'd like to go to bed now.

Always and still here,

Sarah

July 2

Dear Friend,

Day 113.

I downloaded a new audio book. Apparently, I am now one of those people who read whodunnit mysteries with pretty paintings of tea sets and lace curtains on the covers. This one is called *Cappuccinos, Cupcakes and a Corpse*. I don't know what's become of me.

Another new habit I've developed in these pandemic days is buying boxes of cans of seltzer. We used to buy bottles of seltzer long ago. Then I bought a machine that turns water into seltzer to use instead. Because it's better for the environment. I have so much packaging and plastic guilt. And I worry about ingesting aluminum. I don't know why I bought the box of cans in the first place. But having them here made me feel like I was on vacation or at someone else's house. What a luxury and a treat. A guilty pleasure.

I just checked Google to see if drinking from aluminum cans is bad for you. Guess what?! They coat the aluminum with plastic so the aluminum doesn't leach into your drink but the BPA sure does. Foiled again. Oh well. It was nice while it lasted.

Today Desmond finally finished his schoolwork, bringing 5th grade, elementary school and our first whole year of homeschooling to a close. To celebrate I took him to the drive thru at McDonald's for his first ever Happy Meal. That's right. He made it almost 11 years without ever having McDonald's. I managed to talk him into a better meal every time it came up. But we figured it was time. We drove through, ordering off a fancy TV screen menu. McDonald's of the future. He got a hamburger, fries and a vanilla milkshake. The meal came with apples which for some reason grossed us out most of all. Peeled wet apples in a plastic bag. He loved the burger and fries but could only drink half of the milkshake. He said it was too sweet. He tossed it along with the apples. I wonder how many Happy Meal apples get thrown away. He got a minion toy. That was fun. At dinner he said he would like to go every ten years on July 2nd. Sounds like a plan. I told him he'll be 20 next time but I'll be happy to take him.

He came with me to run errands afterwards. It was nice to have his company and have some time to ourselves. I liked having him with me while I shopped because I could make weird noises and sound effects and it felt acceptable.

I got him a graduation snorkel and a Hawaiian shirt.

When we came home, my mural painting friend came over with her daughter for a swim. Sonny couldn't wait to see her again after they played yesterday. Her name is Izzy and sometimes he calls her Dizzy on accident, or he calls her Buddy, which he calls everyone who's name he can't remember. He also calls his friend Violet, Velvet, which I love.

They had so much fun all together. I hope she'll come more often. They live just a few blocks away.

I've gotten lazy about cooking again. Today I brought prepared food home when we were out and about. Salads and wraps. But I did pick enough raspberries from our yard to make homemade raspberry ice cream. I used agave instead of sugar, but I'm not sure if that really makes it healthier or not. I overheard some health food store employees talking once about how agave is as bad for you as sugar. I didn't look into it. I don't want to know. I mostly worry about getting caught in a sugar web that I can't get out of. Agave doesn't seem to have the same pull for me that sugar does.

After dinner, while the ice cream machine was turning, a storm blew in. I ran outside to the back yard and yelled, "We've got to batten down the hatches!" as I cranked down our big navy blue umbrella with the white fringe. Then we ran out to the front porch to watch the sky. The wind was wild, thunder rolled in the distance, a couple of tree branches fell in the street and it started to rain. Desmond gathered a beach umbrella and two rain umbrellas and opened them all on the lawn like a tent and he and Sonny climbed inside. Then he ran inside to grab some snacks and back out he went. As he came back outside, the beach umbrella blew over and revealed Sonny, wide eyed and hollerin'. Desmond covered them back up and they stayed that way until the rain stopped.

It was a good day. A headache found me and is lingering now. It's time for bed.

Izzy and Desmond did make a plan for her to come back at 7:43 tomorrow morning. I'm not sure if they were kidding or not. But we'll be ready just in case.

Always and still here,

Sarah

July 3

Dear Friend,

Day 114.

Things seemed to go sideways today.

Friday is the day I get to go to my studio, the day I am supposed to have a little space and time for myself. A bit of a respite in my week, just to gather myself back together again. And a designated time to paint.

And so I did, I did get there and I did paint. No one is there when I go. I used to see people sometimes but I haven't seen anyone there since quarantine. So it's quiet. I have a room at the end of a long hall. I have a key to the door. In the room is all of my paint and brushes, a desk, a table, two chairs, an easel and canvas. It all waits for me there and is just where I left it every time I return.

It smells like celery there for some reason, I don't know why. I have an air conditioner there that I plug in when I arrive. The on and off buttons don't work so I just plug it in and it starts up. I unplug it when I go.

I am mixing more of my new paint, little by little. I am making a color chart as I go. The color chart of my old Liquitex paints hangs beside the new Guerra paint color chart on my bulletin board. It's amazing to see them side by side. The Liquitex colors look like they were pulled out of an old dusty closet, while the Guerra paints look like they were plucked off a candy shop shelf. So much more vibrant and bright. I wonder if my paintings will look very different now.

Izzy came over this morning. Her mom dropped her off with croissants from the bakery. She did not come at 7:43 as the boys had hoped. She came around 8:43.

Joseph woke up on the wrong side of the bed and seemed angry all day. I was anxious to leave the house. I came back for dinner but it was the same, so I went back out.

I finally cracked and bought a chocolate covered chocolate Haagen Dazs bar.

Then I went to the river. Even though it was cloudy and had been raining so much. Even though the sky was growing dark and everything was mud. I didn't know where else to go. I wished I could go see a movie with a friend in the theater. Or meet someone at the diner. I texted a friend to see if she would come over tomorrow morning with her boys for pancakes. She said yes.

On my way back to my car, I saw a friend just pulling into the lot. We stood and talked for a little bit. It was nice to see a friendly face.

I came home and the house still felt tense. Sonny happy enough. Desmond frustrated before bed when a game he wanted to play wouldn't work. He ran out of time to watch TV before bed. He stomped upstairs. Joseph stomped up right behind him.

I got tired of my *Cappuccino, Cupcakes and A Corpse* audiobook. Mattie and Frannie were flirting more than they were sleuthing to find out who poisoned Mattie's father. So I started listening to Stephen King's *The Stand*, which somehow I have never read. It's the one about a deadly pandemic, so apropos. I don't know how long I'll last with that one either.

I hope tomorrow feels better here. I think the pancake date with help.

Always and still here,

Sarah

July 4

Dear Friend,

Day 115.

Today was the 4th of July. Our town cancelled their annual fireworks display in the park. They changed the annual 4th of July parade to a 5th of July motorcade parade. So it didn't much feel like the 4th of July today. We could have driven to another nearby town to see their fireworks, but it didn't seem right to go crowd another town, or try to find someplace to park, or sit in traffic to find someplace to park, to sit in the car to watch fireworks. So we stayed put. But the town sounds like a war zone now, everyone is setting off their own fireworks. We set some off ourselves before the boys headed up to bed. Just little ones. Nothing fancy.

I stepped outside for a few minutes. The moon is so round and big in the sky. Fireworks are going off in every direction, sirens too. I suspect it will go on a long while. The mosquitoes are out in full force. They got me good.

This morning my friend came over with her boys and I made a pancake breakfast. I made strawberry pancakes, raspberry pancakes, blueberry pancakes, and apple, raisin, cinnamon pancakes (my personal favorite). Bacon and hard boiled eggs too. I had grapes out and she brought sliced oranges and cherries. Doesn't that sound so good? I even ate a couple pancakes. I ate like it was a holiday today.

The boys ran around, sat briefly and ate a bit and then ran around some more. I got to sit and talk with my friend at the table. Then we took the party outside so the boys could swim. Such a beautiful day.

After they left and Sonny went down for a nap, falling asleep in record time, I floated in the pool for a very long time, listening to the neighborhood. The birds and breezes, the wind chime, and then the neighbor's son down the block who performs with his heavy metal band on their front porch with speakers, the volume turned up to 11. Not my cup of tea but I feel like they sounded a little better this summer than last. Our next door neighbor's lawn crew chimed in with a lawn mower. But eventually it quieted down again.

Desmond went off with his friends, came home with a pretty rough scrape on his shoulder from the skate park where they ride their scooters. Joseph grilled some hot dogs, made some salads and cracked open a can of baked beans. We ate inside because it was so hot out. Then Desmond took off again and Joseph, Sonny and I walked to town for ice cream. We wore our masks and couldn't visit the fountain in the courtyard because it was roped off for people dining. So we came home.

My Aunt called tonight and said she will come visit us tomorrow night and sleep over, with her wife and son. They'll spend the day on Monday. That will be a treat. I am missing family so.

I wonder what the motorcade parade will be like tomorrow. I suppose we'll walk down the block to catch some of it. Although I wouldn't mind skipping it. I love to see the marching bands and bagpipers. Cars, trucks, sirens and flying dumdum lollipops is not my jam.

I hope you had a nice 4th, even though it was strange, and even though our country is more bananas every day. It's probably best we skipped it. Maybe next year we'll have more to celebrate.

I hope so.

Always and still here,

Sarah

July 7

Oh Friend,

Day 118.

It's been a few days. I have been feeling a bit blue. I don't know why but that initial feeling of being an animal in captivity has resurfaced. I am the pacing tiger again.

Sonny's attempt at reigning his self-declared kingdom (our home) is in full swing. He rules with great impudence. I feel like I am constantly reminding him to be kind and speak nicely. It reminds me of when Desmond was younger, the phases he went through, when I would think, "Oh no, my child is an asshole..." And then it would pass. I really think children hold the potential to be swayed either way. They are so malleable. Which is good, but also, there's a bit of swimming against the tide. And it's unpleasant to be around a child who is full of sass all day.

The 4th of July parade on Sunday turned out to be five fire trucks that drove around blasting their sirens. We did not attend.

My aunt decided to come visit sort of last minute, with her wife and son who is a year and a half older than Desmond. They came Sunday evening and slept over. It was such a treat to see them.

I wore myself out Sunday, running errands, cleaning and making up five beds so the boys and our guests could decide where they would want to sleep. I think we had gone to the track that morning too and by the end of the day I had walked 11,973 steps, which is a new record.

We set off fireworks again that night, bigger than the night before.

Sonny was so excited and up too late, that he could not, would not go to bed. I had to move him out of his room with the boys, to sleep in our room, because he could not leave his cousin alone. He and I had it out, and he did not give up until after I left the room, feeling like I needed to be committed.

Monday was fun, we took them to our favorite spot on the river, got pizza to go, the kids swam in the pool, we walked to get ice cream and then played corn hole before they took off.

Desmond went out with his friends after dinner and came home late. He was in tears because Joseph was so disappointed in him. Eventually he settled down and he decided to share the air mattress still on the floor of Sonny's room, where Sonny had chosen to spend the night. Sonny could tell Desmond was sad and he laid an arm over him and so Desmond laid his arm over Sonny and they talked their way towards sleep.

I gathered up as many raspberries as I could from the garden this morning and did not have quite enough for a "cuspard" but I pressed on anyway. I added one nectarine, placed it in a smaller pie plate and used a little less sweetener than usual, just to see. It was surely my best custard yet. I'd like to eat the whole thing. But I won't.

We are laying low today. I think I'll cook this salmon dish for dinner that looks nice. Salmon with edamame and avocado. Seems like the right thing to do.

I wish things were different. There's so much to worry about. But there's so much to be grateful for. It's like walking in circles, or pacing, like the tiger in the zoo.

I still miss the zoo.

Always and still here,

Sarah

July 8

Dear Friend,

Day 119.

I am not sure what to say. I've been sitting here for a while. I'm outside and I don't know how long it will be before the mosquitoes find me. I don't know what to do with myself lately. There's so much to process every day. So much ugliness is revealed. The ugly history of our country that is being brought out into the light, the violence that continues, black men hanging from trees, being deemed suicides, the complete ignorance, anger, dismissive attitudes, lack of empathy. The number of cases of the virus continues to rise around the country. But nothing is clear, tests aren't accurate, numbers of deaths reported aren't accurate either. It feels like there is no way to know what's really going on. But everything is a hot mess. Feels like there's a rotting carcass on the lawn. Every day, there it is, more and more foul than the day before.

I feel like I've had an unforgivable fight with someone I love, but I'm locked in the same room with them and I won't be getting out. "I don't even know you anymore," I'd say. Just like in the movies. And then I just pace.

Otherwise, my day "on the inside" was okay. Because we plod along.

Joseph came into contact briefly with someone who is sick with COVID at the hospital, while he wasn't wearing his mask. He is lucky he was even informed and was given a test when he asked for one. He found out today that his test came back negative and we breathed a sigh of relief. He said the cotton swab test felt like wasabi up his nose. It was a day of worrying more than usual. But expecting he'd likely be okay.

At cuspard o'clock, while Sonny was napping, I lay flat on my bed with my slice of cuspard and looked at lake houses for sale online. Just for fun. It felt so good. Sometimes it doesn't take very much.

I cut out cardboard ice cream cone shapes and the boys and I painted them together this afternoon. It was fun to mix ice cream flavors up for them in paint at their request. I mixed pistachio, cookie dough, cotton candy, vanilla, chocolate and strawberry. Every time we do an art project I am the last one at the table, painting away. They wander off pretty quickly. But they seemed to enjoy it.

Sonny and I took a quick walk to the bakery to buy croissants this morning and left Desmond at home. He was on a zoom chat with his friend Joel in England. I told Joel before I left to take care of Desmond while we were gone.

Sonny found a Lego book and Scooby-Doo book in the free book box on our walk home. And I found another big feather on the ground. Everywhere I go now, there are feathers. I give them all to Sonny.

Time to get the boys to bed. I look forward to lying down. Maybe I'll watch a movie or just sleep.

We are going camping soon. Tomorrow I will try to get my camper in order.

If I start now, I may be ready in time.

Sending you love.

Always and still here,

Sarah

July 9

Dear Friend,

Day 120.

I woke up at 4:00 and was in a panic until I fell back to sleep at 6:00. In tears, missing my family friends on Long Island who are like parents to me. Missing the beach. Grieving a normal Summer. I got out of bed and jumped online to look at Airbnb's, motels, hotels, nothing seemed like an answer.

I finally went back to bed and fell asleep. I dreamt that I met Michelle Obama. I hugged her and cried and cried and she comforted me. Makes me cry just to think of it now.

Things feel ruined.

I moved through the day in a sort of haze, like I was moving through molasses.

It was so hot out that even with our AC cranked up to "Turbo", the temperature in-side only dropped from 77° to 76°. But it felt okay inside the house. Downright cold when we walked back in from being outside.

I gave Joseph a haircut and Sonny too. Sonny wanted a haircut like Desmond, shaved short on the sides and back, long on top. But his hair was so long, I was sad to do it. I cut it short but did not shave it. He is happy with it. He looks like a doll. Joseph liked his haircut so much he put on a Speedo and went out to mow the lawn.

We got our camper set up in the driveway so I can clean it a bit and get it ready for camping next week. It's nice to see it opened up again. Our camper is a 1975 hard sided, Apache pop-up camper. It has fiberglass sides and folds up like a pizza box. Well, not at all like a pizza box but it's white and boxy. The sides fold in and the top lowers down flat. It's a sweet little home away from home if it doesn't fall apart on us. I always suspect it might but it holds up again and again.

I called my family friends that I miss so much but it made me feel worse. I miss them more than they miss me.

After dinner I decided we'd go get ice cream, because life feels terrible. But that didn't feel good either. It was too sweet. And now I feel like my bones are made of neon glass tubes, humming and twitching.

Maybe I'll read my Cape Cod mystery. It's nice to be transported to the Cape in the 30's. I think that would be a very nice place to be.

Always and still here,

Sarah

July 10

Dear Friend,

Day 121.

I am enjoying the variety of masks of strangers when I am out and about. I feel like I know things about these people that I would not have known otherwise. Like an older man whose fabric mask is a piano keys print. He must be a musician. Or a woman with a black sequined mask. She must wear fancy underwear.

Sometimes, when out shopping, I suddenly notice I have something strapped to my face and I panic for a second, embarrassed I have walked into a store with something in the wrong place. It's like those dreams when you realize you're naked in a crowd. I have an impulse to pull it off quickly and then remind myself I have to leave it on.

I have also found myself mouthing things under my mask when I'm out. Silently talking to myself. I wonder if I've always done this.

I was in Adams today, food shopping and I kept passing a woman who kept looking at me. I think she thought I looked familiar and that she might know me. She reminded me of someone I know but I decided I didn't know her. But we kept making eye contact and looking away. It's much harder to recognize people with masks on. Even when I see someone I do know, it takes me a moment or two to figure out who it is.

It was a rainy day today. A good day to go to the studio to paint. Joseph and the boys stopped by. It was nice to have a visit. Sonny was so excited it was like he drank a pint of jumping juice right before he got out of the car and came bounding up the fire escape stairs.

I got to show them my cake painting in person. They hadn't realized how big it was. I do hope I can find a place to show all my paintings together so that people can see them in person. It's such a different experience than seeing a photograph online. But I don't know when an art opening would be safe again.

I devised a plan to go to Long Island for a night and asked a friend if I could stay with her. She hasn't responded. I wouldn't blame her if she said no. Nobody quite knows what to do these days. I keep looking at hotels. I found one right on the beach but it's so expensive, of course. Ah, well.

I think I've given up on listening to *The Stand*. It's like listening to the news.

I watched a really sweet movie last night about a writer who rents a cottage on Cape Cod by herself for a year. It was based on a memoir. Makes me think I could do it too. But I'd bring my guys along. Make them dig for clams so I could write and paint.

One of the Joan's in the movie said, "Joy is your duty." She was such a magical character. She made friends with the other Joan, the writer. At her house, she dressed them both in flowing, colorful wraps and scarves like togas and they ran along the beach together, then climbed the spiral stairs to the top of the light house.

I should make joy my duty more often. Instead of laundry. I'm not sure how though. I'll think more about it. Maybe tomorrow I can make some.

Always and still here,

Sarah

July 11

Dear Friend,

Day 122.

Today was Saturday. There was lots to do today and the things that needed doing wove around each other like a braid that I followed through the house. Always on my way to do one thing and stopping to do something else, like shorten Desmond's too long blue shoe laces so that he'll wear his new sneakers, or teach Sonny about the value of coins because he has lined them up across the kitchen floor and is suddenly interested, and I don't know when that moment will come again. I used to feel like a running-back running down the field holding the football, trying to get to the end zone in my home, just trying to get something done. Dodging and weaving. Now I feel more like a dancer, tumbling into one scene, pirouetting into the next.

Eventually I got around to doing the things I had intended to do. I got into the attic and pulled down the bin of slip covers and blankets for the camper. Another very hot day today, the attic like a sauna, the camper was warm too. I cleaned and zipped the covers back on the old cushions and then jumped into the pool with Desmond.

All day I had been thinking I was supposed to be making joy my duty. And that I'd have to do it later. After I finished all the things I had to get done.

When I was in the pool with Desmond I thought maybe if I swam underwater with him, which I never do, that would be joy. So I borrowed Sonny's new swim mask and slipped below the surface with Des. We did handstands and somersaults, back flips and raced from side to side of the pool. The water was really too shallow to do an easy handstand, but I tried. He said we should do 4 somersaults in a row so I did. So much water went in my ears. So dizzy, but also so bright and blue with so many bubbles and the rushing underwater sound of motion, watching my knees turn around upside down and come right side up again. The back flip just about ran my face along the bottom of the pool, almost not deep enough. The races were fun and I was faster every time. He was so happy I was playing with him. It felt good but maybe not exactly the joy I was looking for.

For dinner we told him we'd take him out to Diamond Mills, the fancy hotel in town. We had yet to celebrate his elementary school graduation, so today was the day. Joseph called ahead to see if we could sit outside but there were only tables inside. I felt reluctant to go. But we went in hopes it would feel okay.

When we arrived at 5:30 there was no one else sitting inside. We took our masks off once we were seated at the table. Slowly more people were seated on the other side of the room. By the time our meal was done, tables closer to us were filling in. They were more than six feet away but I was increasingly nervous. We hurried Sonny to finish his ice cream and tried to leave quickly. We had a really nice time, the boys charmed our server and it was a fun celebration, but I wish we had been outside. I don't think I'll do that again soon.

Before we had left for the restaurant, Joseph found his old graduation cap in the attic and I hid it in my bag along with a diploma. At the table Joseph played Pomp and Circumstance on his phone while I handed Desmond his cap and diploma. He was so happy. He so wanted a cap and gown. He ordered raw oysters and calamari. Sonny had pizza.

When we came home, I asked Joseph if I could go for a walk. I headed out and then turned around to come home because it was so misty and drizzly. When I turned back I noticed an enormous, beautiful moth on a tree. I watched it for a while and then went home to bring the boys back to see it. We all stood around watching it, neighbors came out and we all watched together. We looked it up, it was a cecropia moth, the largest moth in North America. I've never seen or heard of one. We were able to figure out it was a female and that they live to be a year old. It was likely just about to lay eggs. I am a little worried a cat will get it if it doesn't fly a bit higher. I hope it will be okay.

By then it had stopped misting, although there was still thunder rumbling around the neighborhood. So I decided to go for a walk after all. As we made our way to leave we noticed a big rainbow arching across the sky. "A double blessing," Joseph said. Indeed. Magic and more magic.

I walked to the track and there was a beautiful cloud show in the sky to watch on my way, turning around and around as I walked. Sunset, clouds and a breeze, another rainbow. More magic.

It was a lovely day. I won't get to go to Long Island tomorrow. But we may go to a lake nearby. I will make joy my duty again. Maybe I'll get better at it each day.

Always and still here,

Sarah

July 12

Dear Friend,

Day 123.

Yesterday Joseph suggested going to a lake today. And the thought of it lifted my spirits. But when I woke up this morning, it was cloudy. I thought the clouds would lift but the morning kept on and the clouds stuck around. It looked as if it would rain.

"I guess it's not lake weather, " I said to Joseph.

"Yeah, not really," he said.

You ever feel like you're on a swing in a playground and you're being turned slowly around and around, the swing chains twisting tighter and tighter? Sometimes I feel like that. Then my swing chain is twisted too tight and I can move less and less. I felt that chain twist around one more revolution tighter when I realized we weren't going.

I went to the kitchen and was in a cabinet down low, Joseph was standing next to me at the sink. There were too many containers jammed in there. I couldn't get one free. I started to laugh, a little maniacally. I reached up and grabbed Joseph's shorts in my fist like a little kid. I looked up at him and said, "I gotta get outta here. We gotta go. Let's go." And I laughed and cried on the floor. "Please," I said as I started to make sandwiches to pack. So he started packing too. Just getting us in motion to go got that chain to start to unwind. The kids ran around grabbing their goggles and bathing suits. We loaded up the car, the sun came out and off we went. By the time I was in the driver's seat, I was calm again. Relieved.

We drove to Colgate Lake, about 45 minutes up the mountain. A small, pretty lake with grassy shores. When we arrived, we remembered it was Sunday, too late. So many cars were parked in the lot but we found a spot. Joseph declared it a bust as soon as I turned off the engine, but I told him to wait and see.

There were a lot of families, but they were spread out pretty well. We found a spot in the grass by the water and laid out our blanket and lunch. We spent four hours there. The boys ran around with other kids catching salamanders and frogs, trying to catch a water snake with nets. They ran along the shore shrieking with the other kids, "A snake! SNAKE! Snake, snake snaaaaake!!" All of them pointing and smiling, looking around to make sure everyone was watching. They made a perfect snake alarm. It reminded me of being in a traffic circle in a car with my mom in England, when I was the designated pointer. "Just keep pointing at Big Ben!" She cried frantically, as she tried to maneuver around the circle, driving on the left side of the road, sitting on the right side of the car. She may as well have also been driving backwards.

Desmond befriended a man in his twenties, swimming in the water, his girlfriend sitting on shore. He asked him if he wanted to race, the young man was a little reluctant, but they raced anyway. The young man won and was very pleased.

Desmond asked me if he could swim across to the other side. The young man said he would swim with him. His girlfriend called to me, "He was a lifeguard!" So I said okay. And then watched Desmond swim and tread water and swim some more, all the way across the lake. It's a small lake, but it would have taken me a few minutes to swim out to the middle. I watched with my heart in my throat. He made it to shore and then swam back again. He stayed in the lake most of the time we were there. When he caught a frog, he was a ways off from the other kids who were squealing and jumping around, slashing their nets into the water. I was not worried about that frog in Desmond's hands. He is very careful and mindful of all creatures. He carried it over to show me, I told him not to show the other kids, to let him loose in the water.

I don't know about being around strangers outdoors like that, spread out. It felt okay but the whole time I kept thinking, "I hope this is okay." I don't know.

We talked about coming back on a weekday when it's likely to be much less crowded, and earlier in the morning. "Maybe tomorrow," we said, and shrugged.

But by the time we were ready to go, I had such a sunburn on my back and down one arm. I hope it rains for days.

My whole back feels like someone just slapped me really hard but the feeling doesn't fade. I don't know what I was thinking. I wasn't thinking, I guess. My eyes were on the kids. I put sunscreen on my shoulders and that was all, but the sun blasted through that anyway. It doesn't matter. It's something different from yesterday, and that's alright with me. If I had been at the beach, I would have put sunscreen on. Lakes are sneaky like that.

I made a nice cod fish dinner with zucchini, little potatoes, dill, and tomatoes in butter. A one pot wonder. I am trying to get incrementally closer to the ocean.

Always and still here,

Sarah

July 13

Dear Friend,

Day 124.

I really enjoy writing to you every night. It's a nice way to end the day. In 12 Step programs, it is suggested that you do a nightly inventory of your day. To take time to think about what went well and what you may have done differently, if you made any mistakes and if you have any amends to make. I have never really done it as a practice, even though I have hung out in a number of 12 step groups. I'm not great at following directions. I wonder if this is what it feels like. It takes some time for me to remember what happened each day, when I sit down to write. I think about what the best part of the day was, the hardest part, and if there's anything interesting to tell you about.

Today was pretty ordinary. My sunburn was a challenge.

Turns out we all got burned, except for Desmond, who is already as "brown as a berry" as my mom would say, when I got tan in the summertime. "You're brown as a berry!" I imagine that saying came from her mom, or grandma. Seems like an old fashioned thing to say, from back in the day, when berries were brown. I don't know what berry she had in mind...but I liked to be as brown as a berry. Sounds like a nice color to be.

Joseph says the sun is stronger up on the mountain because of the altitude. That seems like a Dad thing to say, that you just take in stride but wonder about the rest of your life. Because we're closer to the sun? Because the air is thinner? The clouds are closer?

Sonny's back looks pink like bubble gum. It hurts my heart and makes me feel like I failed him. I am glad it's not as bright and dark pink as mine. I'd like to blame my hormones for the severity of my burn, it's like I'm on some burn increasing medication. But I am not. I'm a sun sponge.

Speaking of great bumper stickers, I spent five minutes trying to get a gay pride rainbow sticker on my car super straight today. Peeled it off twenty or more times and stuck it back on, a little crooked each time. I enjoyed the irony. And in the end, I got it on straight. It looks fabulous.

I've been reading posts about things people love as grownups that no one ever mentions or warned them about. I have recently become aware of one of those things. I love when there is a brand new, empty garbage bag in the kitchen garbage can and I am the first one to toss something in. The way it puffs up and the garbage just disappears. It's so satisfying.

In COVID news, it's not going anywhere and neither are we, apparently.

I was walking to my car, wearing a mask after picking up groceries, again, and said to myself out loud, "A global pandemic!" It still surprises me.

The mask debate continues and a new debate about whether or not schools should open in the Fall is being batted around. The Administration seems to think it'd be worth the percentage of deaths among children, staff and parents to open the schools back up. If it were up to me, I'd keep the school closed and change our gun laws while we're at it. Because I think school should be the safest place in town.

I don't know what they'll do. But I am so grateful I can homeschool my kids.

I think the saddest thing about the virus, and the Black Lives Matter movement, is that it turns out, Americans are not very good at taking care of each other. It seems like that's been touted as an American virtue, that we band together. But now we just fight about everything. There's so much anger. It's been a wild few years with Trump in office. This feels like the grand finale at the fireworks show. Like a grand brawl, fists, spit and sparks flying.

I do hope better things will come. A calm after the storm. Some healing. A balm.

Be the balm.

Another good bumper sticker.

Always and still here,

Sarah

July 14

Dear Friend,

Day 125.

This morning I dusted books and rearranged them. I almost sewed new buttons on an old shirt.

We thought about going to North South Lake today with another family or two but our sun burns kept us home. Mine seems to be shrinking and Sonny's isn't as pink. I hope by Friday we'll be back to normal.

Friday is Desmond's birthday and we are heading up to the lake to go camping for a couple of nights. We go every summer, sometimes twice a summer, to the same spot. It's so pretty up there on the mountain. The air feels different, there's a calm you can feel when you step out of the car. I wonder if it's all the negative ions from the trees. Almost as good as the beach.

I am slowly getting the things we need put away in the camper. Blankets, towels, umbrellas, jugs of drinking water and toys. I did some cooking today. I have found cooking ahead of time and freezing meals in parchment paper and foil is easiest. We throw them on the grill to heat them up. And good food becomes part of the trip, all right in the cooler. I am repeating our menu from last year with a pierogi and sausage dish and a lemon chicken dish. I'll bring a batch of blueberry scones the kids can grab when they need a snack. Oats for the ducks and for breakfast. This year I think I will make an egg, cheese and sausage casserole for breakfast too. Bake it, cut it and freeze it. That might be nice. And we'll pick up a cake for Desmond's birthday at the bakery. Unless I am extra ambitious and have time to make one. But camping is so much prep work. I don't know that I will.

Our friends have accepted an invitation to stay with us in the spot beside ours. I reserved the two camping spots side by side this winter, right along the creek, in hopes that we'd find some friends to join us. They haven't been camping before but I'm pretty sure they'll love it. Hopefully it won't rain and the kids will get along. I'm glad Desmond will have friends there for his birthday. Oh boy, I guess I should decorate a bit at home and there are presents to wrap… Maybe I can recruit Joseph to do some of the cooking.

I think camping should be pretty safe in terms of the virus. Besides our two families being close, we won't really be near anyone else. There are shared bathrooms but masks and handwashing should do well enough. I wonder if it will be less crowded than usual. It's never really crowded to begin with. There is a beach there we'll go to. And we'll have our kayaks and bikes. It will be nice to have a change of scenery for a few days.

Our rose of Sharon tree has bloomed. It always blooms around Desmond's birthday, which was also my Dad's birthday. Sometimes it blooms right on the day, this year it is a few days early. Already the pink flowers are furling then falling from the tree into the pool. They float like little pink cigars. When I was a kid we had an above ground pool too and it was right beside a rose of Sharon tree. Funny how things repeat themselves.

This afternoon our friend Bill came over for a visit. I don't think he's been in the house since the quarantine began. He played with the boys while I cooked and then I sat with them at the table and we played Dominoes while we listened to Herbie Hancock. So much fun, I hadn't played in years. I think my sister had taught me how to play in Florida a long time ago but I had forgotten how.

He stayed for dinner and we started a movie but I ushered the kids off to bed before it was through. Such a party pooper, but I was so tired.

Little by slowly, I think I can get it all done. Tomorrow I begin again.

Always and still here,

Sarah

July 16

Dear Friend,

Day 127.

Tomorrow is Desmond's 11th birthday, and the last few days he has referred to just about everything he's done as "The last time I'll _____ while I'm 10 years old."

Every year he is sad as his birthday approaches. The thought of leaping from one year to the next in one day, unnerves him. Today he said he is so worried about getting older because he is getting closer to dying...Oh my goodness. I told him that I try to remind myself to be grateful when I am sad about getting older. It's a gift not everyone gets. We are lucky to be here at all. I don't know if that's a cheerful thought though, really. It has a heaviness to it.

I tried every angle of pep talk I could think of to cheer him up. My pre-birthday pep talks for Desmond are some of my best. I don't know if they make a difference for him, but I think they make me feel better.

On the news this morning, I heard that yesterday was the highest number of positive COVID tests reported in this country since the pandemic began. Hospitals are filling back up to capacity, are understaffed and there's still a shortage of PPE. Ahhhhhmerica.

When Trump was elected, I started obsessively watching YouTube videos on making your own bomb shelter. I thought for sure he was going to get us all killed. Now I think he might get us all killed, just not in the way I had imagined.

This morning someone on the radio said something like, "In war, you have to be prepared for what the enemy CAN do, not what the enemy MIGHT do. We've been preparing for what this virus might do, instead of what it can do, and that is a mistake." They also said, "This can't be fixed with politics, it has to be fixed with science." I do miss science, and facts. They seem to be in short supply.

I went to pick up a few things for camping today at Adams. The man in front of me at the checkout was wearing a safari hat with mosquito netting over his whole head, instead of a mask. I'm not sure how he got away with it.

People are so angry. I have to remind myself that everyone is scared and stressed. It helps me to have more empathy.

Ahhhhh, I don't know.

127 days later and there are still more questions than answers. It seems like the hot water we're in just gets hotter. I wish I had something better to tell you. I made chocolate cupcakes. I made them with maple syrup instead of sugar. Tomorrow I'm going to make a chocolate ganache with agave. I think it will be pretty good. I was going to get a bakery cake, but Desmond asked if I would bake him something.

I was listening to the radio a couple of days ago with Desmond in the kitchen. Joe Donahue was interviewing a woman who wrote a book about women who do too much. She ran off a list of things like not wearing makeup to the store and buying cookies from the supermarket instead of baking them for your son's birthday, then she said, if you do these things, you'll see you won't lose anything. And Desmond said, "except his love for you." And we laughed and laughed. So I baked.

The next few days we'll be on top of the mountain at the lake, making campfires, swatting mosquitoes, kayaking, and hiking. I think I'll take my laptop so I can write to you, at least until the battery dies, but I won't be able to send you any letters until I get home on Sunday.

Be well, be kind. Be the balm.

Always and still here,

Sarah

July 18

Dear Friend,

Day 129.

It's late Saturday night. We're still camping. I'm sitting in the dark by myself, in front of a pile of glowing embers in the fire pit. It's that living neon orange heat that is the best part of the fire. It looks like magic and is constantly changing as I watch it.

The campgrounds are still lively, even though it's pitch black now. It's quieting slowly and gradually. People are still talking, somewhere a toddler is crying, a bicycle bell rings. The creek that runs through the woods just beyond our campsite has a small waterfall and I can hear the water steadily running, like a bathtub filling in the next room. A dog barks, people laugh.

Joseph and the boys are lying down in the camper, heading off to sleep, I hope. It was a long, full day, after a long full day before that.

Desmond's birthday was a very good day and a very good birthday. He woke up happy after ending the day before almost in a full panic about turning 11. So much worry. Opening birthday presents first thing in the morning is a fine remedy. He loved his gifts and Sonny was disappointed and then pleased with his "Desmond's Birthday gift" that we gave him so he wouldn't feel left out. Birthday waffles and bacon, a dip in the pool and a parade of friends driving by the house, offering Happy Birthday wishes out their car windows, honking and waving, stopping to chat, some with small gifts, one with a handmade sign. Such sweetness, so lovely to see friend's smiling faces, friends we haven't seen in a while and some that we have but are always happy to see more of. This is a new COVID inspired birthday trend. These birthday parades, driving by someone's home on their birthday to honk and wave. Even though it came to be as a strange work around, it is very sweet. I wonder if it will last past these days of quarantine. Probably not. But I think it will be one thing we look back fondly on.

We finished packing to head up the mountain and when Sonny was up from his nap, off we went. Arriving is always full of the hubbub of setting up the camper and getting settled, then making a fire and getting dinner ready. This time followed by birthday cupcakes and s'mores with our friends.

It was late when we got the kids settled in their beds. Joseph and I always get them settled and then sit by the glowing, end of the night's fire. And so we did last night. But Sonny was not going to sleep. I was annoyed and then noticed the stars splashed across the sky and the big dipper grinning at me. I poked my head into the camper and whispered for Sonny to come, I wanted to show him something. And Desmond asked if he could come too. So they both scrambled out from inside their sleeping bags to the door. I carried Sonny on my hip back out into the night to point up at the stars and whisper together with wonder and excitement. Counting the big dipper's stars, four for the scoop and three for the handle. I wrapped an arm around Desmond and we wowed and ooed. Then I led them to the fire to sit with Joseph and I for a bit before they went to sleep. Sonny curled up in my lap, Desmond climbed into Joseph's lap, with his long legs hanging down, his arms folded across his chest, his head resting on Joseph's shoulder. And we all whispered together about the light in the burning wood, the sparkle, spitch and snap of the smudge. I thought that maybe we were sitting in a memory they would hold forever. I think it will certainly be one I keep. I hope so.

I did not sleep much at all through the night. Sonny talked and yelled in his sleep, the camper rocks when someone shifts. I would drift off and then be woken up by something to lay in the dark with my eyes closed wishing for sleep again and again.

Today was a whirlwind of little boys, food, fires, beach time at the lake, the ice cream truck, Desmond and his friend Julian who is just eight years old, kayaking across the lake together. Sonny tried the kayak too as I walked beside him and he was able to paddle around proudly, talking with the ducks. We were fully covered in sunscreen and I stayed in the shade. I followed Sonny around with our umbrella like an obsessive cabana boy, screwing the plastic anchor into the sand to set a circle of shade over him where he was busy digging trenches and then pulling it up again to set it down someplace else when he changed tracks. I am happy to report, no one got sunburned.

Our friend Bill stopped by at dinner time with his Patricia, to wish a happy birthday to Desmond, bearing gifts and homemade spruce and mint ice cream. Wooden bird whistles and a dinosaur shirt for Sonny.

After they had gone, I slipped away for a walk by myself to the lake because I felt like I had been sitting all day long. I caught the sun just as it was setting behind the mountain when I reached the beach. When I got back, Desmond wanted to go for a bike ride so we did, back to the lake. Sonny on his little seat on my bike, Desmond leading the way. Our friends drove over to meet us there and the boys ran back and forth on the sand as the sky grew darker and darker. We rode our bikes back in the dark down the black top and gravel paths to our camping spot.

The bedtime hustle and jostle is always a little charged. Tired grownups who just want to relax and wired kids who just want to keep running. It's like cogs in a clock that stick and grind, bumping forward just the same, but the sound of it makes you think maybe the clock will stop. Then it seems to find its footing and runs along quietly again.

I am glad I sat to write to you tonight. I did not think my brain would work well enough to make sense of the day. But I wanted to catch these last two days before they faded or grew too big by tomorrow to pack neatly in a letter to you.

I am a little nervous the bear everyone saw earlier this evening will come out of the woods and find me here. The woods do come alive a bit after dark with leaves rustling. It's hard to tell how big or small a creature might emerge, surely too close if it were revealed in the light of my laptop. My goodness.

I'll climb into bed now and hope for sleep. Tomorrow is bound to be as long and lovely as today. May we all be ready.

Always and still here,

Sarah

July 19

Dear Friend,

Day 130.

We were all up before Sonny this morning at the campsite. Can you believe it? I actually slept most of the night too, waking a number of times but falling back to sleep easily. Sonny called out in his sleep, "No, Des! Don't take that, it's STEALING!" Right before I woke in the morning, I dreamt I was reading a sentence my mother wrote and it was so beautiful. I thought, man, I wish I could write like that. The only part of the sentence I could remember when I woke was the very end of it, "...tossing out a sunshine lyric." When I woke I realized I wrote that long beautiful sentence but it was gone.

The morning was breakfast then packing everything up. All of the unpacking in reverse. So much work, but I think it is worth it in the end. The boys love it so much, it is a gift for them.

Our friends packed up and headed home. We packed up and headed back to the beach at the lake for a few more hours of the kids digging in the sand, kayaking, feeding the ducks, sitting with our feet in the water and me reading my Cape Cod mystery, a paragraph here and there, sometimes sneaking a few pages at a time. Sometimes I just hug the book to my chest, because everyone in the book is at the Cape, and it makes me feel closer to being there. I imagine my bookcase in my future Cape house and the book on the shelf there. Someday I will look at it there and remember holding it close, wishing for the day when I could look back in the other direction at my longing.

The parking lot at the lake has every other parking spot marked with a bright orange X. There were signs at all the bathrooms to wear a mask. Most people did. At the bathrooms with multiple sinks, there were clear shower curtains hung between the sinks as barriers. It seemed like a good social distancing activity, camping. Other than our friends, we were not near anyone else. Even on the beach, there was room to spread out. But I have never seen a line as long of people checking in as we were leaving. And the lines of people parking up the mountain to hike at the falls! Holy cow. So many people, so many cars.

I have to say, being at the beach and seeing women in bathing suits is always a revelation. I love seeing real women, in their real bodies, all of them beautiful, all of them different shapes and sizes and ages. None of them flawless. Not a one. Well, maybe one, but she was 18 and I everyone is flawless at 18. Sonny told me he found who he is going to marry and make part of our family and pointed right at her. I couldn't blame him. Although, she was with her boyfriend. And he had a man bun.

We tried to stop at Mamma's Burgers on the way home for frozen custard and burgers to bring home for dinner, but the line was so long and it was 90 million degrees out. So we skipped it.

We hit the ground running when we landed back in the driveway, unloading our cars, putting things away until just a few things were left that could wait a day or two. I jumped into the pool which was a little green but a cool 80°. As I walked around skimming the rolled pink cigar roses from the water's surface, a hot 99° wind blew in my face. Felt like I was sitting in front of a heating fan.

Showers and baths, clean clothes, take out and ice cream finished the day. It is good to go away, it is good to come home. I like having a refrigerator full of food and the little light that comes on when you open the door. Little things please me. It's nice when I notice them.

Always and still here,

Sarah

July 20

Dear Friend,

Day 131.

The state of affairs is a load of pants.

I just learned this British phrase from the thesaurus. The word "pants" means nonsense in England. This is probably the best thing I can offer you today. A new turn of phrase for your repertoire.

"A load of pants". Or you can say, "a pile of pants". I can't decide which one I like better.

I am feeling quite glum about it all, the country's pants. I won't bore you with complaining about it. But it does get in the way.

Let's see. Someone in the house was very unhappy all day. And that makes the house feel unhappy for us all.

What else. There was a lot of sugar in the house. So I ate it.

But the worst bit was our pool filter broke. And because of this fancy COVID summer, like toilet paper and bicycles, pool filters have all been bought up.

So, here we are.

Tomorrow might be better.

Always and still here,

Sarah

July 21

Dear Friend,

Day 132.

Today started out sort of rough around the edges but turned for the better. I sort of struggled to get off the ground a bit. Sometimes everything feels very heavy and I'm not sure how to maneuver through it. The news stories online are awful. One is worse than the next. I realized how scared I am. Just in general. Of all of it. It might be best to take a break again from the news online. I'll stick with my public radio station talk show in the morning if I think of it. Try and enjoy my life the best I can.

Morning was chores and news and a pile of pants.

After lunch Desmond took off to visit his friends. Sonny asked if we could make rings with jewelry wire with our crystals from the river. Then he decided he wanted a ring made with amber. So I made him a big amber ring with gold wire and a crystal ring for me. We wore them into town.

We walked to Main St. to see the new mural hung this morning that I helped to paint, and Joseph's paintings hanging in the windows of the old J.J. Newberry building. They all looked beautiful. Art abounds.

Of course, being so close to the bakery, we thought we'd get some croissants, but the bakery was closed for a cleaning.

We bumped into our friend who works in the bakery across the street and it was so nice to see her. She was on her way to her outdoor poetry group, which sounded so lovely. We tried our luck at the health food store for a treat and bumped into another friend and it was so nice to see her too.

Sonny got his favorite cheesy popcorn and I got a cold coconut water.

When we got home, we opened a box that was waiting on the front porch. It was a beautiful book about the ocean for Sonny from another friend. We sat right down to read it together.

I think spending time with Sonny, getting out of the house, and such sweet interactions with friends helped lift me up. At some point, it was like my kite finally got off the ground and then stayed aloft all afternoon, into the evening.

Desmond came home and wandered off to his room. He came back downstairs in an amazing getup. A black velvet hat, mirrored silver sunglasses, a pale blue button-down shirt, buttoned to the top, under a black corduroy blazer, black highwater pants and black socks. It was too much, with his beautiful little face. He's sort of a show stopper sometimes. He has these really inspired fashion moments, followed by dance routines usually. He pulled up a video of dancing pallbearers from Ghana to show me. Then he played the same song from the video and did his interpretation of their dance. And I thought, how can I be sad? Look at what's happening...

And then Sonny did his best to dress up and asked to dance with Desmond. I recorded it and may need to watch it when I am blue.

Now I have to try to recreate the outfit Desmond wore for myself. It's right up there with Holtzman. I loved it so much.

And so, another day has come and gone. It was better than yesterday, as I suspected. Let us suspect tomorrow will be even better. Or at least, just as good.

Always and still here,

Sarah

July 23

Dear Friend,

Day 134.

The first sentence is always the hardest.

I got busy last night adding Desmond's latest birthday hat photo to his birthday hat photo album and did not have time to write you. Glad I remembered to take pictures of him in his hat. He's so adorable. I like our hat photo tradition. My mother had shown me an article she pulled out of a magazine when I was in high school. It was a story about a man who bought a bathing suit for his daughter when she was born and every year he took a photo of her in it and eventually, it fit, when she was 18 or so. This was back in the 50's when people were all still thin. Seems so risky now, to buy someone a bathing suit when they're born that will fit them when they're grown. I'm full grown and I can hardly find a bathing suit that fits me, although it was a lot easier when I was 18. I thought a hat was a pretty safe bet. So when Desmond was born, I had a hat waiting for him. He was a few weeks old in the first hat photo, and then one photo every year followed, usually within the first week after his actual birthday. They happen to all be of him sitting in the same chair too, which wasn't planned at first but now, I can never get rid of that chair. It's fun to look at the photos one after another and watch him change and grow.

I always think I'll have time to watch a show or movie before bed but I never do these days.

Yesterday we went to the river in the morning at low tide and found so many crystals. We heard our first cicadas and crickets of the season.

Tonight, the boys are sleeping in the living room on the pull-out couch. We'll see how that goes. They had a dance party in the dark with our multicolored strobe light, Desmond's microphone and light up rings.

Desmond's chocolate cake and ganache is almost gone. I'll be safe soon.

Our pool filter pump is still broken. But I put a post up on a local generosity group page on Facebook asking if anyone had one lying around. Today I picked one up from a woman who said it came from a small pool 20 years ago, but it looks like it's more like 40 years old. It reminds me of the robin's egg blue Devilbiss humidifier I had in my room when I was little. I regret throwing that away. I loved it so much, the sound it made, the cool mist. I thought it was likely too old and moldy to be any good to run. I have a hard time letting go of objects from my childhood. I have so few connections to that part of my life, and I miss it. Mostly I miss the people who are gone. But there's nothing left of them to keep. Just things.

There are some amazing clouds outside my window right now. I can just see parts of this amazing sky beyond the trees and houses. Isn't that just like life? Getting just a glimpse of something incredible in the distance, but you can't see it all at once because of all the things closest to you.

I always think, if I could just zoom far enough out on this world, it would all make sense.

I put some groceries away today without cleaning them. But that felt weird so I cleaned the rest. On the news radio show I like, this morning they wondered why we weren't quarantining like we had in the beginning, to put an end to the virus. I think the virus will be here for years. Trump has finally started advising people to wear masks. Five months in.

I regret not traveling to all the places I wanted to go before this all happened. Who knows when we'll be allowed to travel to other countries again and if we'll be allowed without proof of having had a vaccine. If there is a window of opportunity in the next few years, I will jump at the chance. I want to go to Wales and Ireland, Hawaii and France. France is a hilarious name for such a romantic place with the most beautiful language. France. How'd that happen.

I also want to go to the Salar de Uyuni in Bolivia since I saw a video this week of people riding bikes on a salt flat covered in a thin layer of rainwater. It made the salt flat a perfect mirror of the sky. They looked like they were riding their bikes through the clouds. There's so much to see. I hope we get the chance to have adventures again.

I'm reading a book called *Write it Down, Make it Happen*. I think I will. Let's write down all the things. The first thing we should write down is that the virus is gone.

The virus left as quickly as it came, sooner than anyone had anticipated.

There, now we wait.

Always and still here,

Sarah

July 24

Dear Friend,

Day 135.

This morning Joseph and I woke up leisurely and amused around 8:30. Instead of one of us getting up with Sonny at his usual 7:15, the boys woke up on the pullout bed downstairs and turned on cartoons. Desmond got Sonny breakfast in bed on a tray. So when they asked if they could do it again tonight, we said yes.

I got over to my studio today to paint. I finished painting the sand in my big beach painting and started painting tiny umbrellas in the smallest one. Somehow, I managed to buy all that paint and not have an aqua blue. There's no way to mix one. I tried.

I got a message while I was at my studio from someone in the Facebook generosity group who happened to be around the corner and had a pool filter pump I could have. So I zipped over to grab it. Joseph hooked it up to the pool and it seems to be running well. What a lucky gift. I was afraid we were going to have to take the pool down. Which would have been awfully sad since we don't have much else to do these days.

My laptop has gotten so slow, when I type I have to wait a few seconds for the sentences to appear.

I just escaped my house and came to the river to write. I'm five feet from the water's edge, sitting on a rock. The sky is the softest of pale pastels, lavender, pink, yellow, green and blue, with little wisps of white clouds. There's one solid pink cloud that looks like it's walking behind the mountains on the other side of the river. Like a cotton candy T-Rex.

Sonny was having a tantrum and following me around at home. So I slipped out. Friday is my day of rest. Sort of.

I think the boys lost their permission for a sleep over on the pullout as I was leaving. Oh well.

Maybe tomorrow.

It's strange to leave home, there's really nowhere to go. Though it's always felt that way, it's even truer now. I thought about going to Barnes and Noble but it closes early. And I am so tired of grocery shopping, although it seems we always need groceries.

It's beautiful out here, but it's buggy.

When I come to the river alone, I always imagine my mother with me. I wonder what that would have been like. She would have liked it here.

Where did the cicadas go that I heard the other day? And the crickets? They are absent again.

What an amazing thing it must be to live by the water.

The woods behind me are growing dark, but the water in front of me is still shimmering like a taffeta gown. Dusk is strange, with its lack of contrast, it's so hard to see. The woods flatten out like a monotone drawing. I'll make my way back now I suppose. I'd love to grab an ice cream on the way home but that's probably not the best idea.

The sky is turning a bright pink, a motorboat is pulling someone and even though they are far off, I can hear them yelling, in fun, I think.

Alright, off I go. I hope you are having a nice evening. It's Friday night. Do people still go out on Friday night? It's been so long.

Always and still here,

Sarah

July 25

Dear Friend,

Day 136.

This morning the boys headed out to the basketball court to try out Desmond's new basketball that my sister sent him as a belated birthday gift. They went in the morning to beat the crowd and the heat. There is always a crowd at the basketball court, even in the days of Corona.

I went for a walk by myself to the track. Listening to the audio book *Educated*. I'm only a third of the way through I think, maybe half, it's hard to tell with an audio book. Seems like a strange title for the book, it's not at all what I thought it would be. But I like it. I think.

I stopped by the courts on my way home, it was so hot. We were all drenched and tired. So good to come home to air conditioning and tall glasses of water.

Everything looks overgrown and scraggly. Every container seems to be overflowing, inside and out. Sometimes my house looks like a disaster to me, no matter how hard I try to straighten it up and clean it. It refuses to be tamed. Like a surly teenager. Spitting dirty clothes back onto the floor, tossing crumbs on the counter like spite confetti. "Take that!" it says. "Whyyyyyyy..." I moan. It doesn't care.

Today, I went through more drawers and cabinets, cleaning out stuff I never use, filling brown paper bags to donate. Some things I don't know what to do with. Like the full bottle of mouthwash I bought as a hint for the ripe mouths of the house that no one used. Three half used bottles of baby powder. Opened containers of diapers we don't need. I hate to throw things away.

Three bags sit on the front porch to donate. Mostly toys. I'd put them out at the curb but the boys would pull them all back in. It is equally satisfying and anxiety producing to let go of these things.

After dinner we sat outside in the backyard. Joseph asked Desmond to bring his trumpet outside to play his newest song he's been working on. The jazz song, "Autumn Leaves". He's playing it so beautifully, practicing it every day. It's in my head all the time now. It took some convincing but he got his trumpet and came out to play it for us. Our next door neighbors grew quiet on their porch as soon as he began to play and when he was done, neighbors in a few directions applauded. So sweet.

Joseph has promised, now that we have a filter up and running for the pool, that he'll have the water clear by tomorrow morning. 'Tomorrow's Pool' would be a great title for something.

After Desmond finished his song, I went inside and sat down with my cello, which I haven't touched in months. I pulled out my book and opened it to page one. My cello synapses just smoke now. But they seemed to light again a little bit as I played. I have been sure for days that I would sit and play. And every day has ended with a dusty cello in the corner. Glad I took the time today. Silently apologizing to my family for the noise, after Desmond's beautiful "Autumn Leaves" performance. You have to start somewhere. Even if you start again and again.

I made black berry popsicles this evening for tomorrow. Between tomorrow's popsicles and tomorrow's pool, it should be a nice Sunday.

Have you written down any wishes yet? You don't have to write them anywhere fancy, or light candles, or conjure spirits. I've been adding them to my grocery lists, since I write so many of them. That feels just right.

Sweet dreams, my friend.

Always and still here,

Sarah

July 26

Dear Friend,

Day 137.

Today's pool was just as cloudy as yesterday's pool. But we swam anyway and the blackberry popsicles were good.

This morning Joseph took the boys to the pool supply store with a test strip and a photo of our cloudy water. He came back and told me about the chemicals they gave him. Told me he would mix a "slurry" and "broadcast" it into the water.

"Is that what the pool people told you to do? Broadcast a slurry?"

"Yes," he said.

All day we spoke about Joseph broadcasting his slurry into the pool. I made him wait until I was done swimming.

I went for a walk in the woods while they were slurry shopping. I haven't walked the long path in a long while. I brought my mask and wore it on my arm, putting it on when I was going to pass someone. I paused just now thinking of what word to use for putting on a mask. You don't slip it on. You sort of hook it on. Our ears have new purpose.

It was so hot out today but it was bearable in the shade of the woods. Glad I went.

While Sonny napped, Joseph went for a bike ride and I floated in the pool. My pool float has a small hole somewhere that I can't find. I blow it up before I get in the pool and it deflates very slowly. I finished my Asey Mayo *Cape Cod Mystery* book. I ordered a new Cape Cod mystery book online. I think this next one will be even better.

I forgot to play the cello.

I talked on the phone, which I feel like I haven't done in a long time. To a friend I can't see because of the virus. Made me sad.

Tomorrow we made plans to go to a lake with our friend and her boys in the afternoon. I am glad we will get out and be with friends.

I'm feeling like my world has gotten very small and fragile. I'm impatient and frustrated.

I know things could be worse. But I think they could have been better. And I thought they would be better by now, but things are getting worse in other parts of the country.

I'm doing my best to not focus on the news.

And still writing down my wishes.

I wish you were here.

Always and still here,

Sarah

July 27

Dear Friend,

Day 138.

When I opened the back door this morning, the air felt cool, finally. I tried to coax the boys to gather themselves up to go to the track, so I could walk before it got too hot. It took so long, by the time we got there, the track was radiating the sun's heat back up at me. It was like walking on a hot plate. But I'm glad we went. The boys brought Desmond's new remote-control car and the car chased Sonny around the track and then Sonny chased the car. So many near misses with the car running under Sonny's feet, we were lucky he hadn't taken a spill by the time we left. The fun for them lasts about a lap and then they fight and whine while I walk or jog three more. Sonny threw Desmond's sandals from the bleachers. I yelled at Desmond from the other side of the track when I looked up to see Sonny in a headlock.

Sonny gets so hot and so tired and just can't go on. I remind him that you can be very hot, or very tired and still walk. I've been reminding myself as well.

Sonny lost a gold coin he was carrying for the last few days in the house somewhere. Not real gold, just a gold colored coin from a turtle sanctuary we visited in Florida last year. He kept asking me to find it. I had had such luck for a while finding things and was really trying to hone my psychic finding ability. It seemed to go away but I think I just haven't figured it out quite yet. So I tried again. When I do it, I close my eyes, ask where the missing object is and wait to see an image appear that is the clue that helps me find it. I tried this for Sonny yesterday. I saw paper. I looked under all the papers and books lying around with no luck. I tried again today. I saw paper again, small white papers and a piece of origami. So I looked again, under papers, and in the playroom where Desmond had had a collection of origami. And then I found it under an empty tissue box full of little white pieces of paper that Desmond was collecting, little notes and things, odds and ends. I thought maybe the tissue box is like origami. Anyway, I was so happy to find it and that my clue was accurate. I anxiously await losing something else.

I got all the morning things done that needed doing and got us packed up for the lake. We went back to the lake where we got the terrible sunburn a few weeks ago, this time with a generous application of sunscreen.

My friend was late arriving and after an hour I had given up hope that she was coming, surrendering myself to hours at the lake with no friend and no book to read. I was glad I had at least brought a float for myself. I was going to have to relax and do nothing. Well, nothing in between waiting for the kids to need me to do other things. Which usually translates into 5-minute intervals of relaxing, which is not so relaxing. And then she came up over the hill in the distance and I was so glad.

I brought two floats so we both got to float around, our boys sort of hovering around us, standing beside us, unsure of what role they were to play in us relaxing. They tried climbing on top of us, swimming under us, pulling us. They wandered off and came back.

The boys had a nice time swimming around, and we got to sit and talk some. We talked about how we are faring and how to carry on. Our conversation was like walking through a museum, passing exhibits, peeking our heads into rooms together and deciding to skip a room here or there, too heavy, too dark. Luckily we were able to find other rooms that were still light and hopeful and we strolled through them gingerly.

The dogs at the lake are interesting. Dogs off leash. They are all of a different character. Running amuck. They are like scattered wild cards.

When dinner time rolled around we packed up and went to a burger spot on the mountain. Picnic tables outside and a take-out window. I had a really good fried chicken sandwich, then watched everyone have an ice cream. I felt certain I would regret it if I had one. I sucked up the last inch of Sonny's melted vanilla milkshake through his straw before I tossed the cup in the can. It was enough.

I found a 1954 penny on the ground while there. Then Sonny and I fought over it after he almost lost it. Turns out it's worth an average of 15 cents. Huzzah!

I was short on patience today. I cursed under my breath a lot and huffed and puffed. It occurred to me that my stress level may be a bit high. And perhaps, I could find the time for more self-care. That's a thing. I need to figure out what that might look like and when I can squeeze that in.

All in all, it was a good day. It's good to get out of the house and be with a friend. I am grateful for these little things.

Tomorrow there may be thunderstorms and I'm hoping for a lazy rainy day.

Always and still here,

Sarah

July 28

Dear Friend,

Day 139.

I don't know why I thought part of a lazy Tuesday could include me highlighting my own hair while my children were awake. I've been desperate to do it and usually do it at night when they have gone to bed, but I haven't had the energy to attempt such a feat at night lately. I thought I'd just do it leisurely in the morning while we were hanging out at home.

Highlighting my own hair is awful. I do it because I can and because it saves me a lot of money. It's really hard to do in a small dimly lit bathroom, two small mirrors acting as guides with a side of heckler, my eyeballs insisting on Olympic level gymnastics to see the top of my head, which cannot be seen, stop it. It's nearly impossible to move your hand the way you want it to when you're looking in a mirror. Why is that? And why is pool water at 80° so much colder than the air at 80°? So many questions.

I mixed the wrong hair dye and used that for a little while before I realized what I was doing. I was frazzled from the moment I started.

Sonny was being a nudge and pushed my patience over the edge into the abyss. At high noon, still in my pajamas, with tin foil folded into tight squares all over my head, the rest of my hair in between the foils wild like a lion's mane, my eyes crossed, my fingertips white with bleach, I stormed at him. I blew him up the stairs with the force of a gale wind. No lunch. No lunch that he refused to discuss, said he didn't want and then demanded. Angry with me for telling him he may not lock Desmond in the playroom. Angry I finally cut the key from his new leather-bound journal because he would not stop asking for me to cut it so that he could wear it as a necklace. At every turn he scoffed at me.

I left him upstairs crying. I shook.

I went back upstairs after I had calmed down. I sat on his bed and put my hand on his back and he crawled into my lap. I apologized, he apologized too. I talked about how awful it feels to get so angry with him and that I shouldn't yell, how terrible it feels. We talked for a few minutes and hugged each other. He said, "You are allowed to be upset with me. Just like I get upset with Des. And Daddy gets upset with me, and I get upset with Daddy. And Des gets upset with me and Daddy and you. And you can get upset too."

So I cried. I hope I am doing it right. Always. I just want to nurture them always. To think I have frightened them breaks my heart wholly. And I don't know if I've broken something when it happens. Another chip in a China plate. It's just the best I can do. And it's not often. I hate getting it wrong.

Seems like it's so hard to get things right a lot of the time. Especially now. Socially, politically, emotionally. I'm always afraid I am offending someone; I am often offended. Everyone's hackles are up. Everyone's choosing sides.

I heard someone say once that difficult people are like spiritual sandpaper. This year is a coarse grit for sure. This country is sanding my spirit to a bloody pulp. I can only hope that the paper is gradually switched to a fine grit and I come out of this buffed to a high gloss.

Road rash of the soul.

Dragged down the highway of hatred.

I'm gonna write a country song.

Always and still here,

Sarah

July 29

Dear Friend,

Day 140.

I sat outside this morning in the shade with my *Write it Down, Make it Happen* book, my breakfast and a mug of tea. I bought a new green tea and I put coconut oil in it this morning, it smelled like horses for some reason, but not in a bad way. I am making an effort to find moments of peace and to give myself some attention. Reading this book outside in the mornings seems like a good plan.

A few pages in and I was crying. A line about a random offer of help that someone accepted. And how it would be nice if when we needed it, we heard a loud voice over a speaker say, "Anyone who needs help, please report to the second floor." That was all it took.

Joseph came outside and saw me in tears and sat with me. I tried to explain my heart aches, opening each one like a tissue paper wrapped fragile thing, spreading them out in front of us. "This...and this...and then this one...and this here... and this one goes with this one..." Then holding up empty palms and gesturing at them and dropping my arms, defeated. "What will I do with this?"

Sonny came out and asked what was wrong. I said I missed my parents. He said he was sorry and gave me a kiss. I asked him if he could go get me a tissue.

He said sure. At the door, he turned around and said, "It's like fish and dogs. They don't live that long. I'll be right back," and gave me a thumbs up. When he came back he told me how when people die they become people you can't see with wings, and they can fly. They are called angels. They surround us. Then he started to talk about zombies and Joseph and I laughed and he got flustered. I think he was saying that it's best not to come back to life if you die.

Joseph said nice things, reassured me, encouraged me. Then he went to go paint. Sonny decided to go for a swim.

I sat beside the pool and read my book some more, making a list of all the things I want to happen next.

I felt so much shame last night after I sent you that last letter. I was afraid that I shouldn't write about my awful parenting blunders. I think I share those things in hopes that you will say, "Me too." You usually do. The admission we share smooths over the guilt some. I do not judge you, and when I feel we are the same, I judge myself a little less.

This morning Desmond played virtual video games with his cousin in Florida, talking on the phone and playing on his tablet. Sonny came to the phone too and talked with her about animals he likes and which ones she likes. She is 15.

I spoke with my sister in Florida on the phone for a little while. I miss her. I wonder when I will see her again. Everything feels so still, I keep having the urge to visit people I haven't seen in a long while, friends and family, because it feels like the perfect time. But then I remember why things are so still and that we can't travel.

I floated in the pool a long while this afternoon. I made phone calls to friends to talk about all that is building up day by day. One friend I called was just arriving at the beach in her car and said she'd call soon. One friend I spoke to for a while. It is so encouraging to be understood and loved.

At some point before or after or in between calls, I dialed my childhood phone number, what would have been my mother's house, were she still there. The phone number is still not in service after all this time. When I dial, a recorded woman's voice says, "The number you have dialed is not in service," and then there is the softest hiss of a sound, not silence, not static, just a held line. I floated in the pool with my eyes closed, feeling slightly dizzy, listening to the quiet hiss, straining to hear...anything.

When I was little, my father used to turn on a radio in our kitchen and tune it to static. I thought at the time, he was listening for aliens. Maybe it had something to do with outer space, I don't know what it was he told us he was listening for, but whatever he said, I interpreted as listening for aliens. I wish I had thought to ask him while he was still alive. I wonder if my sister remembers. I never heard anything but static.

When I went ghost hunting, they used a "Spirit Box" which is basically static and then supposedly catches some fluctuation in frequencies and spits out words. Just random radio words maybe. Sometimes they are words that make sense, sometimes they don't.

So I listened intently, just in case. And I whispered into the phone, in case she was listening.

After dinner, I took the boys out to the craft store to look for a key necklace charm and red jewel for Sonny. It felt nice to go out after dinner, like a date, a summer night outing, so out of the ordinary. Sonny picked out a big locket with a glass window that opens, Desmond picked out a package of gold chain. We stopped at Target across the street to see if I could find something I needed. I did not find it, but I did find a box of three Haagen Dazs chocolate covered, chocolate ice cream bars, so we bought those. That was very exciting. We ate them in the car on the way home, laughing and talking all the way.

It was a day with tears but also a lot of tenderness. I am lucky to have my three guys who love me. I am glad for nighttime, that comes at the end of every day and tells us to rest, so that we can wake in the morning to the light of a new day and begin again. Isn't that something?

This day is done and it was done well enough.

I hope your day met you with tenderness too.

Always and still here,

Sarah

July 30

Dear Friend,

Day 141.

When I wake from a dream and lie still until I fall back to sleep, I usually reenter the same dream. If I roll over, the dream vanishes, as if me turning in bed has wiped the slate clean, like an Etch A Sketch. I can't remember what I was dreaming.

I've heard that changing your bed's position in your room so that your head points in a new direction, can cause you to have more vivid dreams.

I find myself climbing into bed excited to go someplace else. We could try moving our beds around to be better entertained while we sleep.

This morning I made a point to bring my breakfast and book outside again to read, but Desmond followed along and sat with me and talked, which was nice too. He wore his gold chain necklace, bracelet and ring that we managed to make from his package of gold chain from the craft store. I told him he looked like a prince. He said he's channeling his inner gangster.

After breakfast I went for a walk in the woods alone again. Shortly after I entered the trail I spotted a cache of golden oyster mushrooms. I walked back out to my car to grab a bag. I pulled them carefully from the log they were growing on. I've never found or harvested mushrooms before and hope I did it right. I left as much of the base as I could and did not take them all. But the bag was heavy with my mushroom treasure for the rest of my walk and I enjoyed its company, the fabric bag swinging at my side.

I passed a man on the trail twice. The same man I passed the last time I walked this trail. He was older than me, 50's, 60's maybe. Tight white tank top tucked into his denim jean shorts, white tube socks and sneakers. Balding, no mask. And no smile. He looks me in the eye, he says hello, but he does not smile.

I thought about and imagined saying hello to a stranger and not smiling. It makes me uncomfortable just thinking about it.

It bothers me now that I smile at strangers and they can't tell because of the mask. It has occurred to me that I don't have to smile now, but I can't help it. I try to smile harder so that my eyes will wrinkle well enough to make it obvious I'm smiling. I've started adding a head nod. If I wore hats, I'd tip my hat.

I ran errands today too, seven stores. I came home so tired. I did not remember to buy everything I wanted to get and could not find everything I needed. I haven't found rubbing alcohol yet. I think I'll try the pharmacy.

I had mixed a batch of my homemade disinfectant, filled my new glass spray bottle to the brim. The other day I was cleaning the bathroom drawers and left it on the floor. Sonny knocked it over and the glass broke. So I cleaned the floor. And have been cleaning my groceries with window spray. I'm hardly cleaning them now though, I am just going through the motions.

I read today that Dr. Fauci says it's not a bad idea to wear goggles to prevent catching the virus.

Part of me is excited I may be able to wear steampunk goggles and really take my Holtzman to a new level. But also, that feels like adding another OCD level of fear and I'm too tired.

I did finally manage to find pool noodles today. I bought enough of them that I could cut open the back of my pool float and fill it with noodles so that it will float forever. Then I sealed it back up with duct tape. I immediately regretted it. It works perfectly of course, but now I have a float full of pool noodles with a strip of duct tape across its back. I don't know why I do the things I do. It looks like I found it in a dumpster. But it will last the summer and then maybe someone will take it from the curb and appreciate my ingenuity.

I swam with Sonny and then showered and put on my pajamas.

I made spaghetti and salad for the boys, a salad for me, then dozed off outside on the loveseat, my legs hanging over one side.

Tomorrow is Friday and I'll go to my studio. I chopped vegetables and put together more salad for the week and one for lunch tomorrow.

The new paint colors I ordered came in the mail too, three blues. Cobalt bermuda blue, pthalo blue green, and pthalo turquoise. I hope I have one that will be just right for the aqua blue umbrellas in my beach painting.

I finished listening to Educated today, which it turns out was perfectly titled after all. It was quite an emotional roller coaster. I was glad to have heard it all but am glad it is done.

I've started listening to Shirley Jackson's *We Have Always Lived in the Castle*. So far so good.

I look forward to painting those blue umbrellas tomorrow, with Shirley and my salad.

Always and still here,

Sarah

July 31

Dear Friend,

Day 142.

I noticed last night I haven't written in my calendar all week. We had no plans that needed remembering and I did not cross off the days. I usually jot down a thing or two to remember what I did, in case I am ever accused of murder, I'll know where I was.

This morning the air outside was cool and we opened the windows. The fresh cool air coming into the house on a breeze felt so good. We have not had a cool morning in so long. I was up early and out for a walk on the trail soon after. I started off listening to Shirley Jackson's novel but only for a minute or two before the sound of the woods persuaded me to turn it off so I could hear the wind in the leaves, the cicadas and birds, and my steps on the packed dirt of the path. I walked into the woods and felt the energy of all of those tall living trees surround me and I felt, or imagined I felt, that they were happy I was there. It was so sweet. I stopped to put my hands on a tree and it was like putting my hands on the strong, solid leg of a horse. Taking a minute to think about how alive the woods are when you're standing in the woods, is magical.

After I walked the loop, I walked down to the river beach on the trail. I was walking too quickly and took a funny step onto some tree roots that were like stairs down to the rocks and was thrown onto my hands and knees, swiftly and painfully. My first thought was, "I should not fall down when I am alone," and then I hoped for the best. I turned myself around and sat on a log to survey the damage. Nothing terrible, just scrapes on my shins and knee. My palms burned. I stood up right away to walk it off and was fine. So glad. I've got a nice egg on my shin.

At the end of the trail, I looked up and there was the man in the white tank top and jean shorts. He was looking at me and I smiled, he said, "Good morning." No smile.

I made breakfast when I got home and sat outside with the boys. Sonny has asked me a few times if the leaves of the rose of Sharon trees are edible. I told him I didn't think so because I've never heard of anyone eating them. So today when he asked for the third time, I looked it up. Indeed they are! The new softer leaves are good for salads, the older leaves are just tougher although you can eat those too. And the flower is edible as well and has a "nutty flavor" according to the internet article I read. So we all had a taste of the flowers and the leaves. And they were pretty tasty. How wonderful to discover a new food and to have such an abundance in our own yard.

When I got to my studio this afternoon I mixed my new paint, spilling the medium all over the bottle and then one of the blues all over my table. I pushed the blue immersion paint to the edge of the table and let it drip back into the bottle, with a square flat brush like a little broom. So clumsy today.

Sadly, the blues I bought could not match the aqua blue of the umbrella on my computer screen photo. I wonder if there is a paint that can. Now I just have a lovely variety of blues, which will serve me well with all the Cape Cod beach paintings I will make.

I spent three hours, after I mixed my paint, just painting tiny umbrellas and tiny people on the beach. I finished the smallest of the three beach paintings. By the time I get to the big one, I should have these umbrellas, towels, beach bags and people really nailed down. They are so tiny in the photo it is hard to see what's what. But I don't have to paint it all, just the best bits.

I decided to stay out on my own for a while after I was done painting. I bought a burrito and piece of carrot cake from the health food store, which I can't decide if I regret or not, and then drove up the thruway to my favorite antique center that is open again and open until 8:00 every day. I was glad I could go but there was nothing good really and everything seemed more expensive than it used to be. I thought it would be fun to drive there and walk around. It was not as fun as I wanted it to be. Everything feels strange. But it was nice to feel a bit of freedom and watch the sun slip lower in the sky, driving in and out of the long shadows.

And now here I am again, thinking of you.

Always and still here,

Sarah

August 2020

August 1

Dear Friend,

Day 142.

Last night I stayed up late so I could write a letter to an advice podcast I listen to. I am hoping they read my letter and just tell me I am okay. And that no one I know listens to this podcast. I should have used a nom de plume.

Every morning I make the same cup of medicinal tea. It is organic green tea, two teaspoons of coconut oil, a half teaspoon of raw honey, a teaspoon of powdered mushrooms, some milk and in the summer, some ice cubes to cool it down. I have tried to drink it with almond milk but it is just not the same. I have it every morning without fail, even when we go camping. It is a loving way to start the day. I am always so happy to have my tea.

On this morning's walk through the woods, which is now also me attending a large gathering of my tree friends, I ran into a human friend I know from the gym. We stopped to talk for a while, agreeing to forgo our masks but keeping a distance all the same. He was walking his dog, a black lab mix with white around its sweet eyes and muzzle, the telltale sign of age in a dog.

He told me his mother-in-law had passed from COVID and his wife who had been caring for her caught it as well but has recovered. The dog had been his mother-in-law's and was now his and he walks her every day. He said his wife is still struggling with some health issues but is otherwise okay. I wondered later if her struggles now are a result of the stress of the ordeal and the loss of her mom.

When I was home again, I made my breakfast and brought it outside with my book and notepad. In the spot where I always sit to write down all of my wishes, was a single milkweed seed. The kind you blow on to make a wish. As if my yard had been listening and left me an encouraging whisper.

I whipped up some new popsicles. I have not made the same flavor twice. Today I made a layered pop with peanut butter, chocolate and banana flavors. I had one tonight and the peanut butter layer was so good. It was as creamy as ice cream.

I was hoping to visit a friend today but I was rapidly overwhelmed by my kids and felt like my brain was broken before noon. I felt a wave of exhaustion and nausea. So decided to lay low.

I ate lunch and floated in the pool, reading my book and soaking up vitamin D. I am doing my best to keep up with everything and mend myself at the same time. It is a seesaw, busy and flustered ups followed by bumpy landings to rest.

For dinner I cooked up some chicken and my oyster mushrooms with garlic and butter which were pretty good. Buttered spaghetti for the boys, bright red sweet cherry tomatoes and a sliced cucumber from a friend's garden.

Joseph has some art hanging in town and he said the opening was this evening. I was so glad to have something to attend. I wore a pretty white sun dress I just bought and the boys rose to meet me with ironed button downs and gold chains. I had walked halfway and had to turn around because I left my mask at home, placing it down somewhere as I was getting myself ready to go. Sonny came with me because his polyester Transformer costume was too hot. I found my mask where I had put on my shoes and he changed into shorts and a t-shirt. Joseph called to say the opening ended at 6:00 and that we were too late. Of course it did.

We walked back to town anyway. The boys got ice cream at Alleyway. There seemed to be a lot of people walking around but not the usual line at the ice cream shop or people at the tables there. No one at the outside dining at a spot that is usually full when I drive by. Strange for a Saturday evening. I wonder where everyone was.

Feels a bit like we're in a *Truman Show* bubble. I'd like to find the doorway out. I feel defeated today. But today is done. Another chance arrives with the sun. See you there.

Always and still here,

Sarah

August 2

Dear Friend,

Day 144.

I had no idea how attached I am to this mask I made and have been wearing since the quarantine began. I sewed two different masks for myself but the one I wear is easier to breathe in than the other. I made it from a vintage embroidered tablecloth. It is a soft white cotton, with pink cross-stitched flowers. It is my best and favorite.

I thought I lost it tonight.

First off, I learned I should not go food shopping at dinner time when I am hungry. I felt miserable, starving, waiting to get home to eat. I walked all around Hannaford, a big supermarket, because they have most everything I need. I was irrationally completely crestfallen when I came upon the organic bananas that were all the same solid bright green. Sometimes they just don't turn yellow, and I did not have the energy to go to another grocery store tonight.

They were still out of rubbing alcohol. I can't find it anywhere, even Walgreens was out of stock.

When I left I mustered up enough energy to drive to the next parking lot up the road and stop at CVS to see if they had any. I drove over there and parked the car, then could not find my mask. I searched everywhere it could have gone and it was not there. Devastated, because I was hungry and tired, I drove back to Hannaford like a drag racer. No mask lying on the blacktop where I expected. I stood in the rain, puzzled, dumbfounded, staring at the shopping carts. Why would someone take my mask? There are literally masks all over the ground, everywhere you go. Disposable masks, and cloth masks that have all been trampled and driven over. But mine was gone forever.

Now I had lost my mask and could not go to CVS, so I went home. I shoved food in my face. And I took out my fabric to try to make a new one. I cut enough fabric to make a few new ones, so that I might wear more and not get so attached to one.

I went outside to my car to get my headphones so I could listen to my audio book while I ran my sewing machine. I took one more look around the car, incredulous that it could be gone. "It doesn't make sense!" I said out loud, to my car.

And then there it was. Between the console and the passenger seat. This small bit of soft white and pink fabric, like a tiny blankie, curled up in the dark.

I felt sort of relieved but, how had I lost hours of my night to not having lost this thing?

I folded my cut fabric for another day. I had no elastic anyway.

My throat hurts. I'm so tired.

The next three days are just me and the kids. At least we have groceries.

I am already exhausted just thinking about Thursday. I told Joseph we should drive to the beach for the day. 2 1/2 hours each way. I don't know if we'll make it.

But it's bedtime. Every night, I am spent. Glad for the next day already in its revolution to meet me. I get to have my morning tea again. I wish I could make you a cup.

Always and still here,

Sarah

August 3

Dear Friend,

Day 145.

This morning I heard on the radio that the United States is number one in COVID cases. And that if we could quarantine for three weeks, we'd be over it. Which does not make sense to me, but if that's true, that's wild to think about. It feels like American's love of their freedom will keep this virus moving for a long while. Blues music and apple pie.

Do you know that Americans walk differently than people from other countries, according to the FBI? They kick their feet out when they walk. We also smile the most. And when we're standing still, we rest on one foot or the other. So if you ever change your identity and go hide out in another country and the FBI is on your trail, walk weird, stand straight and stay tight lipped.

Joseph has been missing his brown belt for a week or so now. He told us the other day he'd give whoever found it, $20. I thought, oh good! Something is lost! I sat down and covered my eyes with my hands to make the theater very, very dark. And I asked where it was and waited. Eventually, I saw a spiderweb and a soda can. I relayed this to Joseph and it was not helpful and I thought, man, I used to be good at this.

This morning I was straightening up the backyard and I moved a plastic basket of Sonny's toys that was under the back stoop. When I lifted it, 6 crickets scurried out from underneath. I shouted out to Sonny that there were so many crickets and he came running to see. But they were all gone. I lifted it again to see if anymore where underneath and noticed the basket was attached to a screen of spider webbing that spread to the stoop. So many spiderwebs, I thought. Ah ha! I leaned in to peek under the stoop and what did I find? Joseph's belt. And, it was draped over the aluminum gutter, running along the ground from the house. Not a soda can, but aluminum. It must have fallen off of the stoop railing and was hidden in the row of rose of Sharon trees.

I was so excited. Desmond came to see what the fuss was all about and I explained it all to him with mounting excitement and volume until I was laughing like a mad scientist which surely left my neighbors wondering if I had finally snapped.

The boys were very upset that they would not get the $20. Se la vie.

I had a friend and her daughter over this afternoon for a backyard play date. The kids swam and jumped on the trampoline, back and forth. My friend and I sat in the shade, the sun falling through the leaves and landing in little circles and heart shapes of light on her face. Talking about our families and our tender and stubborn hearts. So nice to find a friend who is so easy to talk to, to be understood and understand.

It occurred to me that banana splits are really a thing of the past and they hardly make sense anymore. Why would you put ice cream on a banana? Do people still do that? I used to think it was a good idea. I may have tried it at some point, but now I think it's absurd. Lunacy.

I thought about the next popsicle I want to make. Two flavors, maybe vanilla and chocolate in stripes. And I'll drop a maraschino cherry in first so there's a cherry on top. That will be a beautiful popsicle.

Would you believe they make organic maraschino cherries? I have a jar of them in my fridge. I'm sure I paid about $8 for that sucker too.

Tonight, Desmond was complaining of his foot hurting. He could not remember injuring it and has no marks anywhere, but it is puffy, sore to touch, and by the end of the night he could not put pressure on it. I hope it's better tomorrow.

I'll try not to worry.

It is supposed to rain tomorrow. Maybe we'll have a relaxing day. Didn't I just say this about last Tuesday? I will not highlight my hair this time. Maybe we'll bake scones and watch that movie about how smart trees are. Put all 6 of our feet up.

Tomorrow is a secret only for a little while longer. Meet me here again tomorrow night.

Love you.

Always and still here,

Sarah

August 4

Dear Friend,

Day 146.

I liked today alright. It really was a lazy rainy Tuesday for the most part. Turned out we were in the path of hurricane Isaias. I'm always the last to know. We were sort of at the tail end of the storm, we had heavy rains all day and some wind but nothing exciting. Desmond kept checking the news online to see what damage was done where. We did not even lose power, just some puddles in the basement but that is to be expected.

This morning, when we came downstairs, there was a light rain falling. Desmond looked out the back door and said, "Why is the pool half empty?" I had not even had my tea yet.

I was afraid he had dealt our poor pool its final death blow the day before with his big waves he made atop his enormous white swan float. I watched the sides bulge and move, water splashing over its edges. I said, "If Dad were here, he'd tell you stop. This old pool might not survive those waves." So he stopped.

I went outside to investigate and checked the hose that I had noticed was leaking a bit yesterday and had forgotten about until just then. The hose had come clean off and the pool water was pouring out into the grass. I reattached the hose, running back into the house for pliers to loosen and then tighten the clamp that holds it in place. Down to the basement to unplug the filter pump. And then throwing the hose into the pool to fill it back up.

Then I told Sonny to come out and see the pool. It was the perfect depth for him now. He did not need his puddle jumper floating device. He was so pleased, he got right in, even though it was drizzling and cloudy. The water was up to his armpits instead of his chin on tippy toes. I let him play in the water for a bit until it started to rain harder and I then had him come in so we could have our breakfast.

He was so disappointed later in the day when he said he was going back in, and I told him I had filled it back up.

I hope all of our grass doesn't die from the pool's saltwater. Maybe all the rain will help dilute it and wash it away, deep into the ground, past the roots of the grass and clover.

The pool in repair, we stayed inside, warmed pancakes from the day before and tried out some paint pens a friend had given us on our collection of rocks. We colored all the rocks we had so that we could return them back to the river shore where we found them to leave for someone else to find.

Desmond painted one white and put a little face on it like a ghost. I think I will keep that one.

This afternoon I made a big bowl of popcorn and we put on the documentary about the wisdom of trees. Sonny did not last long, but Desmond and I liked it. Desmond agreed to watch it with me later and we decided to put on a movie called Troop Zero.

I so wanted us to learn about trees together but this movie about a rag tag group of girl scouts trying to fit in held lessons just as important. Not about trees, but about people. A really beautiful movie. At the end I had to sit very still to keep from out-right sobbing. Tears just pouring down my face. So lovely. Ah, life. People. Kids. Heartache. Stars...sigh...

I decided I do not have the energy to prepare us for the beach Thursday and then sit in a car for 5 hours in one day with Sonny and Joseph. Desmond is no problem, he is easy breezy. The other two have opinions and stuff. Huffy and Puffy.

I was sad to make the choice not to go, but I didn't feel it would be worth the stress and knew if we went, it would take me a long time to recover.

So guess what I did? After looking online several times over the last month for Airbnbs and possible hotels near the beach, all of them unappealing or too expensive, I booked us a room at one of the too expensive fancy hotels and I could not be happier about it.

Spoiling us for one night and having two days at the beach is worth every penny right now. I won't get to see my Long Island almost family. But at least I will get to go down there and be by the ocean and watch my boys dig in the sand and chase seagulls. Oh, my heart does love the beach. Thank you, thank you hotel for having a room and being fancy.

Tomorrow, I'll have to pack and prepare for a long day or two at the beach and a night away from home and the first long car ride we've taken in a very long while.

Always and still here,

except for Thursday,

when I'll be at the beach,

Sarah

August 5

Dear Friend,

Day 147.

My children tried to break me like a wild horse today. Keep yo saddle.

Good Lord.

What time is it? So tired.

I am mostly packed for our beach and fancy hotel adventure tomorrow. I took my toiletries bag out of the cabinet to look for my toiletries bag and was dumbfounded that it was not there. "What does it MEAN??" I asked out loud. And then noticed it in my hand.

I have been listening to a lot of Shirley Jackson books and today started listening to a book about Shirley Jackson. Man do we have a lot in common. I just haven't written my horror novel yet. She wrote "domestic comedy" and horror. I've been listening to her domestic comedy although I didn't realize it was comedy. Because what she writes about is just truth, pure and simple. Like when her kids told her over and over again in a restaurant that they want spaghetti and she told them there is no spaghetti on the menu, when the waitress finally came, she ordered them the veggie plate and the chicken salad and spaghetti for herself on accident. It's just what you do. That's like moving your toiletries bag out of the way so you can find your toiletries bag.

I can't remember all that happened today, but I do know I asked Desmond at least 20 times to fold a basket of laundry for me. That lasted from 10:00 to 6:00.

I gave Sonny and Desmond haircuts. Sonny's first haircut with a buzzer all around the sides and back. Now he looks like this rotten kid who used to come over and break stuff in our house all the time.

No matter, tomorrow we will be at the beach. And I will fall to my knees and weep, holding handfuls of sand, streaming from between my fingers up to the sky.

No I will not.

I will spend 10 minutes opening up my beach chair that I can't open and then sit in it and stare at the ocean like Jack Nicholson in *One Flew Over the Cuckoos Nest*.

Or something in between the two.

I'm very excited.

Wish you were coming too.

Always and still here,

Sarah

August 6

Dear Friend,

Day 148.

Well, well, well. Here I sit in the dark at a desk in our room at the fancy hotel. Joseph in one full sized bed, Desmond and Sonny in another. We made it.

When we left the house this morning, it was sort of cool out and cloudy. The drive was also gray. From the backseat, I started messaging Long Island friends about the beaches. I heard Jones Beach was closed because their electricity was out from the storm a couple of days ago. Wondering what other beach we could go to. I thought surely we could go to one of the many other beaches in the area but as I looked, I read over and over that the beaches were only allowing residents of the county due to COVID.

A friend messaged back, "It's raining on Long Island! And there's lightning, the beaches may close because of the lightning."

I felt my beach day crumbling like a cookie that wasn't baked right at all. I did it all wrong.

Our fancy hotel, which we paid too much money for, was nonrefundable. So even if we had to sit in a parking lot somewhere until it was time to check into our room, we were going.

Robert Moses was open and it's a state park beach, no county discrimination there. So we decided that would be our best bet. We drove on in the rain and gloom, steadily advancing towards the sand and sea, by hook or by crook. I checked the weather, rain until 2:00 and then a little graphic of the sun peeking out from behind the clouds. 20% rain. As long as it stopped raining, I thought, it's not the perfect beach day, but it's my beach day and I will love it no matter what.

For a few minutes I listened to a podcast that had music like the theme music from *Stranger Things*. I watched the trees rush by the car, the gray sky behind them. I started to wonder if we had bewitched the skies, summoned rain and clouds, lightning, power outages, so that we could freely drive, right to the sand, to park the car, and then the spell would release the sun from its cloudy shroud as we stepped onto the beach.

When we pulled into Robert Moses, field 2, at 1:00, the collector booths had white handwritten signs that said, "No Charge". The windows were closed, no one inside.

We drove on through and right up to the beach. When we stepped out of the car, it was windy, cool, the ground was wet, but it was not raining. I pulled on my car sweater and gathered our things.

We smiled and laughed and high-fived and then settled ourselves on the beach. When we had our chairs opened and our blanket spread out on the sand, the sun came out. Then not only was it my beach day, it was the perfect beach day.

What perfect beautiful luck. When I thought that the universe was conspiring against me, it was really working so closely with me.

We wandered down to the water and seagulls ripped open our bags of pretzels and popcorn. We shooed them away and ate our popcorn and pretzels anyway.

The boys collected pieces of clear jellyfish from the sand. The lifeguards promised me they don't sting. They filled their hands with squishy jellyfish bits. Sonny scrambled down the beach with Desmond like it was an Easter egg hunt. "Look! More gelatins!" When they rinsed them with sea water in their bucket, they were crystal clear like glass.

An old man was walking down the beach with a metal detector so Sonny and I asked if he was looking for treasure. He smiled and said he was. I asked him what the best treasure he ever found was. He told us that one time, he found a wedding ring set. It was worth $14,000.00. So he put a post on Facebook to try to find its owner. The initials of the woman who owned it had been inscribed in the ring. 4 hours later, he found the woman who had lost it. He said, "She was the best thing I found."

I took a long walk by myself and made up a song about moving to Cape Cod.

We stayed until Sonny and Joseph were cranky and tired and then we came to the hotel to clean up for dinner.

We met up with a family friend who lives nearby. The town here closes its little Main Street from cars in the evenings in Summer. We walked there and ate together outside. Finishing our meal with macaroons and pistachio cake from a French bakery.

She walked us back to our hotel and we wandered around inside a bit. Sadly, the pool is closed because of the virus.

It looks like rain tomorrow. And since there is nothing to do inside, I suppose we'll head home before too long. I am tempted to go stare at the beach through the rain from the car.

What a glorious place to be. At the beach. It was a gift to be here today. I am so grateful, especially for the sunlight sparkling on the water. It's my favorite.

Always and still here,

Sarah

August 7

Dear Friend,

Day 149.

Our magic worked as well today as it did yesterday. We woke to rain and dark gray skies. I turned my phone on to check the weather. My weather app said at 10:00 the chance of rain would go from 40% down to 20% and the sun would peek out from behind the cloud. Google's weather report said the sun would peek out from behind the cloud at 11:00. Either way looked like a potential beach day to me.

It stopped raining by 10:00 when we checked out of the hotel. But it was still very gray.

We had breakfast down the block, Joseph and I grabbing omelets to go and then sitting in the French bakery where the kids got fruit cups and croissants. Before we left, Joseph and the boys headed to the bathroom and I sat alone. I took a minute to really look around me. There was a pretty good sized group of people there. 6' apart and all wearing masks, unless they were sitting at tables. It was noisy, with its high ceilings, marble counters and tile floors. And I realized how much I had been craving this feeling, being around people. Besides the masks, it looked pretty normal. And I almost missed it, I wasn't really paying attention. But when I did, I got teary, just so glad to have it be so. There we were. Just like on TV. Almost.

After breakfast we headed to the beach. Back to Robert Moses, because it's now Joseph's favorite beach. Even though Jones Beach was open today. We thought we'd go back to field 2 where we were yesterday. It was a short walk to the water and there was a concession stand there with food for lunch and maybe even dinner if my guys let me stay that long. I imagined us staying until the sun set, or the bugs came out, whichever came first.

The concession stand never opened but we had enough food to last until dinner.

It was mostly overcast with the sun peeking out from behind the clouds now and then. But it didn't rain. It was so beautiful. The gray sky with pale clouds and a slate blue ocean. Everything else looked day glow in contrast with the muted blues and grays.

I communed with a huge seagull and wondered if the seagull is my spirit animal. Ripping open bags of chips with its beak, living at the beach eating fish and watching people. I don't know much about seagulls. I've decided I will get a book about them and read it. I read a book about pigeons once and it was one of my favorites. I wonder if seagulls are as interesting as pigeons.

Yesterday was a day for jellyfish. Today was a day for clam shells. We made a fine collection.

The lifeguards said that field 5 may have their concession stand open so we thought we'd drive over there at dinner time, park and eat on the beach. But when we got there, that was closed too. Joseph found a place on his phone that was very close, on the beach, lobster rolls, all the things, on Fire Island. But what he discovered was that you cannot drive there. I thought he knew this. So we had to decide. Should we park and walk 1.6 miles for an estimated 32 minutes at 5:30 to Kismet, then walk back before dark to drive 2½ hours home? The obvious answer for me was yes. It was not the easiest plan and I didn't realize how long 1.6 miles was, or that Sonny was not going to walk much of it on his own, but it was more time at the beach and a walk to Fire Island to add to our adventure. So we went.

It was so beautiful. And tiring. But we made it. The restaurant was overpriced, like food at the airport or the movie theater. But it was nice to sit and see the bay. We had lobster rolls and calamari. And then trekked back the way we came, passing the beautiful black and white lighthouse again. The sun was setting and making an orange line of haze across the sky over the bay, pink and lavender between the clouds over the ocean. Two thirds of the way back, Joseph saw lightning in the distance.

We got to the car and got everyone settled and as soon as we were on our way, it started to rain. Two days of the rain directly catering to our plans like something out of *The Witches of Eastwick*. I can't say how grateful I am for these two days of such beauty, being outside in the sun by the ocean, the soft sand, the cool saltwater, the clouds in the sky, the seagulls.

Living upstate has given me such appreciation for nature. It wasn't something I thought much about growing up on Long Island. It wasn't something anyone talked about. Upstate I am closer to nature than I had ever been growing up and closer with people who are intertwined with nature.

To come back to the beach as a grown up with new eyes, I see every seashell as a different specimen of the living creatures in the sea. The life that abounds in the ocean and in the sand, on the shore and in the dunes. Everything's alive. I want to learn more about everything that is there.

I read my book very little on the beach. I mostly looked out at the water, felt the sand, looked at shells, watched the people and the sky.

We squeezed every beautiful minute out of the day today.

I needed this so much. I feel like I'm filled back up and can carry on.

Tomorrow we'll be home all day. Joseph will pass out on the living room floor. The kids will be their usual busy selves. I walked 16,000 steps today, so tomorrow I can rest. I'll be glad to float in the pool if the sun is out.

Always and still here,

Sarah

August 8

Dear Friend,

Day 150.

150 days! Remember in March when we thought it would be two weeks of quarantine and then we could go back to normal? We are still so far from normal.

Do you ever go down the conspiracy theory road? Even for a minute or two? It's terrifying. Population control is terrifying. The profit this virus has brought to the richest in this country is astounding. I worry. And I practice not worrying. Whatever the truth of this virus is, I'll likely never know it. And if I did know it, there wouldn't be anything I could do about it. So I try not to think about it. Do you think about it?

When we came home last night, there was a box of vegetables on our porch from a friend. The box stayed outside overnight and in the morning we realized there were home made cookies in there too! Thank goodness our neighborhood menagerie of animals didn't notice them. Or unanimously agreed to leave them for us.

It was so late when we got home, Desmond crawled up to bed and Sonny cried while I brushed his teeth. I wouldn't have pulled him sleeping from the car to brush his teeth, except that while we were at the beach, I noticed his bottom teeth looked like they were yellowing, like rotten Garbage Pail Kid teeth. But when I looked again today, they looked fine. Must have been the peanut butter he was eating.

There was mouse poop in the kitchen sink, the peaches we had just bought were moldy and the plant in the bathroom was wilting. "We're gone two days and it's like *Grey Gardens*," I thought to myself.

So nice to be in our own beds. Sharing a full-sized bed in a hotel with Joseph is like trying to sleep on a balance beam. My parents had a full-sized bed while they were married. That may have been why they divorced.

Them and Bob Marley, sharing his single bed. No thanks. But if someone wants to share your single bed with you, that IS love, Bob, yes it is.

I can't remember what all happened today. It's a Groundhog's Day blur again. Back to our usual shenanigans. But with a couple of beach days under my belt, I don't feel like I'm missing out on as much.

Our town hung up banners on Main St. while we were gone. They say, "Welcome to Saugerties! Stay safe. Stay open. Wear a mask." I don't really get the "stay open" part. Am I supposed to stay open?

I have so many banner ideas, but the town does not ask me.

Probably just as well. Me and my big ideas.

Always and still here,

Sarah

August 10

Dear Friend,

Day 152.

Sorry I didn't write yesterday. I went to bed early because I wasn't feeling very well. Probably hormones or some vitamin deficiency, I am boosting my magnesium and should get some B vitamins, I think. Do you take B's? I'll have to find a good one.

Yesterday was Sunday. The highlight of the day was Desmond taking us out to dinner with the money he's put into his savings column from his allowance. We walked to town to eat at Bella Luna. The guys all had pizza and he let me order a salad. I thought we'd spend more time down in the square with the water fountain he used to love to run through. It's been closed mostly, open only to patrons of the two restaurants there. After dinner Desmond ran through it once, not with the abandon he used to, drenching himself head to toe. This time he stayed perfectly dry. Sonny ran through a few times, avoiding the water blast each time. A drunk patron nearby smoking cigarettes kept yelling, "You're a winner! You're a winner!"

Today Joseph was back to work and the boys and I drove to Delmar to our pediatric dentist to check on Sonny's teeth. We had to wear our masks and they took our temperature at the front desk before our appointment, writing down our temperatures on a yellow post-it note.

We'd been monitoring some cavities he's had but haven't been in a while because of the virus. We got X-rays today and things don't look so great. He'll need to have some repairing done. It's hard not to feel guilty and ashamed, like I've failed on some basic parenting level. But we haven't done anything differently than we have for Desmond's teeth and Desmond never had cavities. The dentist says Sonny's teeth are "very white and powdery" whatever that means. He says they didn't absorb enough calcium and something else... and that there are so many reasons why that may be the case, there's no way to know exactly why. Could be hereditary or it could have happened when I was pregnant, if I had a cold.... And that it doesn't mean his adult teeth will have the same issue. Sometimes people say things that surprise me and I just listen. I should ask more questions. Why would having a cold when your pregnant affect your baby's teeth?

Sonny was a great patient and has no idea what's in store. This dentist office is supposed to be really great so I am just going to trust it will all go well without it being traumatic for him. It may be more traumatic for Joseph and I.

I've been googling all of the pros and cons of the procedures they recommended and all of the options available. Life is overwhelming.

Tonight, Desmond made tomato soup to add to our dinner. He served it in the big clam shells we found on the beach, floating a single basil leaf in each one and placing the shell on a fancy white plate with a gold rim. So pretty. Even Sonny ate the soup.

Joseph came home early and we sat together to eat dinner. Desmond had put on some jazz music which never fails to make me feel like I'm living the life I want to be living. After dinner I said if I were home alone, I'd go lie on my bed and read a book. Joseph said I could if I wanted to.

I did want to, but first I stretched out beside him in the living room. He had a patient die today. Not COVID related, just a hospital death in the ICU. I don't know what that's like to hold a stranger's hand while they die. And then come home for dinner. I am glad Joseph was there and that he held his patient's hand.

I went up to my bed and read some of my new Cape Cod book. It's called *Cape Cod* and it's by William Martin. It's a NY Times bestseller. The book moves back and forth between the pilgrims and Native Americans and a modern-day Cape family who are descendants of the pilgrims. Two story lines. The pilgrims sound like pirates when they talk. The "Saints and the Strangers" be liking to set up camp in the bay.... but the Nausets won't let them wipe out their tribe with the diseases other white men brought before them, like they did to other tribes. Arrows vs. guns.

I read for a little while and fell asleep. Joseph put the boys to bed and I woke up a few hours later, thinking of you.

I wanted to write to you before another day went by. Now everyone's sleeping. Another day is done.

No plans tomorrow but a meteor shower is on the calendar for the next two nights. Hopefully the skies will be clear. Maybe we'll spot a few shooting stars, zipping by, over this crazy, crazy world we've made for ourselves. Man, oh man.

Always and still here,

Sarah

August 11

Dear Friend,

Day 153.

I'm thinking a lot about Shirley Jackson. Still listening to the book about her. We have so much in common, me and Shirley.

My best moments today were outside. Walking around and around inside the pool, skimming the leaves and flowers. It's like a zen rock garden, that pool. We had such a heavy rain, was it just yesterday? The pool was filled to the top, with green leaves resting at its bottom.

Our power went out for a little while. It's exciting when the power goes out. There's a mystery. Is your power out? Yes, mine is out, is yours out too? What happened? When will it come back? Nobody knows. Sonny tried all the light switches. "It's out in the playroom too!! It's out in the bathroom!!" And when it came back with a hum, he checked all the switches again, so exciting.

I took a shower before I made dinner. Being fresh from the shower or bath before I have dinner always reminds me of being little. I don't know if that happened often or if it was just one time that stayed with me. Sitting at the table in clean pajamas, damp, washed and brushed hair, eating spaghetti and meatballs with a glass of milk. Such simple pleasures. Being cared for so. Perfect comfort.

I hope you found some moments of comfort today.

I'm feeling quiet and still.

I'm going to crawl into bed and read about the pilgrims and the Nausets. Oh, but first I have to check the sky for shooting stars....

Always and still here,

Sarah

August 12

Dear Friend,

Day 154.

Woke up this morning to another power outage. It really makes it feel like the end times when there's a power outage on top of a global pandemic. I wondered if it were. I wondered if this was the new normal, no more power. What would that mean? What if they let loose a virus to wipe us out and then took our electric away and watched from their highest towers.... But it was just a transformer that blew on the corner. My neighbor across the street told me when I wheeled our garbage cans to the curb in my pajamas.

We ran through the, "Do you have power?" "No, do you?" "No, I wonder what happened." But he knew, he heard it blow and called Central Hudson. So all there was left to do was wait. Neighbors from the corner were outside. "You're power out?" "No, is yours?" "Yep, transformer blew."

Then my next-door neighbor came outside. "You're power out?" I asked. "Yeah, you?" "Yeah, Jim says it was a transformer." Then Jim chimed in, giving his report and I went inside to wait.

The house was warm. The kids found plastic animal snouts I left on the counter the night before when I opened a package from a friend and put them on. They tossed around hacky sacks that came in the package with the snouts. Felt like a dream.

I used a match to light the stove to make my tea and oatmeal for Sonny. It made the kitchen warmer, but I really wanted my tea.

I sat outside where it was slightly cooler, but not much. There are so many crickets now. They are loud and there's such a variety of cricket sounds around the yard. Are they different crickets? Or are they just doing different things?

The sunlight was falling at an angle through the yard, sneaking under the umbrella and landing in the seat beside me. I placed my hand in the sun and realized my hand looks like my Dad's hand, but my thumb curves like my Mom's thumb. I tucked my thumb beneath my palm and I felt a tenderness for my father that I have not felt in a long time.

I wandered around the yard and pulled weeds, trimmed things that were taking over, put tomato cages around flowers that were flailing about and cut a bouquet of flowers for the table.

When I came inside the power came back on to greet me. The kids cheered. I made my breakfast and listened, halfheartedly, to the news.

While Sonny napped, I floated in the pool and read my book. Desmond was bored and only wanted three things—a friend his age to play with, to watch YouTube and something sweet to eat. I told him to eat an apple and read a book.

When Sonny was up, I drove us to Adams so we could pick up some food for dinner. A lobster roll and Cape Cod chips for Desmond, chicken nuggets and chips for Sonny and sushi for me. Then we headed for the "beach" in town to eat our food and swim. Our beach is a creek beach. The "sand" is dirt. There's lots of tiny green leaves growing in the water. The water is brown and warm. This is why we must move to Cape Cod.

I sat on the dock with Desmond and Sonny as they took turns getting in, being tickled by plants and scurrying back out. Desmond said, "I'm not swimming in this waste bucket!" But he didn't want to go home, he wanted to swim. Eventually he adjusted his spirit to the water before him and was cannon-balling off the end of the dock, swimming to the floating dock a little further away. Sonny climbed up and down the ladder with his puddle jumper on, in and out of the water, following Desmond, swimming to the dock and back, shrieking at the leaves, and then ignoring them completely.

They made me laugh.

It was too hot, I wanted to go home.

I noticed before we left a friend of mine was there too and we chatted a bit. It was nice to see a friend.

It was close to 7:00 when we got home and we all got in the pool. The pool was cool and clear.

Then bubble baths and Shark Week! When the show started, it was very dramatic. I asked Sonny if it was too scary. "I love it..." he whispered.

And so, another day comes to a close. I feel like my edges are a bit frayed. I wonder if there will be meteors tonight. Have you seen any lately?

Life seems tricky enough without the virus. This really has put a damper on things. There still seems to be no end in sight. With schools opening next month, I imagine they will close shortly after they open. I am reminded again of the old adage, "Half measures avail us nothing." We'll be right where we are forever at this rate.

Always and still here,

Sarah

August 13

Dear Friend,

Day 155.

Yesterday was 6 months since my first day of quarantine. I never imagined this would last so long. Although we are not in quarantine, we certainly are limited. I suppose it's just social distancing now and wearing masks in public spaces, still lots of hand washing, wipes in the car, cleaning groceries. I used to like grocery shopping.

I miss the zoo. I miss museums. I miss birthday parties and BBQs. I miss my family. I miss traveling on a plane, airports, and trains. I miss knowing I could travel to another country if I was brave enough. I miss movie theaters, plays and live music. I miss Desmond's community band practice and Desmond's trumpet instructor coming to the house. I miss people's faces, smiles and noses. I miss eating in the bakery, at Adams, at friend's houses. I miss big play dates and hugs. I miss the lighthouse trail, the water fountain in town, first Fridays.

The anxiety that follows me gently through the day is tiresome. It's like a rabbit that stays by my feet. Nothing happens but I am afraid I will step on it, or it will bite me.

I went for a walk this morning in the woods. Forest bathing. I saw the man in the tank top on my way out. He was coming in. Today he was wearing a navy blue tank top and although he still did not smile, there was almost a smile in his voice when he said, "Good morning."

Last week I found what I think is a fossilized fish poop from the river. I had to keep myself from looking for more today. How much fossilized poop does a girl need?

I think the highlight of my day was eating tuna fish in my car in a parking lot for dinner. This speaks volumes about my day.

I placed a podcasting microphone in my cart on Amazon today.

I still cannot find rubbing alcohol anywhere. But when I stopped at CVS tonight, I asked the pharmacist. She said the truck was coming tomorrow and she'd hold some for me. Something to look forward to, I guess.

No meteors last night. It was cloudy again. Have you seen any?

Sometimes during the day, I think, what I need is to watch a movie tonight and start a knitting project. Doesn't that sound nice? And then night falls and I just feel like leaning on a wall.

Tomorrow's Friday. See you there.

Always and still here,

Sarah

August 14

Dear Friend,

Day 156.

Last night before I went to bed, I checked for shooting stars again. I braved the mosquitoes, stepped out onto my front stoop and looked up into the sky but the streetlight was too bright. I went upstairs and opened the door to our deck in our bedroom, sliding the screen door open and stepping outside into the dark. It was hard to see anything. But from there I could see more stars in the sky. I watched and waited. I could see bats flying in circles over the house, and then there was a bat flying in circles over the deck, circling closer to me with every round swooping lap. "BAH!!" I yelled and pushed the screen door aside and jumped back into my room, in a panic that I would not get the screen door closed in time and the bat would follow me in. I slid it shut. "Ew, ew, ew, ew, ew..." jumping around my room in the dark, trying not to wake Joseph. I stood by my bed with just enough light from the nightlight to see, looking around the room, afraid the bat did come in. I unplugged the nightlight. I plugged it back in and checked again. No bat. No shooting stars either.

It reminded me of being little in our big yard on Morris Avenue at night in the summertime. Watching bats fly in big arching circles high in the sky above our yard at dusk. How big the sky seemed, how mysterious those bats were to me.

A package came in the mail today with a pop-up beach tent for our trip to Cape Cod. We leave next week! For 6 days. So exciting. The end of August felt so far away and suddenly it's almost here.

The pop-up tent is pretty amazing. You can just drop a strap on it and throw it in the air and ta-da! A tent! With screened windows that you can button up for shade or leave open for air. Metal L shaped pins to secure it to the ground.

I also got matching straw sun hats for the boys with a snazzy blue and red ribbon band. Makes them look like an old fashioned acapella duo. They seem to love them now and I do hope they'll wear them at the beach. We shall see.

I went to my studio to paint for a little while. I ran out and bought new paint brushes yesterday. Tiny little brushes for tiny people and tiny beach umbrellas. So much easier today with fine points for fine lines.

I came home in time to walk to town with Joseph and the boys for dinner out. We went to the Dutch Ale House, a few blocks away. The boys wore their new hats. They have a big tent set up in their parking lot out back behind their building. Just because of the virus. They've done such a nice job creating an outdoor space. It was so sweet to go out to eat in town and to be someplace new. I felt uncomfortable talking to the waitress without my mask on. The servers all keep their masks on all the time. We wear them to and from the table. I felt like I shouldn't face her when I spoke and said so, laughing. She said, "It's fine, I'm used to it." I can't get used to any of it.

I've started ironing clothes and folding them to pack for our trip. I hope this week doesn't go too fast. I want our trip to come but I don't want it to end. May it arrive slowly and last a while.

I want to go back to the place I took the photo of the pink coconut cake and eat one. I want to find the kettle ponds and look at houses for sale. I want to go to another pirate museum. And buy a gold doubloon. Oooo, I can't wait.

Always and still here,

Sarah

August 15

Dear Friend,

Day 157.

I went for a walk this morning at Ulster Landing where I have been before but have never walked the longer trail. I thought a change of scenery would be nice. 9:30 on a Saturday morning and my car was only one of three in the parking lot.

It started off well enough, I did a small loop I have done before and then headed off on another trail. It was a lot of uphill walking on a dirt path. I walked and walked, listening to my audiobook, one earbud in and one tucked away so I could listen to the woods. I walked down a trail that sort of petered out, doubled back and went down another trail that ended. I found another way to go and walked a long way until I came to a gravel road. I made a right turn instead of a left so that I'd be walking back in the direction I'd come. I walked down a very steep hill, feeling more doubtful with every step. It took a sharp left down to the river. I didn't want to walk back up that steep hill but I was so curious where it was headed. It went to a spot called Turkey Point. There was a kiosk with faded posters hung inside, one about being cautious and watching for snakes. I did not want to know. I turned and trudged back up the hill. You know when you are on a bike and you can't peddle up a hill so you get off and walk it? I wanted to get off of myself and walk myself up the hill. It was so steep and long. Up I went, back to the trail entrance with it's blue circle trail marker nailed to a tree. Back the way I came. I walked so far.

I did find a little sand beach that looked like a perfect spot to bring a beach chair. With a wooden picnic table, its feet in the water. Close to the trail entrance.

On the way out, I checked the kiosk at the start of the trail. The map made no sense and lied through its teeth. That trail did not make a loop. It was like a trail warp in there. I walked 7,000 steps. Lost in the woods.

As I walked through those woods, it struck me as a disheveled sort of forest. I wondered if forests were like people. This is where Sonny got bit by that snapping turtle. If this place was a person, it'd be someone very complicated that I am deeply unsure of.

I had brunch when I got home and waited for a friend who was coming to visit. I sold my smallest beach painting to an old friend and he was coming by to pick it up and have lunch.

He came a little later than expected and skipped the lunch part. We bumped elbows and sat outside and had iced tea and talked while the boys splashed in the pool.

When he left, Desmond was starving and wondering what happened to the "getting pizza" part of the visit? So I ordered from Slices in town and took a walk to pick it up.

I thought, I'll have a salad and they'll have pizza. Always with good intentions. My tombstone will say, "She meant well."

I did not have salad. I had two slices of pizza and two chicken fingers. It was so good.

I've been eating so well. Not tonight, but the other days leading up to it. I feel much better when I do. The scale still doesn't really care though. I'm still doing that Metabolic Renewal diet and exercise program and I really like it. I look better, to me. When I pass a mirror, my heart doesn't sink anymore. I think, I look okay. I look more like myself. The way I used to look. Before I got old.

I fell asleep in the living room reading. I couldn't keep my eyes open. But my legs hurt from my walk and kept waking me up.

Tonight, I sat out on the deck while Joseph watched a movie with the boys. When it was time for bed, Sonny came out to the deck to look for bats. We waited until he saw one, flying fast and jittery around the darkening sky with pulled cotton clouds behind it, passing so slowly.

Desmond has developed a weird tick with his eyes. He makes his eyes get real wide. Often and for no reason. It's making me nervous. I wonder if it's the captivity. His computer brain is malfunctioning. Or the motherboard of this virtual reality we're in is glitching.

My neighbors next door got a Tesla car and it sounds like a hover car when it takes off down their driveway. I feel like I'm in the Woody Allen movie *Sleeper*.

The windows are open tonight for the first night in a long time. It's finally cool out, there is a breeze and the crickets are humming their summer tune.

Today I learned that seasons are not capitalized and the movie *Groundhog's Day* is actually *Groundhog Day* AND *Ghost Busters* is one word. *Ghostbusters*.

I also learned that your fingers and toes turn to raisins in water to give your hands and feet better gripping abilities in water. They create channels for the water to move through. That seems like a stretch but if the internet says so.... it could be true.

We bought stamps today, to save the USPS.

Tomorrow is Sunday. Which doesn't mean anything at all. I'll still be here.

Looking forward to it. You never know what will happen next.

Always and still here,

Sarah

August 16

Dear Friend,

Day 158.

It is dark outside and the windows are open. Joseph is out in his studio painting, the boys are asleep upstairs. There are two cricket sounds. One is like sunlight glittering on the water, the other is like a string of pearls that begins and ends, 20 pearls long each time. We've had the windows open all day. Such a treat.

This morning I sat outside, reading with my breakfast in my lap. My *Write it Down, Make it Happen* book says we should write down what we want to happen, but we can also write down all of our fears about why the things we want to happen won't, then we write down why those thoughts are false, cheering ourselves toward victory. Let's try it.

Desmond noticed the neighbors had a tent set up in their yard and wished we had one too. I told him we did have one, in the basement. So we pulled it out. Its box was moldy and the tent was dusty and smelled like mildew. I bought it when I moved upstate, 19 years ago. I have never used it. I loaned it to a friend once. It's in perfect condition, but I should have stored it in the attic where it's dry. We put it up anyway, I thought it would do it some good to get some air on it. I will look up how to clean it and see if I can spray it or scrub it or even just hose it down. It's exciting to have a tent. Of course the boys wanted to sleep in it. I told them we should wait until it's not so stinky, even though they did not mind.

It ended up getting rained on later in the day, so its cleaning began without me.

I had yellow grape tomatoes from the garden on my salad for lunch. Finally, our tomato plants are bearing fruit.

It took me so long to get to my studio today. I was so easily distracted, but I did get there eventually. I spent a couple of hours painting more tiny people on the beach. It's so joyful to look at. SO tiny!

Yesterday I grabbed an old copy of *Jaws* from a free cart outside the bookstore in town, on my way to pick up pizza. There were two of my mom's favorite books there too, both on my list of books to read, both I have on my bookshelf at home. *Moby Dick*, which was her favorite and *Lonesome Dove*. Today I looked to see if either were available as audiobooks on my library app and they are both there. I downloaded *Moby Dick* and started to listen to it a bit today. It made me nervous I might run away and board a ship that's setting out to sea.

Once, when I lived in Catskill, before I had children, I had a girlfriend visit from the city. She slept over. Joseph was away somewhere, I don't remember where. Her father had recently passed and we decided to try to make contact with her father and my mother. We made audio recordings, trying to catch an EVP. But heard nothing, besides what sounded a little like someone eating potato chips.

I had recently attempted to read my mother's copy of *Moby Dick* and had had it out on my night table. I could not follow along well unless I read it out loud, but I only read a few pages before I lost interest. Anyway, the next day, after she had gone home, I went up to my room and found the book on the floor. Far from the nightstand. I tried to debunk my hope that it was paranormal. I put it back on the nightstand and tried bumping into it in every which way that may have made it fall that distance, but could not recreate the landing. I called my friend to tell her I thought maybe we had ghost activity. I told her what happened and that it was my mom's favorite book. She said, "That was my dad's favorite book...."

I like to imagine her father and my mother working together to throw that book off my nightstand.

I think my mom would really like me to read it. Have you read it?

My list of things to read and paint, make and do, is so long. It feels longer at night. Everything is more nerve wracking at night when I'm tired. In the morning, nothing seems so bad. Just sitting here thinking about all the things is making me nervous. All...the...things...We have a million hats. My cello is leaning in the corner and I never play it. It's all very upsetting.

I thought tomorrow would be Tuesday, but alas, Monday still comes after Sunday. So Monday it is. I think I'll take the boys out somewhere in the morning. It's supposed to rain in the afternoon. What will you do tomorrow?

Always and still here,

Sarah

August 17

Dear Friend,

Day 159.

I'm outside hiding with the crickets. So tired. I have spent the day serving my children and I quit before quitting time. I'm letting them fend for themselves. I've done all I can do. Luckily we have a television, and Joseph will be home in time to put them to bed in a little while.

I got them out of the house early to go to Mother Earth. We used to like to go in the morning sometimes, to pick up food and get breakfast and sit and eat in their little cafe. I miss that. Today we got breakfast and just ate it in the car. I forget how insane it feels to take them to a store, I don't do it very often. I felt winded by the time I got Sonny buckled in his seat and closed his car door, both kids inside. I just realized I forgot to clean our hands with wipes when we got in the car like we always do now. Ah, well.

We drove across the river to Poet's Walk, a trail we've never been to before. They were all, "Thank you Mommy for taking us here to this new place!" But it was only a matter of time, not very much time at all before it turned into, "Why did you bring us here?? This was a terrible idea!" Desmond hurt his foot running and was limping and could not go on, Sonny wanted to walk all the way to the river, we were at a stand still for a bit. We turned to head back and suddenly and without surprise, Sonny was too tired and too hot. I kept giving him water to drink. He couldn't wear his T-shirt anymore. I poured water into my hand and patted his back with water to cool him down. When the car was in sight, I insisted all complaining cease. "You can SEE the car now. There is no reason to complain!"

I rummaged around in the attic looking for old coin collecting books my mother had given me. They were her brother's, or mother's or sister's or hers, no one knows for sure now. But I think she told me they were her brother David's. He may have gotten them first and then the family all participated in filling them the best they could. Desmond fell into a streak of penny collecting videos on YouTube, he learned all the very rare and valuable pennies to look for, so I thought I'd pull out those old books. There is a penny from 1910 and 1911. So great.

Then I realized it was my Uncle Dave's birthday today. Hugs and kisses to Uncle Dave, who has passed over. Thank you for the coins...

I cleaned the tent and put the rain fly sheet on top in case it rains. I jumped on the trampoline with Sonny.

I made dentist appointments at a new dentist's office for cleanings for the kids. While I was on the phone with the receptionist asking if they had anything sooner than November, Sonny was yelling at me about Desmond's old underwear in the garbage pail. Underwear I had taken down from the attic, with its elastic waist bands so cooked, they just cracked when you pulled on them, stretching out with a hiss, never to return to their original shape.

I cooked dinner, did laundry and washed dishes. I handed them boo-boo packs and wiped tears. Gave Sonny a bath, washed his hair.

When Sonny was in the bath, he asked for the baster. I gave them one once in the bath to play with so they could suck up water and fill cups and things. When I came back to wash his hair, he said, "Get ready, MOM!" And I followed his gaze to the bathtub faucet where he had it covered with the black rubber bulb of the baster. The hot water was running. As I reached for it in a panic, it shot off, spraying water around the room and in my face. It was only slightly warm, but I was terrified scalding water was going to spray us both.

Sometimes I feel like a nanny.

I still thought it was Tuesday all day. I feel like maybe we missed a day. Are you sure it's Tuesday tomorrow?

Sonny just came out to look for bats with me....

Always and still here,

Sarah

August 19

Dear Friend,

Day 161.

Today was much better than yesterday. Yesterday was much like the day before. I could not figure out if it was better to take the kids out of the house or keep them at home. Either way, they seemed to complain and argue on a loop that we could not find our way out of.

The solution, which I am surprised I had not thought of sooner, was taking them to someone else's house to play with other children. What relief.

This afternoon we went to a new friend's house with another good friend and her boys. Five boys all together, jumping on a trampoline, playing Minecraft, building with Legos, and then pizza and roasting marshmallows. I got to sit and talk with grown-ups and I hardly saw my children at all. I felt like I was talking a mile a minute, it had been too long.

What a beautiful home too and cool people. I miss people. New people and new places. It's extra exciting these days. Newness.

Yesterday I over computered. But I did complete my 22.5 hours of continuing education for my realtor's license, so we still have that in our pocket. Online courses, Facebook, Instagram, Pinterest, Amazon, Gmail, it was too much, even though I stumbled on a hilarious video of bats hanging upside down, turned right side up in black and white, with Goth club music. It was bad. I was outrageously bored. Nowhere to go and nothing to do.

We did go to Falling Waters yesterday morning to leave the rocks we painted. It was like setting up an Easter egg hunt along the trail. But the beaches where we look for crystals were covered in the invasive water chestnut weeds that grow in the river. They had spread close to shore and the hurricane we had with all the rain, brought the tide in so far, it deposited the weeds on the shore and now they are stuck there. They carpet the rocks and you can't move them or see beneath them. I did not hear the end of complaining about this travesty as we walked. I don't suppose we'll see crystals there again for a long while.

We walked past a shed and there was a terrible stench like a dead animal or fish. I told them it was probably a dead body locked in the shed. This quieted them for a few seconds.

Last night we did some tiny colorful rubber band weaving. Sonny impressed me by being able to do it on his own. I made a chain for my mask, so I can keep it attached to my neck like little kids have clips on their mittens and a ribbon that runs through their coat sleeves. I'll never lose my mask again.

It's not very comfortable though. It feels like another thing on my head that shouldn't be there. One more thing to get used to.

Yesterday I found a half full bag of organic jumbo flame raisins in the cabinet that I eat every day with my 100% dark chocolate. I thought we were all out. It was so joyful. I could hardly believe it. A small bright spot.

And when I went to bed, I found an email from a friend who I have known for a few years. She just realized she knew my mother. She had worked with her on her books in the 80's at Harper and Row. I think I must have met her then too, when I was a teenager. It's so rare to meet anyone that knew my mother. I've moved away from where we lived and no one in my life here knew her, not even Joseph. Sometimes I feel like I made her up, or it was truly another life. I love finding this connection to the past that links with my present, like a neat sailor's knot, so satisfying.

Tonight, I was reading to Sonny before bed and I handed him a tissue and said, "Please don't pick your nose." Which I say to him every night when I read him a book because it is a perfect time for nose picking apparently. "Sorry," he says and holds the tissue. A minute later he was wiping something on the arm of the chair. I said, "Please don't wipe your boogers on the furniture." "I'm not!" he said, "I'm wiping the mud from under my fingernails on the chair!"

Desmond was afraid to go to bed. He whispered in my ear a story he read today about a cartoon monster that is covered in ears and makes a high-pitched scream. Anyone who hears it starts to grow ears all over their body until they can't breathe. He was worried this would happen to him, in his room. I told him I was positive that would never happen. To anyone. But that is super creepy.

Sweet dreams.

Always and still here,

Sarah

August 21

Dear Friend,

Day 163.

You were so kind not to correct me when I told you it had been 6 months since quarantine began, when it had only been 5. I suspect I could have told you it was 10 months and you would not have bat an eye. Maybe you hadn't noticed my blunder. Either way, I stand corrected. But don't worry, 6 months will be knocking on our door in no time flat.

Tomorrow we head to the Cape and we are all in a flurry. I've been packing for two days straight. I thought I could start packing on Monday but that seemed like jumping the gun a bit. I did iron some things and made a few piles. I should have kept going. Packing for me and the boys, for a week, with food and beach equipment is quite a task. Thank goodness Desmond is able to pack his own clothes with little overseeing. Both kids try to bring random items that make no sense. Like 4 dominoes, very small basketballs, spy goggles, and fish food. I try to pay it no mind. Every man finds his comfort in different treasures. As long as it fits in the car and there's room for rocks and shells we'll collect from the beach, mementos from gift shops and frozen clam chowder from Chatham's fish pier.

I am pretty sure I've over packed myself. I am fully prepared. I will have lots of costume changes, an outfit for every event. Beach wear, dinner wear, walking wear, casual wear, shopping wear, and layers for cool evenings and mornings. My OCD really kicked in when I packed our toiletries. It involved tiny containers and a label making machine. I was careful not to make humorous labels, as not to confuse Joseph. "KID SHAMPOO" instead of "KID POO".

Anyway, I think we're all packed and should be able to head out in the morning before too long. I was even able to get to my studio for a couple of hours today to paint.

Sonny did not want me to go to my studio today, because he loves me so much. I told him it's something I really love to do and makes me happy, so it's nice for me to be able to go for a little while to sit quietly and paint. He suggested maybe Daddy could go and paint for me.

I feel as though I've been on a hamster wheel for the last two days but am glad I was able to get off before the day was done. Now I can rest and begin again tomorrow as we set off towards the sea once more!

The first time I went to the Cape I felt as if I was returning home, and it was hard to leave. Now I find myself perpetually waiting to return again. It will feel so good to be waiting in motion, instead of waiting in stillness.

I wish you could come. I will report back with our adventures and findings and bring you a golden doubloon.

Always and still here,

Sarah

August 22

Dear Friend,

Day 164.

I'm sitting on a couch in Harwich Massachusetts. Did you know that the

Massachusetts were a Native American tribe? I never thought about it before but it seems obvious once you do. I like being here and thinking of the history of this place. Thinking of the pilgrims and natives. I like the rocking chair in the corner that looks like it's from the 40's.

We meant to leave at 9:00 this morning but rolled out of the driveway at 10:15. A little traffic at the bridge to the Cape, which I was very excited to sit in and look forward to becoming better acquainted with. People sure do like to talk about the summer traffic. Like people in LA love to talk about the traffic on the freeway.

We got to the house at 2:50, 10 minutes before check-in time. There was a woman inside still cleaning and she said she'd be another hour before she was done. So we drove to town to find coffee for Joseph. I got a $10, 12 oz smoothie, and Sonny got a $7, 20 oz watermelon juice that he drank ⅓ of. The black paper straws were the diameter of a dime.

We stopped in the general store and I bought myself and the boys each one golden doubloon. I forgot to get one for you, but I can go back tomorrow.

Our friends that we are sharing the house with got stuck in traffic and arrived at 5:00. I ran outside and played Barry Manilow's "Looks Like We Made It" on my phone for my friend, my best friend from college, my Shelly, as I flung open her car door with great dramatic flourish.

By the time we all made it out of the house, it was high dinner time, we were all starving and every place was packed with a long wait to sit. We ended up at George's Pizza and ordered two pies to go. The woman took our order, handed us our receipt and said, "Just so you know, your pizza will be ready in 45 minutes. Go walk around."

We chewed on our knuckles for a bit and then walked into an art gallery next door. The Nines. The gallery is owned and run by a woman artist I've been following on Instagram, she paints mostly glass bottles and water. It was lovely to talk with her. I told her I'd like to move to Cape Cod and paint here too. She said she did not know many other artists and was so glad we stopped in.

It was odd to introduce myself to someone I had wanted to meet, with a mask on. I wanted to take it off just for a second to say, this is my whole face, here, it's a much better face without the mask on.

We shoved piping hot pizza in our mouths in the car on the way back to the house. It was not the seafood we longed for, but it was pretty good.

Everyone is settled into bed now. When I put the kids to bed, I pulled out a calming essential oil. I put a drop on each of their palms, had them rub their hands together and then cup their hands over their mouth and nose and take a deep breath in. Long day. Sonny was in and out of the bed like a jumping bean.

Tomorrow we'll find the beach, seafood and ice cream. Adventure still awaits.

Always and still here,

Sarah

August 23

Dear Friend.

Happy day 165.

Tonight, I rock in the old rocking chair in the corner. Everyone's gone to sleep. It was a long beautiful day in the sun and water.

I started my day in the outdoor shower. I wouldn't mind if all my days started this way, at least when the weather is mild enough. To take a hot shower with the sun on your face and the clouds overhead is bliss. To close your eyes and open them to pinecones in the trees, watch the mist and steam from the shower float away. I reached my arms, hands and fingers straight up towards the sky. I felt like I could just shoot into the atmosphere. I thought, I am a creature of the Earth, isn't this somethin'.

We got our week beach pass stickers for our cars at the Chamber of Commerce of Harwich, $68 cash or check. And spent the afternoon at a little beach, full of people. I tried to see if I could tell who was a local and who was a tourist but it was hard to say. Only a few really stood out as tourists, with their tattoos and accents.

The beach was on the Nantucket Sound so the waves at the shore were very gentle. Perfect for me and Sonny to find our way slowly into the water which was not cold at all. We walked in holding hands and pointed at the seaweeds, picking each one up to look at them and see how they felt.

The sun lit the water here and there, like fistfuls of sequins thrown onto its surface, where they floated, bobbing and lighting, flashing on and off. Yards and yards of the prettiest deep blue silk, fleeting and free.

Golden horseshoe crabs washed ashore, lay in the sand.

Desmond and Milo slipping under the water and reappearing again and again like seals.

I stood next to Joseph in the water and he pointed to two people not far away. "Isn't that Jenny and her husband from around the corner?" Yes, it was. So I called out and waved to our neighbors from Saugerties, who stood nearby, in the water, in Harwich. We moved towards each other through the water and talked for a little while. They mentioned their daughter wanting to see seals. I told them about the Chatham Pier Fish Market.

Joseph and Jeffery swam out to the buoy, where they said it got very quiet. We joked that just beyond the buoy you can hear the theme to *Jaws*.

We left after everyone save Jeff and I, seemed to get stung by something in the water. Jelly fish or a plant? We couldn't say. But those who were stung were left with a few painful and itchy red splotches on their skin.

Outdoor showers at the house and off we went to the fish pier, where we saw our neighbors again, who were on their way out after a happy visit with the seals. We all ordered fried fish dinners at the window. Fried fish sandwiches, fried clams, fried calamari, fried shrimp and fish and chips. All with fries and coleslaw. It is really one of my favorite meals, their fish sandwich. It could not be improved upon if they tried.

We stood on the observation deck and watched the seals that like to hang around the pier waiting for the fishing boats to come in. They are big and black with whiskers and long faces. They float effortlessly like anti-gravity creatures in a dark sky. They float on their backs with their bellies in the sun and then bend their heads back gracefully and disappear into the dark water without a sound.

There are fishing boats anchored in the water. It's not enough to say they are beautiful. And I am not exactly sure what it is about them that is so striking to me. They delight me completely. They excite me, they make me want to pump my fists in the air. I took so many pictures. I am going to paint them. Boat portraits. I cannot wait.

I am wildly in love with this place, those seals, those boats, the light, the sky, the gulls. I could stand on that pier for hours and watch the light move, the seals swim, the boats float. I am so enamored with it all. Slapping my hand on the rail of the deck, gesturing at the water. "I can't get over this place," I say. "Can we get ice cream now?" they ask.

We scoped out a beach for tomorrow and then headed to Sundae School ice cream shop. I haven't had sugar in a while but had a cup of ice cream. It was worth it. Cookies and cream and mocha brownie. Amen.

Always and still here,

Sarah

August 24

Dear Friend,

Day 166.

There is some fuss and bustle when you travel in a group to a beautiful place with lots to do. What to do first, most, later, today or tomorrow. Who is in the mood. The morning was this way with thoughts being thrown around, ideas slipping between the bread of a peanut butter and jelly sandwich, notions shaking out in a container of crackers. Which beach should we go to? Applying sunscreen to faces and limbs, passing out breakfast between stacking lunches.

Nauset beach was the popular choice, the ocean, big waves, lots of soft sand, last summer's spot. Then Milo got itchy and wanted to go shopping instead. So we parted ways for the afternoon. We were beach bound, and our friends were off to explore.

I have a second cousin who lives on the Cape. She is married and has a son Oscar, just Sonny's age. She invited us to meet them at Nauset beach parking lot and jump into their pick-up truck to off-road to a stretch of Nauset only accessible by car, and only by cars with a season pass sticker. We would not have all fit so I had declined, but when our friends decided to skip the beach, I messaged my cousin to see if she would meet us today and much to our delight, she said yes. So off we went.

It was a real adventure and just what I was longing for. To see a part of the Cape hidden from the tourist's ice cream and lobster roll eyes. I want to see the Cape after she comes home and lets down her hair, staring off towards the water. I want to know what records she plays and where she finds wild berries. I want to know what time she wakes up and when she goes to bed.

When you drive off-road through the sand, you have to let air out of your tires so you don't get stuck.

My cousin, my boys and her little boy all piled into the back of their truck, Joseph and Corey, her husband up front. We bounced along the winding sand path through the marsh and dunes. In the marsh there are blue boxes that look like mailboxes but are plain and square. They are fly boxes, the blue color attracts the biting green flies and traps them there. The short evergreen shrubs growing on the dunes all lean away from the ocean wind that has trained them to grow this way. Even when there is no wind, they look caught in a great gale of sea air.

The ocean was a striking blue, the sand pale and soft. At every "cut", every entrance to the beach, there is a shark box full of medical supplies to treat deep flesh wounds. Two years ago was the first fatal shark attack on Cape Cod in 82 years.

A white pick-up truck with a purple shark flag drives up and down the beach, warning beach goers when there is a shark sighting. A spotter plane flies overhead, looking for sharks.

"Does the pilot just see the sharks with their eyes from up there?" I asked Corey.

"Yeah, they see their shadows in the water. They are 10' to 18' long so they're easy to spot."

No kidding.

There was a shark predation the next beach over. A shark was spotted eating a seal....

The seals swam so close to the shore. If we had been swimming, we could have swum nose to nose. But we all stood on shore, looking out at the water, watching the spotter plane, eyes on the water. We did not see any sharks, but lots of seals.

The water was cold, the waves were not big but powerful, like fat fists, the water clear, carrying bits of seaweed rolling in the surf. The waves would land on shore and you could see how easily they could just snatch your feet out from under you and pull you in.

A fog rolled in along the horizon, a cool wind blew with pockets of warm air mixed in.

Desmond was sad he could not swim as much as he wanted to. Sonny and Oscar played and played. Two peas in a pod.

We stayed until it was pushing the limits of dinner time landing on the kids plates before they became ticking time bombs. We climbed back into the truck and bounced our way back through the dunes. That ride was as brilliant as the beach itself.

I texted our friends who were still shopping in Chatham and they picked up seafood to bring to the house. We promised our cousins we'd meet for lobster rolls for lunch tomorrow by the water in Dennis and headed back to wash the salt and sand from our legs and necks and inside our ears.

The outdoor shower is one of my favorite events of the day. Twice on beach days. I wondered if I shouldn't be taking nighttime showers too.

Now I want a pick-up truck. I will write it on my wish list.

Always and still here,

Sarah

August 26

Dear Friend,

Day 168.

Everyone's gone to bed just now and I am rocking in the old rocking chair. It was a long beautiful day. I stayed up late last night planning the day and it all worked out almost as planned, and exactly as it should be.

Yesterday we did the rail trail, which we love, in the morning and moved our cousin lunch date to another day. We came back to the house and Sonny very agreeably had a nap. Joseph and I got to drive around Harwich to drive by houses that were recently for sale, to get a feel for the area and an idea of prices and sizes. It was the first time we'd been alone anywhere together in a very long time. I guess I should formally tell you we are planning on moving here when we are able. We had been planning before COVID came along, but that really put the breaks on any forward motion. Luckily though, the timing seems to be working in our favor. If we had moved before, it is likely Joseph would have been furloughed, as the Cape Cod hospitals, as well as many other hospitals across the country, furloughed a lot of their nurses. This way, things will have settled down some hopefully, by the time he finds the perfect job at the hospital here. And our property values have gone up, with so many people moving up to the Hudson Valley from the city. Especially in our county. I think things will line up nicely in due time and in perfect order. Like the rain that came and went with our beach days on Long Island. When it is time, the rain will stop. Rainbows are back stage nervously bouncing up and down, waiting to sashay into view. I just know it.

We all went together to Hyannis yesterday afternoon to walk around and had dinner at Spanky's Clam Shack on the harbor.

Today we got out of the house relatively early and drove up to Wellfleet to hike the Atlantic White Cedar Swamp Trail and see The Marconi Wireless Station Site which is the site of the first transatlantic wireless communication between the United States and Europe, in 1903. Pretty cool. They are side by side and right at the ocean's edge.

The trail was so beautiful and so different from the trails where we live. Lots of scraggly pines, and trails covered in pine needles and white cedar trees. A windy path with trees growing right in the path, up out of the sand, that you have to walk around. Wavy ground beyond the path covered in moss. So, so lovely.

There was a lot of whining and sighing going on, hand gestures and nonsense, but I saw through it all into the woods. Zen calisthenics. Deep breaths and forest bathing. Every last thing is thrilling to me and the thought of living near all of these wonders just about lifts me a foot off the ground.

From there we attempted to go to the Great Pond of Wellfleet but it was for residents only, which if you ask me, should really be relayed on the pond's website. But a quick Google search sent us to Mayo Beach which is free and requires no permit.

The tide was out and there were fishing traps set across the beach. Small anchored boats lay resting on the sand, waiting for the water to return. The beach changed from a light colored soft dry sand with white shells to a wet brown mud-like sand that was cool and smooth as clay on our bare feet and nearly covered with tiny black snails. We walked to the water's edge. Sonny shrieked and clung to us, afraid of all of the tiny snails, really as tiny as a pea, until he put on his shoes. Michele reached into the sand and pulled out a clam! So Desmond did too and so did Sonny. They filled a bucket and then put them all back in the water since none of us were going home and none of us have a shell fishing license. I wish I had pulled one out of the sand myself but I was too busy watching them and taking pictures.

Then we went our separate ways and we headed to Provincetown and our friends went off kayaking.

Provincetown is a real touristy, fun summer town. A busy Main St. with lots of shops, lots of people. Everyone wearing masks. Signs everywhere saying masks are mandatory. We went to the Whydah Pirate Museum. Do you know this story? This guy Barry, when he was a kid, his dad told him there was a pirate ship sunk out in the ocean that no one could find, right in Wellfleet. He decided he would find it. So he grew up and became a diver and he did find it. The only pirate treasure EVER found! Plenty of pirate ships have been found, and he has found more of them than anyone else, but this is the only one with treasure. They've uncovered about 20% of the treasure since they found the ship in the 80's. We spoke with a woman in the museum who is part of the diving team. She said they've only been twice this year because of COVID. And they found more coins. Rumor has it there is a ruby the size of a hen's egg down there. I don't know why they don't just say an egg, I guess it sounds better than a chicken's egg, specifically. Makes me feel like it's bigger than an egg, a HEN's egg. Maybe a very big hen.

Desmond asked how old you have to be to dive with them. She said 12 ½. His eyes almost fell out of his head.

We walked around the shops and went back to where the restaurant was that I took the photo for the pink coconut cake I painted, but it was a different restaurant now and although the case was still the same, the cakes were not. I was hoping I could buy a pink cake and try it. But it was not to be.

I got some amazing homemade ice cream before we jumped in the car though.

From there we went to Duck's Harbor Beach in Wellfleet, on the bay side to watch the sunset. There were people arriving as we were, carrying chairs and blankets, to watch the sun go down. It was really perfect timing. People left their sandals at the entrance to the path over the dunes, like we leave our shoes at the door in our house, so we did too. We sat on towels, the boys ran in circles around us, dug in the sand, jumped up and down. It was so beautiful. When the sun was down, I pointed at the sky and told Sonny the sun had gone down. He looked up and asked if it had gone into the water. No, not really. I tried to explain where it was. He takes it all in stride.

And then we piled back into the car, put on our ghost story podcast and headed back to the house.

We were able to add an extra day to our stay. We are the luckiest.

I've decided I'll become really good at giving tours of the Cape by the time you come visit us. I'll know all the really amazing spots and show you the best time. I can't wait.

Always and still here,

Sarah

August 29

Dear Friend,

Day 171.

I just wrote you a long letter and then it disappeared. Now I am left with crumbs floating about. Let's see if I can sweep some back together...

I think the best parts were telling you about our last day at the beach on the Cape yesterday. Most important, my cousin and her husband and son met us at Red River Beach in Harwich for the afternoon and her mom stopped by too. Her mom is lovely and funny. She came with a chair and a swimming noodle and a walking stick. She swam out in the bay on her own with her noodle and motioned for her daughter to bring her her walking stick when she was done. Her stick was tall and light wood with a groove carved in it that wound around and around.

I wrote about how finding family in Cape Cod feels so lucky. I like them so much, and they seem to like us too. It's like instant soup, all the ingredients are already in place. Could be luck, could be genetics. We seem to fit together easily.

I wrote about our adventures the last two days there. The sand flats of Brewster were something to see, stretching a mile to the bay at low tide. We had rain, we had seafood, I bought books at the general store, a mystery, a book about pirates and a book called *Cape Odd*.

I wrote about staying up late with my friend Michele on the last night so we could talk. So much hustle on our vacation, we hadn't been able to sit and connect. How nice that was to make time. How grateful I am to have a friend I've known for so long.

I ate a too big piece of cake on the way home and passed out.

I cleaned out my car today before I went to my studio and found a container of cole-slaw in my glove compartment that Desmond left. Its lid had ballooned up with gases. I'm lucky it had not burst. I handled it like a ticking bomb.

Joseph bought two bottles of rubbing alcohol this morning at Stewart's. He was going to save them as a gift for our wedding anniversary which is in a few days, but he didn't want me to have to wait. I've been looking for rubbing alcohol for over a month. COVID victories.

The lost letter was much better, and longer. But it is late now and my laptop is working in slow motion again.

Tomorrow's letter will be better. Maybe. We'll see what tomorrow brings. Probably not a beach or seafood dinner.

It is strange to be home. I am a bit blue, summer's winding down. But fall is not so bad. Before I get there, I'm just gonna do Sunday tomorrow. See you there.

Always and still here,

Sarah

August 30

Dear Friend,

Day 172.

What can I tell you now that I'm home, after being in a magical land for a week? We are back to the old routine. Everything is as it was, once again. Groundhog Day has crept back in.

I didn't have my pedometer in Cape Cod and found it this morning after closing my eyes and searching for it with my witch powers. I thought I had likely lost it for good whilst out and about but found it on the table beside my closet after I saw what I thought was my closet shelves but may have been the white wainscoting beside the table.

Did I tell you I had another success giving a friend clues when his girlfriend lost her wallet? It was in her car. I hope someday I can say, "It's in her car." Instead I told him random things I saw that turned out to be very like the things her wallet was lying beside, under the car driver's seat. I was still impressed, but I hope to really fine tune this parlor trick.

I realized today that I left some things in a drawer in the Airbnb on Cape Cod. I am hoping the host can mail them back to me. Or my cousin said she could grab them for me. I am waiting to hear back. I suppose that's like leaving your sweater in the house of the boy you like so that he'll have to see you again.

I picked flowers from the yard for the table today. And a whole bowl of cherry tomatoes from our garden.

I went for a walk this morning in my usual spot, saw the guy in the white tank top, we exchanged pleasantries. Today I asked how he was, he said "Very well." Still no smile.

The beaches are still covered with the water chestnut weeds. It's like a curtain has closed on the crystal hunt for good. Like all the other theaters, closed until further notice.

I've been listening to Shirley Jackson's short stories. Man, are those sad. Each one a study in the meanness of humanity. It's like we're living in a Shirley Jackson story these days.

Did you hear about the four year old who floated out to sea on her unicorn float in Greece last week? A strong current swept her away from the beach where she was with her family. She floated a half a mile when a ferry spotted her and picked her up. I watched a video of four men at the back of the ferry, reaching for her float. She was quiet. And the ferry passengers were quiet too. They pulled the float on board and one burly man lifted her, her back against his hip, his big arm wrapped under her arms, like a sack of potatoes, she hung there in her bikini and water wings, silent. A smattering of applause. Talk about a Shirley Jackson story. Super bizarre.

I vacuumed my studio.

I saw some friends in a zoom meeting, that was nice.

Desmond spent the day making a stop motion animation video I was excited to see it, until I watched it. A very well crafted video of a Lego crook breaking into a bank, shooting a guard who bled on the floor and then climbing out the way he came and shooting someone else in a chair. I didn't watch the rest.

I don't know how that even happens. In a home where guns and violence are not celebrated or even allowed. The violent gun culture in this country is so prevalent, it doesn't even matter. It's still what he thinks is cool.

He said he made it because he wants to be a famous YouTuber. Makes me want to give up. Sort of.

That was depressing.

We had an interesting talk about it, but I don't feel much better.

I am the crazy mother who hates guns, buys organic food and won't let them drink soda every day. Things could be worse.

I saw some very pink clouds tonight. Very, very pink. And almost shaped like an elephant's head and a lizard. Floating by, so slowly, right to left. I felt like they were going the wrong way. It made me a little dizzy.

Oh well. We made it through the day. I had to eat some ginger snaps right at the end.

I'm going to crawl into bed and read. I'm worried about tomorrow. Not sure why.

Always and still here,

Sarah

August 31

Dear Friend,

Day 173.

I'm in my backyard, back under my umbrella with the crickets, birds and squirrels. It's a bit cooler now than the last time I sat out here, but it's still beautiful. Still in short sleeves and short pants, which I like to call shorts. Somewhere someone's mowing a lawn, a screen door banged shut, a short and polite car horn honked.

I have to go to UPS when Sonny's up from his nap. I have a mountain of boxes to return to Amazon. Things I ordered were so backed up arriving, they all came at once like Christmas. And the things I am returning are all going to different warehouses and need separate boxes. I'm a little embarrassed to go to UPS with so many boxes. If I make Desmond and Sonny carry a few each, and we act like we don't know each other, no one will suspect I have a problem. In my defense, they sent me a rubber dinosaur head two times, when I ordered a rubber alligator head. I won't be ordering one again, I tell you what.

Sonny's birthday is coming. I think I have bought him enough nonsense to make him happy on the day. He would like me to make a blue mosasaur cake. A mosasaur is a dinosaur that looks like a scary whale. Wish me luck.

I'll have to bribe the boys to come with me to UPS to do my bidding, with a treat from the health food store, which is in the same shopping center. I'll buy them liver tonic. Just kidding, they'll probably pick out a muffin. And I will likely cheat and buy dinner there or at Adams instead of cooking.

When Sonny went down for his nap he asked if when he got up, we could go to the Museum of Natural History. I told him that was quite a ways away and would take more planning. "Then how about the Bronx Zoo?" he asked. "Just as far," I told him. We'll have to plan a day.

I was thinking of taking him to Kelder's Farm for his birthday, but I am not sure if jumping on a bounce house is fun with a mask on. Or maybe the Teddy Bear museum that has a cafe, for brunch.

A blue mosasaur cake....

Our wedding anniversary is tomorrow. 13 years. Joseph is working so we will celebrate on Saturday since we married the Saturday of Labor Day weekend all those years ago. I will bake a small version of our wedding cake and I think we'll go to the spot where we got married with the boys, across the river at the Clermont Historic Site. My mother-in-law sent us a DVD recording of the day that her father took. The friend that I had taking video that day, lost all the tapes. I've never seen a video of our wedding, just still photos. I'd been asking about his video for years and it was finally found. We'll watch it on Saturday while we eat our cake. I hope it's really true and there's something to see.

Can I tell you what kind of cake we had at our wedding? It was banana-lime cake with lime and ginger curd and marshmallow frosting (so it wouldn't melt), and shredded coconut on top. I was a real weirdo about picking out my own recipes and having a bakery make it. But now I have the recipe and can make it every year. All's well that ends well.

Sonny's up. We'll be heading out sooner or later.

I'm going to try to relax some today. We'll see how that goes.

Always and still here,

Sarah

September 2020

September 1

Dear Friend,

Day 174.

Today is my 13th wedding anniversary. Joseph was supposed to be working but was on call last night and was called in at 2:15. He came home at 6:00, so he didn't go in today. He slept a bunch trying to catch up to being awake again.

While he slept, I figured I'd make our wedding cake today instead of Saturday since he was home. I made the ginger-lime curd and then a simple whipped cream frosting, because it's easy and the best and there was no summer, outdoor heat to worry about. I made elderberry syrup in between, because we were all out. And then the cake.

Sonny was very excited I was making our wedding cake but he became confused by how small it was. He said, "You forgot to make my mosasaur cake!"

"It's not your birthday yet, Sonny!"

I ran out in the afternoon once Joseph was up, to pick up a few things. I finally found a comforter for our bed that is 100% cotton and bought it. The traditional 13 year wedding anniversary gift is lace, but the modern gift is fur or textile. I figured this falls under the textile category. Perfect timing.

We went out for dinner in town, on the patio of the tavern at Diamond Mills. We all dressed up. I put on the silk flower and feather headband I wore on my wedding day. I thought it looked nice until we took pictures and I realized I looked like an eccentric old lady. I put it on Desmond who looked like a gorgeous exotic bird boy.

We came home and had cake, which was delicious. The boys made Lego wedding figures to put on top. Well, Desmond made wedding figures and Sonny put Santa Claus with a walkie talkie with them for good measure. Desmond said Santa was the officiant.

Then we watched a DVD of Joseph's Grandpa's video he took at our wedding. We have not seen any video of our wedding before. It was wild to see it. I looked beautiful, young and skinny. Joseph looked so young.

I worked so hard on that wedding.

It was so strange to see. I thought for a second I saw someone wearing a mask in a crowd of people dancing. But my brain had just suggested it, of course there were none.

We all sat together on the couch to watch. Sonny climbed all around and Desmond held onto Joseph and I with tears in his eyes. "I never thought I'd be able to see your wedding!" he said.

"Neither did I," I said.

My father wrote a speech to read at my wedding. He didn't read it but he handed it to me after. There were so many speeches that went on so long. I don't know if he felt like there were too many speeches or if he didn't read it because he wasn't asked to say something. I wish he had read it.

I wish there was video of my father and I dancing.

It all made me feel a bit sad.

The news made me sad this morning too. The country is such a mess. I am really worried.

I am grateful for Joseph and our 13 years together. 17 years all in all. I am glad we still love each other after all this time. And for our boys, who make us a family. They love me so much, it fills me up and scares me. I wish we could all live forever. Worry has a way of leaking from one air tight compartment on my submarine to the next. It's like those magic vapor fingers in cartoons that can unscrew bolts and go where they want.

Worry smoke. Ghost fears.

Tomorrow's a new day. I'll be happy to be there.

Always and still here,

Sarah

September 2

Dear Friend,

Day 175.

Oooo, I ate too much dinner. The cake is nearly gone now. Tomorrow I should be safe and get back to healthy eating. It's dangerous to have a cake in the house, and delightful.

This morning we went to see an eye doctor for Desmond. He's been widening his eyes frequently and without much reason. He says sometimes his eyes bother him, sometimes they feel tight, sometimes they feel itchy, but sometimes it just happens. I wonder if it's a nervous tick he's developed from the strangeness in our lives. I was afraid it could be neurological. But the Dr. said his eyes look fine, she didn't see anything wrong. She said to try eye drops and that it may just be allergies.

He was pretty adorable with the technician and the Dr. It's fun to see him interact with other people in the world. We spend so much time on our own and with our small group of friends. It's nice to see him in action. He is polite and brave. He asks questions and answers questions thoughtfully. He makes jokes. He wore a jacket and tie, a straw fedora and a bandana as a mask. With blue Birkenstocks.

They dilated his eyes and he came out with disposable sunglasses that added a little extra something to his ensemble.

After Sonny's nap we went to a friend's house to play. They organized a ceramics class at the house which was nice.

There were two new moms there and three new kids. The teacher wore a mask. I practiced not worrying.

I liked seeing new moms. One laughed a lot and had energy like an electric current, tiny sparks flying from her hands. She reminded me of an old friend of mine. The other was older than me, which is rare in mom groups, since I had Sonny at 40. She had a small curl that lay flat on her cheek in front of one ear. A perfect open circle. I hoped she had the same curl on the other cheek, but she did not. I liked her nose and her gold earrings. She had a quizzical way of talking, with lots of space in her speech somehow. The other mom's speech was tight like a drum.

When it was time to go, the moms became like ushers and herded their children out the door. Then it was as if someone had snapped their fingers and made them disappear. I didn't see them go. I ushered my own out, nudging them toward the car.

We picked up pizza on the way home. This is really the last hurrah for bad eating. Until Sonny's birthday, I should be safe.

Carrying a hot pizza box is a real thrill though, isn't it? I drove by the pizza place one night at 9:30 and a couple was coming out of there with a pizza box and a full bag of food. I wondered what incredible sort of life they were living that they would pick up pizza at 9:30. I still think about it. They were young.

Tomorrow is Thursday. I think I'll try to get some painting in. And go for a walk. See how ol' tank top is doing. Or maybe I'll go someplace new. We'll see what the day brings. All good things I hope.

Always and still here,

Sarah

September 3

Dear Friend,

Day 176.

Hello you. Hello, hello, hello. I miss you.

Remember when life was simple? I miss those days. Maybe it was never really simple, but simpler. I miss simpler.

Let's keep it simple tonight. Me and you.

This morning I walked my usual walk in the woods. Shortly after I started walking, I saw the man in his white tank top, jean shorts, white tube socks and sneakers, and no mask uniform. I did not pull the other side of my mask over my left ear, I let it hang on my right ear where it was. "Good morning," I said, smiling.

"Good morning," he said and just before I passed him, I thought I saw a flicker of the beginning of a smile on his lips.

After maybe 12 steps or so, I turned around to make sure he was going on his way and not doubling back after me, as you do. And he was gone. It may have been possible that he had come to the top of the sloped trail and turned out of view, but it did not seem to me that I had waited that long to turn around. I think I should have seen him. I stood still and waited but did not see or hear anything.

I walked on, turning around every once in a while to check, listening for footsteps. Nothing.

I am here for the strange. I'm all about it. I wondered how likely it would be that he was a ghost this whole time. Every time I saw him on the trail and he returned my greeting of "Good morning," without a smile, could he have been an apparition?

I walked a while until I came to the inlet to a pebble beach at the rivers' edge. I walked along the beach a little ways, when I saw him walk by again, above me, on the trail. He walked above and I walked below. I could hear his footsteps on the path. I thought he must make this loop more than once to see him again on the trail, as he had been walking the other way when I saw him last. And then even though we were walking in the same direction, there was silence from the path above, as if he had disappeared again.

He could be a ninja. He could be a time traveler and there may be a portal in the woods. He could be a psychopath hiding in the trees. Or maybe he can fly and I forgot to look up. I heard that 90 something percent of people don't look up when they are looking for someone. So if you're running away, climb a tree. Maybe he climbs trees..

It's the perfect set up for murder, isn't it? I could turn your letters into a murder mystery if you'd like. If I go for a walk and don't come home, turn these letters into the police. I'm carrying mace next time and Lord help the man that comes after me, I have so much weight of the world angst and mother bear fury, I pity the fool.

Or I'll just walk somewhere else.

After Sonny's nap we went back to our friend's house where we had visited yesterday. Before we left I put together a healthy dinner to come home to.

Just their little boy there today. His mom and I sat and talked, about the virus mostly. So many questions. So much information and misinformation.

I'm feeling the heaviness of it all now. It's so intense. It's a lot to sort through and think about. It's hard to find the truth in the mess of it all. Harder still to accept how ugly the truth may actually be. It leaves me rattled and frightened.

Sometimes I think these battles are better left to stronger citizens than myself.

I have a better chance winning a fury fight with a strange old man in the woods.

I could just weep. But I don't.

I pretend a bucket of confetti has landed on my head, I stand up, and wipe the confetti from my body from the top of my head to my feet, clearing the energy. Tonight it feels more like sap though and will stick a while. Maybe a hot bath can melt the sap.

I have been placing drops of essential oils in my boys' hands at night to breathe, as a calming ritual. I need it too.

Calling in all healing light, sounds, scents, foods, touch. Gather up what's good and hold it in your lap. Breathe deeply. I feel my mother nearby. I found a pink feather today on my walk.

Always and still here,

Sarah

September 4

Dear Friend,

Day 177.

I woke up early today with Sonny. I used to wake up to him calling me on the monitor that's in his room. He has a clock that turns from a glowing blue face with stars to a yellow face with a sun every morning at 7:15. He waits until the sun is up on his clock to wake us up. He used to call over and over, "Mahh-mayy, sun up, Mahh-mayy, sun up, Mahh-mayy, sun up..." until we'd push the button on the monitor on our end and tell him we're coming. But I asked him recently to just come into my room and wake me. Now I wake from a deep sleep with him tapping me on the forehead. I open my eyes to his expectant face and he smiles. It's much better, but also strange.

I left the house early today to go to a friend's estate sounding yard sale. I drove a long way and it was such a beautiful day and a pretty drive past farms and houses, so much green, so lush. It was nice to see her, it had been a long time and I got to see my friend Bill briefly too. I got to hug them both and he gave me a pair of steampunk goggles he thought I needed, with interchangeable lenses, one pair a light green. And then he was off to an appointment. I did indeed need a pair of green steampunk goggles.

I felt funny wearing my mask after talking with my friend yesterday who presented me with literature about how ineffective they are. I often feel as though I've been blindfolded and spun around and let go. Blindly stumbling through these days, dizzy and apologetic.

I wandered around and found a small end table of a fabulous shape and a less fabulous finish that could use a coat of paint. I brought it home for $5. Except I didn't actually have $5, because the $40 that was in my wallet had disappeared. So I'll owe Bill $5 who she said she'd get the money from. It's still in my trunk. I don't know where I'll put it but for $5 and its 50's curves, it will find its way somewhere useful.

I got over to my studio this afternoon and finished my two beach paintings with their tiny people. Sometimes I get so absorbed in my painting, time flies by so quickly. I seem to check the clock only once an hour, surprised so much time has gone by each time I do.

Before I came home, I spoke with a friend on the phone while I walked the length of the parking lot outside my studio, pacing back and forth, in and out of the late day shadows and sunlight. Then I drove down the street to a park alongside the river and sat on a picnic table, watching the water and the sky turn pink and lavender while we talked some more. We talked about COVID, politics, our youth and this utterly baffling future we live in. What will happen? How did we get here? We agreed to hang tight and survive, whatever comes.

Last night was the first night with our new blanket on our bed. It felt so good. Little changes for the better are so sweet. I appreciate them so.

Always and still here,

Sarah

September 5

Dear Friend,

Day 178.

This morning I was thinking about Desmond and I learning to scuba dive, so we can dive with the team that hunts for the Whydah pirate ship's treasure off the coast of Cape Cod. It occurred to me I would probably be very useful with my psychic finding skills and could lead them right to the ruby that is the size of a hen's egg, and all the other buried treasure there too. I may sit and meditate on the shipwreck and see if I see anything from my couch. Then email them some clues.

I met up with a friend at my studio today. It's only the second time a friend has come to my studio to look at my paintings. It was so nice to see her, the last time I saw her was before the virus arrived. And a treat to show someone my work. I am always relieved when people like my paintings in person. I have such doubts.

Someone asked Joseph if they thought I might like to hang my paintings in a restaurant in town. I don't. They always come back with sauce on them. I want to hang them in a gallery. I don't know when that will be worth pursuing. I guess when you say you'd come to the opening.

I stayed for a while after she left and started a new painting. A commission that I hope to complete quickly but we'll see how it goes.

I came back home at dinner time and ate some old chicken, potatoes and golden beets from the back of the fridge. It all smelled okay, but it was not much fun to eat. I was worried it wouldn't end well, but so far so good.

Then I talked my guys into taking a ride to the park by the river where I sat last night to see the sky turn pink. The boys played on the playground and another couple showed up with a little boy Sonny's age and they all played together. Sonny was so happy. Joseph and I talked with the parents, they all wore masks, so we put ours on too.

It is funny to meet someone new when they are wearing a mask. So much less information than we are used to. A big void where 2/3 of their face should be. I spoke with the woman about home schooling and admired her eye makeup and her very back hair. They were from Bangladesh, moved to New York, then Nebraska and then back to New York. Next month they are moving to New Jersey, I think they said. They were just here for the weekend. We tried to give them ideas of things to do in the area. I could hardly think of anything to do at all.

As we were leaving, I turned to say goodbye again and caught a glimpse of the woman's face without her mask on, as her husband took her picture. She looked so different and whole. I think my brain was glad to have a glimpse of her completed face.

On our way home we drove by an old wooden lamp stand on the side of the road. I almost stopped when I passed it on my way to my studio today to look at it. I almost turned around to go check it out with everyone in the car, but I kept driving.

I had such a craving for ice cream, I dropped them all off at home and headed back out to buy some. But first I drove back to investigate the lamp on the side of the road. I guess it's a 1960's lamp stand, with dark brown turned wood and a circular table halfway up the base. It said, "Old Cape Cod house," to me. I took it home. I cleaned it off and sanded its little table shelf. It needs paint. I took the little coffee table out of my trunk and cleaned that too. I have nowhere to put either of them and they are sort of ugly, but I'll paint them anyway and see what happens. If they stay, something else has likely got to go.

I talked myself out of buying ice cream and decided to have a peanut butter and jelly sandwich and a small glass of milk instead. Which is also not on my diet, but it's not ice cream.

We forgot to go to the Clermont Historic Site where we got married as we planned to do today. Maybe tomorrow. The boys are asking to play mini golf in town, which sounds like a really nice idea too.

I think I have general COVID malaise. Do you too? Malaise and melancholy mixed with fatigue. Melanaisigue... Fatancholaise...

Blah.

Always and still here,

Sarah

September 6

Dear Friend,

Day 179.

I woke to Sonny's little face this morning, I swung my legs out of bed and we walked into the day together.

I made the boys strawberry pancakes for breakfast. I love when they want pancakes, I don't eat them but I love to make them. It's so satisfying. I know the recipe by heart, from the same recipe book my mom used to make me pancakes when I was little, except I add an extra egg. More protein. I loved apple pancakes best when I was a kid and still do. My kids only like berry pancakes. My favorite to eat now are apple with raisins and cinnamon. I'm sure I'm not the first to make them but it felt like a stroke of genius when I thought of it. The best. But I so rarely eat pancakes these days, only on special occasions, because of the getting old and not being able to eat carbs without gaining 15 lbs thing. The worst.

If there's a heaven, I will eat so much bread. And cheese. And cake. I will sleep in a bread bed, with a cake pillow.

We actually got out of the house at 11:00 and went to Puttin Plus to play mini golf. Joseph immediately started throwing down some serious mini golf rules and standards with golf lingo I had never heard before. I panicked. I didn't know what was going on. I jumped in with a very shrill shut-it-down verbal karate attack. I don't know what came over me. But he continued to play like he was in a PGA tournament. I guess we don't get out much.

Sonny played any which way but loose. Left handed on the wrong side of the ball, holding the club upside down, swinging it like Ray Charles on a baseball field. That was more my speed.

I was so overdressed in a long sleeved shirt and pants. It got hot really fast today. It was so cold this morning. Somehow, we made it through the 18 holes together.

When we got home, I walked to a few yard sales around the block. Labor Day weekend is historically a yard sale weekend. I nabbed a free plastic watering can that is round and bumpy like a cantaloupe but pale pink, like saltwater taffy. It's awful and beautiful at the same time. I also got free vintage cloth napkins, two are a forest green linen with chartreuse stitching around their edges and the other two are white with pale yellow hand sewn applique edges. I bought a vintage spatula with a red handle for $1.

Not only did we play mini golf, we made it to Clermont, the place we got married 13 years ago, on Labor Day weekend. The boys loved seeing "where it happened". It is a beautiful place. We stopped on the way and bought dinner at Adams at their hot bar and brought a blanket so we could have a picnic dinner.

When we got to the structure made of tree branches that we stood under when we said our vows, I looked down to find one milkweed seed in the grass. A wish. Joseph had hidden my engagement ring in a milkweed pod full of "wishes". When we got married, I folded pretty paper into origami place cards for each guest and inside each one, was one wish seed. So I held it up and the four of us made a wish and blew it into the air. Sonny and Desmond kept blowing it higher and higher, trying to keep it off the ground. It lifted to the height of the sun and glowed for a second or two and then floated away.

The boys ran around the garden barefoot, laughing and falling over each other. They drove us crazy and we had moments of relaxing mixed with moments of aggravation. Mixed perfectly like pancake batter, no delineation, no lumps, just even steven. Thisisnice, You'redrivingmecrazy.

We took some nice pictures and watched the sun set and then came home. I ran out and got ice cream! It was totally worth it. I ate if after the kids were in bed because I ate all my dinner and they hadn't.

I had too many sweet moments today to have them ruined by worry. And I was reminded, when we listened to *Jim Harrold's Campfire* ghost stories in the car, that maybe there's a lot more to life than we see. That's comforting to me. There seems to be some extra magic in my days lately. Bits and baubles of light in the gloom. I hold them close, they are a treasure.

Always and still here,

Sarah

September 7

Dear Friend,

Day 180.

Happy Labor Day to you! It is nighttime now, the day is done, and so is summer, sort of. We have just 15 days left until the fall equinox. But summer vacation has come to a close. Tomorrow we start our first day of school. Desmond as a 6th grader and Sonny as a kindergartener. I am a bit overwhelmed by the thought of schooling them both and am not ready for summer to be done.

I hated to let go of our school routine when it ended and now I am reluctant to go back to it.

There's a bit more of a workload for Desmond this year and making time to sit with Sonny to teach him his letters and numbers feels daunting. Although I do think it will be fine. Probably.

Desmond is very excited for tomorrow. He sat looking at our chalkboard in the playroom tonight that lists each subject and what is expected every day, squealing with delight. Go figure.

Today was a day for preparing. I took Desmond shopping for new socks and underwear, because these are important school supplies. If you can't sit still in your seat, it's a problem. I bought new sneakers for Sonny which reminded me of getting new school shoes in September when I was little. The timing was just coincidence but nice all the same.

The boys had bubble baths, Desmond cleaned his room, and we cleaned the playroom that doubles as our school room. I spent time figuring out how to structure our days and then filled in our chart on the chalkboard with our list of to-dos.

When the boys went up to bed, I steam cleaned the rug in our kitchen and mopped the floor. So prepared.

That rug was so dirty, the water that I emptied from the machine was like mud. So satisfying.

When I was a teenager sleeping the day away, my mom would come into my room and say, "It's the most beautiful day of the year!! And you're missing it!!" Today was one of those days. It was a real stunner. An incredible breeze blew through the house all day.

It was brought to my attention that I don't know how Labor Day started or what it's for. Other than the end of summer and a day for laborers to rest. But I don't know it's history. Do you?

Also Desmond was wondering out loud what the year 3 must have been like. And we started to talk about A.D. and B.C. which I also know little about. I just learned that A.D. stands for Anno Domini, which means "In the year of our Lord" in medieval Latin, which is more familiar than Anno Domini. I always think of it as "After Death" which I had a hunch was not accurate but works anyway. And then I couldn't remember how B.C. years work, I thought maybe they count backwards from year 1 A.D. but that seemed really bizarre. It reminded me of when Desmond was small and he would ask me questions I thought I knew the answer to until he asked and I had to put it into words. Like, "What is blacktop?"

I started to describe what year 3 looked like and realized how ridiculous I sounded. "People wore robes and sandals," I said. "They had SANDALS?!" he asked. "Yes, and stone houses and pottery. They had robes and used ropes as belts."

"Were there Native Americans?" he asked. "Yes, but they were in America. Jesus in the robes was in Israel." No idea what I was talking about.

Anyway, I am looking forward to learning and relearning things I learned and immediately forgot. May I retain this new information for at least a week or two. We are going to study oceanography this year. In theory. And work on getting through a whole 6th grade Social Studies book. Oh boy....

I hope your summer was the best it could be. I am glad we got to do the things we were able to, but there sure was a lot I missed.

I am worried about Halloween. I guess it's canceled, the trick-or-treating I mean. I can't see how that would go on. Desmond and I have been talking about maybe having a party at our house in the yard for a few friends. It's one of our most favorite days. What will you do for Halloween?

I hope you rest easy tonight. The air is so cool now and the crickets are still singing. I'll miss them when they go.

Always and still here,

Sarah

September 8

Dear Friend,

Day 181.

Up and at 'em this morning for our first day of school. So grateful we are not trying to "learn remotely" or "e-learning" from a public school. We are carrying on with our homeschooling and I am so grateful for the flexibility and ease of it.

I thought Desmond's upper lip looked a little darker than usual this morning. I had him come close to me so I could inspect it. Then he inspected it. Maybe it was just the light. "I better go read that 'Guy Stuff' book you bought me." "Yeah, hop to it," I said.

He read a page or two. I asked him what he had learned so far. He said he learned he should watch out for pool hair. "What's pool hair?" I asked. "When your hair turns green from swimming in a pool." Sounds like I'll be getting my money's worth out of that book.

Sonny and I sat down together and breezed through 40 minutes of schoolwork which we both really enjoyed. I was shooting for just 15 minutes but he wanted to do more and more. On one page, he had to color in all the stars that had the letter "m" inside of them. He spent so much time coloring in the stars with a yellow and orange colored pencil to look like fire and shooting stars. Adding silver to some. The apple didn't fall far from the tree with that one.

Desmond started in on his new online math program, assuring me he could do it without me, while I worked with Sonny. He ended up doing 5 pages of the wrong section and had to begin all over again, but he was a good sport about it.

We had a friend and her son over in the afternoon and the kids played for a few hours and then we all walked to town to get pizza. It was very sweet. They are new friends we are getting to know. I love new friends, there is so much to ask and learn about them. So much to tell them. The little boy let out the loudest whistle I ever heard in the pizza parlor, which may or may not have been a scream, it was debatable, as well as surprising and sort of enjoyable. He got his long hair caught on a rose branch thorn as he was leaving our yard. His mom set him free. She is easy to talk to and very smart. She taught reading and history and has so many great suggestions for books and methods of teaching. I took notes.

I am glad the day went well and I am glad it is done. I think as the days go by and we settle into a new routine it will feel more comfortable and trustworthy. Like breaking in new shoes.

Always and still here,

Sarah

September 9

Dear Friend,

Day 182.

Last night I was watching a show that I found online, on my tablet in bed, in the dark. It was late. Joseph was falling asleep next to me. The windows were all open, the ceiling fan was moving the air around the room. I had earbuds in and the volume low.

There was a scene with a beautiful young woman, running barefoot through a field. In Australia. There was dramatic music playing. She ran and ran and the music played and played. And I thought, what if the state of affairs is all much worse than we dare to admit? What if we're all pretending things are okay enough and there's light at the end of the tunnel, but there isn't really? It certainly feels sometimes like we're on the Titanic. The ship is at a full tilt and we're just going about our business expecting it will right itself. Will it? Or has it already split in two?

Desmond was up early and got straight to his schoolwork, but somehow did not finish until 7:30 at night. It's a bit more work than last year. Today he took too many breaks. Tomorrow we begin again.

Sonny woke me up this morning and told me to get up for school. His little face was so serious. He managed to wait a little while, until I made myself some tea and then we sat down and got to work. He did not last as long as yesterday. Writing is hard. His little hand trying different ways to grip his pencil, wanting to use two hands to move it. When he doesn't get it just right, he erases and tries again. He is very excited when he gets it right, but then does not want to do more. It is very tricky. I try to encourage him without pushing. Tomorrow I think I'll let him skip some things if he wants to. Or do some wooden puzzles and magnet letters instead.

We had plans for a play date but my friend asked to reschedule due to feeling over whelmed by the first days of remote learning for her three kids, with a baby in tow. I can't imagine trying to juggle so many kids for this circus of a school year, with virtual school. It seems all of the parents, kids and teachers are struggling. Our town is due to be back in the classrooms next month. But I think you can opt to learn virtually instead if you choose. I know this is so in some places but I am not sure about my town. In some towns the kids will go in for a couple of days a week, alternating days to keep the classes small. When half the class is at school, the other half of the class will be at home watching the school room from their computers. I imagine it's all very temporary, at least that's the hope. But so strange. School has always seemed strange to me, but this takes the cake.

I thought we could head out to Kingston at 3:00 but Desmond was not done with his schoolwork, so we waited until 4:00 but he was still not done. At 4:30 I cooked dinner and thought we'd eat early and then go out. I told the boys we could go get a new fish today for our fish tank. We've had just one fish for quite a while and I thought he might be lonely. Now that the fish tank is in the playroom downstairs, I notice the fish more, sorry, John, I notice John the fish more, and I worry about him. I thought his name was Jerry all this time, but I was corrected.

So after dinner we went out to Petco to see about a fish. They did not have the same fish and we wanted to get one just like the one we have. A neon blue dwarf gourami. Nor did they have any fish that would get along with our gourami. So we tried PetSmart just down the road and they had a golden gourami so we got one of those. Sonny carried the bag with the fish all the way home, holding it in his lap in the car. He held the fish up so it could look out the window. "This is our world," he said with a sigh.

Sonny was going to name the fish Frank but decided to call it Jennifer. So now we have John and Jennifer (again) who are named after their Uncle John and Auntie Jennifer on the Ferm side. We had a John and Jennifer, but Jennifer died. Now they are together again. Desmond really likes to name his fish after family members, which is sweet, until they die.

We got Jennifer in the tank and I watched the two fish swim around each other for a while. And then watched John poke at Jennifer repeatedly. I hope they get used to each other and settle down. I immediately wanted to flush Jennifer down the toilet, it made me so nervous. Maybe John was perfectly happy alone and I went and ruined it with my big ideas and this golden gourami.

Sonny was eating a Greek yogurt and peach popsicle this afternoon and started to jump up and down, complaining of his cavity hurting, so I called the dentist to see if we could squeeze in any earlier to get his teeth fixed. His appointment was still 3 weeks away. They said they didn't have anything sooner but would call if they had a cancellation. When I hung up the clock said 3:33. That reminded me of something I had read recently about the number 3. Spiritually it's supposed to represent your angels working on your behalf. Then I thought, oh yes, a friend told me that you need to ask your angels or spirit guides for help because they don't like to interfere but will if you ask. I thought maybe if I ask my angels to help, they could get us there sooner and that maybe if I did, the office would call back and say they just got an opening and could see us right away. And then I got distracted with other things. A few minutes later though, the office called and said they would be able to see us tomorrow at 4:00 after all. That was quick, I thought. It is nice to imagine there are beings behind the scenes that are helping us along. That there is a behind the scenes. Oh God, please let there be a behind the scenes.

Always and still here,

Sarah

September 10

Dear Friend,

Day 183.

"Sonny was amazing, such a trooper, so brave and the dentist was so fantastic, it could not have gone better. His worst spots are repaired and he has more work in the near future but the hardest bit is done. Such relief. We celebrated by stopping at Target and buying him a new toy of his choosing."

I typed that bit last night as a wish for what our experience would be today. And it is exactly right. What I didn't know last night was that I would plug the wrong address into my GPS and drive an extra 20 minutes North and have to drive 20 minutes back down to the right office, in a panic that they might cancel our appointment because we were so late. But they took us in right away and straight into the dentist's office and went right to work. The dentist worked quickly. I was able to be in the room and hold Sonny's hand. He never once flinched or tightened his grip. He moaned a little towards the end, his nose was itchy and it got uncomfortable for him to hold his mouth open and the gas mask on his nose was heavy.

As soon as they took everything out of his mouth, he raised both hands to give two thumbs up. He sat up and smiled when they took the mask off his nose and jumped off the chair, turning to offer the Dr. a high five. He had a mini root canal and a crown put on one molar, a cavity filled on the tooth behind it.

I am still a little shaky.

He was fine until we were about to walk out the door and he said his tooth stung. So they said they'd get him a popsicle. The dentist said, "Have this popsicle now and that may help by making the tooth cold and then later mom can take you to Stewarts for a milkshake." The tech came around the corner holding one of those frozen blue ice stick popsicles. My eyes got wide and I smiled dumbly. He was happy and stopped complaining of the pain and they sent us on our way.

We went straight to Target for Tylenol and a Lego set. I had given him homeopathic pellets before and after, I took some calming ones for myself. I applied calming oils to my hands and wrists, and valor oil for bravery. I offered him the oils but he declined. I put some in my mask and breathed deeply. None of it stopped me from getting a chocolate chip cookie sandwich with my dinner at Whole Foods to settle my nerves. Which just made me feel gross.

My pre sugar brain can justify whatever I want and nothing else will do. My immediate post sugar brain is pure regret. I never feel better. I always regret it. Well, most of the time.

Sonny showed the cashier at Whole Foods his tooth. She was so friendly and excited. She said her son just got the same crown last week! With such enthusiasm! I asked her if he had pain after, she said, "Oh yes! For about a day and a half!"

A handful of times between when we left the office and when we got home, he howled in pain saying he wished he had never gotten his cavity fixed. I was afraid it would only get worse. But halfway through our drive home he stopped complaining and hasn't made a peep about it since.

On our ride home he watched a show on his tablet. I listened to a Stephen King audio book. The sun was setting and the sky was so beautiful. We drove over gullies and streams where clouds were resting. "Sonny, look!" I'd say and he'd turn to look out the window. "Wowww!!...." he'd say. The clouds had come down from the sky. The sky was falling and it couldn't have been more beautiful. And that felt just right.

When we got home, Desmond came running out of the house to hug Sonny. He had been so worried about him, teary when we left, wishing he could come along. But only one parent was allowed to accompany a child because of COVID. Sonny showed Desmond his silver crown. "Wow, Sonny! You look like a pirate! You need an eye patch!" We came inside and Desmond looked at Sonny's tooth again and cried. He was sad that Sonny was different now. I sat with them for a bit and comforted Desmond. I told Sonny that change is hard sometimes for Des. Sonny comforted Desmond and Desmond put his hand on Sonny's leg and said, "I'm just glad you're okay, buddy."

I'm glad we're all okay and in one piece. It's good to be home again. I think I will take a hot bath and breathe in some more oils. Oh man. What a day.

Always and still here,

Sarah

September 11

Dear Friend,

Day 184.

Did I tell you that after you told me to be careful of the man on the trail, one day I picked up a rock while I was walking and carried it in my hand so I could bean him if he jumped out from behind a tree? But as I walked, a family approached and I had to drop the rock to put my mask on. I remembered to bring my little keychain can of mace. It is linked to a whistle and the little ball in the metal whistle made a tiny rolling sound in my pocket. I did not see the tank top man. It also occurred to me that I may know him from somewhere, he is sort of familiar. Not sure if I should ask.

Our gourami fish, John and Jennifer seem really happy together now. They are fun to watch. They swim around each other and stay close to each other, even touching their fins and tails as they pass by. We've never had fish that do that before. Usually they give each other a wide berth. I am so glad.

Sonny is feeling in tip-top shape after his dental work yesterday. He hasn't complained at all since we got home, slept through the night and has been fine all day. I am glad for this too.

Before I left the house for my studio today, I teased the hair on top of my head and my bangs, so it was pretty high and wild. I tried it out last night and thought it was a great idea. If I could get it together to do that AND wear face paint at the same time, I'd be in business. I don't know what business exactly but that doesn't matter. As I was leaving, I checked myself in the mirror by the door and I looked like a lunatic. So I went back into the bathroom to tame it a bit. I told Joseph he should not let me leave the house looking like an insane person. He said, "I thought that was what you were going for." This coming from the man who yesterday when I turned around was wearing multicolored splash paint leggings, bright aqua blue King Tut socks, pulled up over the bottom of the leggings, and a navy blue Bob Ross t-shirt and new his black sneakers. I need to ask Desmond to be my fashion guard, and Joseph's.

When I got to my studio I got a text from a friend who thought I could whip up some drawings to land an illustration job with a time crunch at *Cosmopolitan* magazine. I thought she was nuts and went into a panic trying to make that happen. Somehow I did it. I think I may have gotten the gig. We'll know tomorrow. Keep your fingers crossed for me, will you?

After dinner I sat on the stoop eating strawberries and watching Joseph pitch a wiffle ball to Sonny and Sonny hitting the ball more often than not. An Airbnb guest next door had a golden doodle dog which is the breed I have my heart set on if we are ever brave enough to get a puppy. We got to say hello and it was the sweetest, softest, cutest dog I ever did see. He actually looked like our old wheaten terrier who we loved so. This dog's name was Teddy. The woman was from the city and she did not wear a mask and neither did we and the whole time I felt like I should have one on and worried she was thinking the same. But she had offered to come to us so we could meet her dog so I guess it was okay.

I sat on the front stoop when Joseph and the boys went into the back yard and leaned my chest over my lap, turning to look at the long green grass of the irises that are gone now, resting my head on my knees. This COVID lifestyle has made life very ordinary. It is odd and unusual, but it is also very bland now. It has taken away so much of the extras, the toppings, the accoutrements, the variety. It's boiled things down quite a lot. There's not even much to say about it these days. There have been 52 cases reported in the last two weeks in Ulster County. New York's line on the graph has come steadily down and continues to hang out near the very bottom. The Country is a zig-zag toothy line that went up in April, leveled out, came down some and then shot much higher in July and is coming down again but still jumps up and down like shark's teeth. 36,000 cases now they say. 193,000 deaths in the US in total so far. Although the testing is pretty bad and the reporting not accurate so who really knows. It feels like the worst is behind us for now and we're holding tight to see what's around the corner. With schools opening up, people suspect the numbers will shoot up again. I don't know what to think, so I don't think too much. Just minding my own business.

When Sonny and I came out of Whole Foods yesterday, we walked right into a wish. A seed floating in the air. I caught it in my hand and held it up for Sonny. "Make a wish!" I said. He thought for just a second, and even though he was in and out of pain from his tooth just moments before he said, "I wish the Corona Virus would go away." And he blew the wish into the air and it floated away as he smiled after it. I was surprised. It was a good wish. I hope it comes true.

Always and still here,

Sarah

September 12

Dear Friend,

Day 185.

Today, for real this time, today is 6 months since my first day of quarantine. Wednesday March 11th. I was out at Adams for our usual Wednesday night dinner after Desmond's acting class. Our friends met us there. We talked about the upcoming quarantine that was to start on Monday. I had a sore throat. I decided the next day to stay in, to start my 2 weeks of quarantine early, just in case my sore throat was COVID so that I wouldn't spread it around. "I don't want anyone to die on my account," I thought. And here we are 6 months later.

I did not imagine it would affect the following school year, or Halloween, or even the summer. I thought, in America, it was so odd it had gotten here at all, surely, we would be able to put a swift end to it. Mysterious times. Let's not think too hard on it. Our hair will turn gray and the circles under our eyes will grow dark and ominous. Then we'll be nearer to the zombie apocalypse and Halloween is still weeks away.

I spent the day today working on this illustration for *Cosmopolitan* which I guess I am still not sure if I'm hired for, come to think of it. But it was nice to sit and draw most of the day. Joseph took most of the kids requests and they let me work at the dining room table. My studio doesn't have internet so I set up a spot at home, in the middle of the fray. But they were kind to me.

It is hard to sit so long. I am so tired. I stayed up too late last night watching this show from Australia about a plant that makes people young again. I stay up late because I like how quiet is and no one bugs me.

Joseph cooked a lobster bisque soup for dinner from a base we bought in Cape Cod, frozen at the fish market. It was so good. The house smelled like a seaside restaurant for a little while.

Nothing at all unusual happened today, no stories to tell.

I sort of miss the heightened bustle of the early days of quarantine. We were all put on lockdown, but everyone was singing from their rooftops. It was like we all stopped in our tracks and lifted our heads up to see each other. But we've slowly put our heads back down and have gone back to trudging along, alone. Does it seem that way to you, or is it just me? That quarantine felt like a weird virtual slumber party in a way. Now we're in some other sort of purgatory.

Or I'm just tired.

That is all. I still love you. I think you're grand. You're doing a very fine job.

Be kind. Be the balm.

Always and still here,

Sarah

Acknowledgments

I felt like you had to have achieved something great to have the honor of an acknowledgments page. Like thanking people when you receive an Oscar. So therefore, I was not going to have one. It felt too self indulgent. I haven't had a team of people helping me along that I should thank, like an agent, editor, publisher, publicist or anything as sophisticated and grown up as that. As I do most things, I was comfortable doing it "by myself", forever reluctant to ask for help.

But in the end, you would not be reading this book if my very dear and generous friend, Michele Walthers, had not asked for my Amazon Kindle password so she could take the reins when I found myself hitting wall after wall, trying to upload my manuscript and turn it into a book. I would be remiss not to thank her, profusely. She spent countless hours, with the help of her husband, Jeffrey, figuring out how to create a paperback and an ebook. And all of this right after she got me hired and then coached me through that *Cosmo* illustration job, step by step. She has championed me, pushed me, and given me a great deal of help and love through both projects and I still don't know what I did to deserve it. Thank you, my dear friend, Michele, I'm taking you away for a weekend to celebrate. Give Jeffrey a hug from me.

I also would not have kept writing if I didn't have anyone encouraging me to keep going. To my friends who read my daily letters and left their little blue thumbs up symbols, hearts, hugging hearts, open mouthed wow emojis and most of all, comments. Comments that made me feel that writing these daily letters was a worthwhile endeavor and that what I had to say might just be interesting, helpful or comforting. Your encouragement kept me writing and lifted my spirits along the way. I felt your presence and your love, thank you, thank you.

Thank you to my husband, Joseph, who let me sit in the living room late at night in my requested silence so I could concentrate, forgoing turning on the TV and sitting at the desktop computer with headphones to watch Cobra Kai, without complaint. Thank you for your support and encouragement to keep writing and giving me the time and space to do it. Your love means the world to me. You believe in me, and so I try.

A big thank you to my sons Desmond and Sonny who kept me company all of these days, entertaining me and giving me stories to write about. You bring so much joy to my life and make all of my days richer and more colorful. You are both magical humans and I am so lucky to be your mom and your guide through this crazy world we love so much.

And a very special, magical, fly through the dimensions that separate us, thank you, to my mom, Pam Conrad. Or just a whisper over my shoulder thank you, I can't be sure which one. But thank you, for instilling in me a love of listening to stories and telling stories, of crafting words to create images and setting the creative bar really high, because your writing was and still is brilliant. I know you'd be tickled to see me writing so much and sharing it with the world, or Amazon, which feels like the same thing. I hope you can see it all and in case you can't, it's okay, because I know that your voice is woven with mine in my writing, my love of words came from you. Thank you.

SARAH CONRAD-FERM lives in the Hudson Valley of New York with her husband, two young sons and two dwarf gouramis. She has not heard the mouse in a while, so it must be gone. A graduate of The Cooper Union, she holds a BFA in Fine Art, a cosmetology license, a real estate license and a driver's license. She can paint you a picture, cut your hair, sell you a house and take you for a drive all in one day, and then write a letter about it. Her greatest joys are being a mother to her two boys, painting and writing.

Made in the USA
Middletown, DE
27 July 2024

57989387R00166